AF352439

THE CANDIDACY CALCULATION

Challenges to Running for Elected Office in Canada

The Candidacy Calculation examines how perceptions of barriers to candidacy in Canada differ by social, economic, and political backgrounds. Through semi-structured interviews with 101 individuals from diverse social backgrounds, geographical locations, and political ideologies, this book uncovers both new and previously overlooked challenges, such as online harassment and social media scandals, while also offering a deeper understanding of traditional barriers like financial constraints, work-life balance, employment issues, partisanship, and family responsibilities. The findings demonstrate that individual considerations regarding candidacy are much more complex than previously thought.

Drawing on an intersectional approach, the book analyses how factors such as gender, race/ethnicity, sexuality, age, and other social attributes intersect to create unique barriers to political careers, thereby presenting a nuanced view of the candidate emergence process in Canada. By rigorously testing the role of political ambition in fostering diversity in political representation, *The Candidacy Calculation* compares the experiences of women and men, various social groups, and individuals who have become candidates with those who have not. The book aims to assist policymakers and activists in identifying solutions to overcome barriers and enhance opportunities for increasing candidacy among under-represented groups in politics.

ANGELIA WAGNER is an adjunct professor in the Department of Political Science at the University of Alberta.

The Candidacy Calculation

Challenges to Running for Elected Office in Canada

ANGELIA WAGNER

UNIVERSITY OF TORONTO PRESS
Toronto Buffalo London

ISBN 978-1-4875-5875-8 (cloth)   ISBN 978-1-4875-5879-6 (EPUB)
ISBN 978-1-4875-5876-5 (paper)   ISBN 978-1-4875-5878-9 (PDF)

Library and Archives Canada Cataloguing in Publication

Title: The candidacy calculation : challenges to running for elected office in
  Canada / Angelia Wagner.
Names: Wagner, Angelia, 1972– author
Description: Includes bibliographical references and index.
Identifiers: Canadiana (print) 20250130203 | Canadiana (ebook) 20250130300 |
  ISBN 9781487558758 (cloth) | ISBN 9781487558765 (paper) |
  ISBN 9781487558796 (EPUB) | ISBN 9781487558789 (PDF)
Subjects: LCSH: Political candidates – Canada – Social conditions. |
  LCSH: Politics, Practical – Social aspects – Canada.
Classification: LCC JL193 .W34 2025 | DDC 324.971 – dc23

Cover design: Val Cooke
Cover image: iStock.com/MicroStockHub

We wish to acknowledge the land on which the University of Toronto Press
operates. This land is the traditional territory of the Wendat, the Anishnaabeg,
the Haudenosaunee, the Métis, and the Mississaugas of the Credit First
Nation.

This book has been published with the help of a grant from the Federation
for the Humanities and Social Sciences, through the Awards to Scholarly
Publications Program, using funds provided by the Social Sciences and
Humanities Research Council of Canada.

University of Toronto Press acknowledges the financial support of the
Government of Canada, the Canada Council for the Arts, and the Ontario Arts
Council, an agency of the Government of Ontario, for its publishing activities.

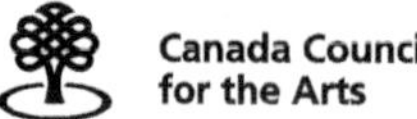

This book is dedicated to my parents,
R. Doreen Wagner (1949–2003)
and
Gary C. Wagner

Contents

Figures and Tables

Figures

Tables

Acknowledgments

This book was inspired by a simple question: Is the news media really a barrier to political candidacy? I had begun to have my doubts after studying media depictions of women politicians at the national and subnational levels. I certainly found examples of media sexism but not at the level of intensity that I thought necessary to depress women's political ambitions. This question led to another one: If media sexism might not be a barrier, could the same also be true of other factors identified as obstacles to elected office? I would not have been able to find the answers to this question without encouragement, support, and guidance from so many people.

A Social Sciences and Humanities Research Council of Canada postdoctoral fellowship at the Centre for the Study of Democratic Citizenship (CSDC) in Montreal enabled me to launch this project. The CSDC, which is based at McGill University, provided additional funding for research trips, computer software, conference travel, and skills training, but more importantly, it offered a welcoming and collegial environment of scholars from across Quebec and the rest of Canada, whose insights deepened my analysis and whose friendship made my stay in Montreal more enjoyable. Frédérick Bastien, Holly Ann Garnet, Thierry Giasson, Allison Harell, and Dietlind Stolle especially stand out for their support. However, my greatest praise must be reserved for my postdoctoral advisor, Elisabeth Gidengil, who was always ready with advice as I worked through the challenges of such a large project. I would also like to thank the 101 individuals who selflessly gave their time to answer my questions about political candidacy. Finally, I extend my appreciation to the Government of Quebec for its commitment to and financial support of the CSDC (and other such centres across that province), which made this collegial environment possible.

My research journey continued during a second postdoctoral fellowship with Linda Trimble at the University of Alberta. She allowed me to continue working on my own project while assisting with her research on the gendered mediation of women premiers in Canada and Australia. Her generosity was not unexpected. Linda has been a stalwart supporter since I began my graduate studies under her supervision at the University of Alberta some years earlier. She is a generous collaborator whose obvious love of research is inspiring, but she is an even more generous friend whose laughter, baking, and vitality continually remind me that life is about more than just academia.

Other scholars also generously provided their feedback on different stages of this project, including Louise Carbert, Joanna Everitt, Brenda O'Neill, Alex Marland, Meagan Auer, and Jennifer Curtin. Chapter 6's review of LGBTQ individuals' concerns about public scrutiny was previously published in *Politics, Groups, and Identities*, while Chapter 7's discussion of online harassment of politicians previously appeared in *Feminist Media Studies*, and I am grateful to the journals' respective anonymous reviewers for critiques that strengthened the research and its presentation. I also extend my gratitude to the three anonymous reviewers who took the time to review this manuscript and offer suggestions for its improvement. I commend the dedication and patience of Daniel Quinlan at the University of Toronto Press, who has been committed to this book from the very beginning. Finally, I would like to thank Cressida Heyes and the Department of Political Science at the University of Alberta for sponsoring the book's index.

Writing a book is a solitary endeavour, with countless hours spent in front of a computer trying to put words on the screen. Online writing groups have been vital to completing this manuscript: Bailey Gerrits' pandemic-era group emboldened me to start crafting it, and Yasmeen Abu-Laban's ongoing collective cheered me on as I put the finishing touches on it. Along the way Megan Aiken, Chadwick Cowie, Judy Garbert, Shannon Sampert, and Victoria Woodman have offered kind words and constant encouragement. My most heartfelt gratitude, however, is reserved for my parents. My mother Doreen Wagner was not able to join me on this research journey as she died of colon cancer in 2003, but her desire for me to embrace life's opportunities led me to academia. In her place, my father Gary Wagner has been a constant source of moral support, home repairs, and A&W mozza burgers. Each one has imparted wisdom that has shaped me in indelible ways. It is to them that I dedicate this book.

THE CANDIDACY CALCULATION

Challenges to Running for Elected Office in Canada

The Initial Calculations: Importance of Descriptive Representation in Canadian Politics

Regardless of the positions I have held – whether school trustee, cabinet minister or premier – I have always had the same goal: to make a contribution to society and to help improve the lives of the people of Ontario. This drive was instilled in me at a young age. I was raised in a supportive, social justice–minded family, and was encouraged early on to stand up for my beliefs, and to pursue my goals with determination and conviction. This support gave me the confidence and resolve to seek out a career in politics, and set me on the path that led me to the position I proudly occupy today.

– Kathleen Wynne, premier of Ontario (2013–2018)
(Email communication with author, 22 November 2016)

Hannah Bell has been fascinated by Canadian politics ever since she immigrated to this country with her family as a young child. Her mother quickly became an active volunteer in their new home of Prince Edward Island, working with women's advocacy groups before eventually getting involved with the federal New Democratic Party (NDP) to help it establish a local presence. Bell was introduced to campaigning when she was about 10 years old. She recalls going on road trips around the province with then NDP leader Ed Broadbent and working with her mother's federal campaign in the mid-1980s. These experiences helped Bell to understand the role of government and of individuals within it. Bell continues to follow politics as an adult. She believes everyone has a civic responsibility to know what elected officials are doing on their behalf. "The onus is on individuals to be informed if you want to be able to have an opinion and then impact those outcomes," said the white woman, who has worked in the non-governmental sector. But despite her strong interest in politics, excellent community connections, and extensive qualifications, Bell had not run for elected office at the time of our interview. The primary reason was that she didn't "actually have an affiliation with any particular party. I never really have. I don't feel incredibly strongly about any one party enough to say, 'This is it. This is who it is.'" Running as an independent isn't feasible at the federal or provincial levels.

Marni Panas, a transgender woman who works in the health care field in Alberta, first got involved in Canadian politics as a teenager when a friend ran for federal office. Doing as her parents did, Panas voted Conservative for many years until she got involved in the transgender community and witnessed the difficulties that people had in accessing services and support. "Then I started to look at things more critically … and my university [education] helped [me] just to understand that there's other ways of looking at things." Panas has given serious thought to running for elected office but has put it off to focus on her son in the aftermath of her gender transition and divorce. "I've worked really hard to bond with him and I am worried about how that would impact our relationship at this age." If Panas ever runs, she expects it to be several years down the road.

Christopher Matthews, a Black gay man, definitely wants to run for elected office, just not yet. At the time of our conversation, he was focused on settling down with his fiancé. He needed to plan a wedding and buy a house, both expensive propositions that suck up a lot of time and resources. "I'm thinking more deeply this week if that's a thing I will actually say yes to or would that be something later on." The Toronto banker has assessed the possibility of a provincial run, and if his personal circumstances hadn't changed, he might have tried to become a Progressive Conservative candidate in the 2018 Ontario elections. For him, it all comes down to timing. In the meantime, he is deeply involved with ProudPolitics, an organization that seeks to encourage more LGBTQ individuals to run for elected office.

Canadians have a variety of reasons for not seeking elected office at the federal, provincial, or municipal levels. They include concerns about raising enough money to fund a campaign without going into debt, securing enough voter support to win the election, and navigating party politics once in office. Others believe it isn't the right time to run because they are finishing a university degree, establishing their careers, or starting families. Many Canadians cannot afford to take time off from work to campaign 24/7 during an election. They have a mortgage to pay, and election regulations don't allow campaign funds to be used to pay the candidate a salary. Canadians are also hesitant to deal with the public scrutiny and loss of privacy that all politicians must endure, which has become a constant phenomenon in the social media era. In this book, I investigate why Canadians of different genders, races/ethnicities, sexualities, socio-economic circumstances, and partisan affiliations choose not to run for elected office.

On the surface, it might not seem important that some Canadians opt out of a career in politics. More than enough individuals become candidates in each electoral cycle. Aside from some rural and small-town municipal councils, government officials don't have to issue a second or third call for nominations to fill all available seats. Competition for federal, provincial, and big-city seats can be fierce. The problem is that the majority of candidates have been white heterosexual men. Women, LGBTQ individuals, ethnic minorities, and Indigenous peoples have made important strides in seeking and achieving political office over the last few decades, but their progress remains slow because of enormous challenges in becoming candidates.

A person's decision to run – or not run – is a rational calculation based on evaluations of personal, professional, and political circumstances and not because of any shortcoming on their part. The problem does not lie with the individual but with structural, institutional, and societal factors that make it more difficult for women, Indigenous, racialized, and LGBTQ people to run for elected office than for white heterosexual men. A diverse legislature requires diverse candidates for elected office. To ensure our legislatures reflect the characteristics and lived experiences of the Canadian population as a whole, we need more Indigenous people, LGBTQ folks, racial/ethnic minorities, and women to become candidates. We need such candidates to decide that politics is worthy of their time and effort. But why should we care that Canadian politicians come from all walks of life? That is the focus of the next section.

The Importance of Representation

Elected representatives play an important role in Western liberal democracies. As policymakers, representatives determine government priorities in areas such as the economy, education, health care, housing, immigration, policing, reproductive rights, and taxes. Their decisions thus have the potential to affect the lives of millions of citizens. Yet citizens vary in their life experiences and their policy needs. A few examples will suffice to demonstrate the point. Women, often the primary caregivers in their families, seek well-run, affordable daycares and long-term care homes so they can earn a living while taking care of children and elderly parents. Indigenous peoples seek self-governance to regain control over their own lives and undo the horrendous damage that colonialism inflicted on their children, cultures, and communities. Black citizens are fed up with police brutality and want an end to Black deaths at the hands of police. LGBTQ individuals seek legal protections related to sexuality that heterosexual individuals do not require, without which they could be fired from their jobs, denied adequate health care, or discriminated against in innumerable other ways when others discover their sexual orientation or gender expression.

Despite these real examples, the reality is that the majority of Canadian politicians are white, heterosexual men who do not experience these realities or share these concerns. Government initiatives are unlikely to adequately address the needs of different social groups when policymakers represent only a small section of society (Newman and White 2006; Schwindt-Bayer and Mishler 2005). Effective public policy relies on the participation of political actors who contribute a range of perspectives, ideas, and expertise (Young 2000).

The nature and quality of political representation is important in a democratic system where a small number of individuals are elected to represent the concerns of citizens in political institutions at the federal, provincial, and local levels. Scholars making normative arguments in favour of diversity in politics routinely build off Hanna Pitkin's (1967) groundbreaking book *The Concept of Representation,* in which she conceptualizes four types of representation: formal, descriptive, substantive, and symbolic. Formal representation focuses "on the formalities of the relationship between a principal (voters) and an agent (a representative)," with authorization and accountability being key factors in this relationship (Tremblay 2022, 38). Of greater relevance to this book, however, is Pitkin's other three concepts as well as Jane Mansbridge's (2003) concept of surrogate representation.

Pitkin defines descriptive representation as "standing for" voters. Also known as numerical or mirror representation, descriptive representation is achieved when members of an elected body possess the same social characteristics like gender, race/ethnicity, and sexuality in the same proportion as their voters (Newman and White 2006, 101). For example, under descriptive representation, if women make up 50 per cent of citizens, women are expected to make up 50 per cent of candidates and of politicians. But gender parity does not exist at any level of government in Canada. For example, Table 1.1 shows that in federal office, women only comprised about one-third of candidates between 2008 and 2015, increasing to 41.4 per cent in 2019. Media reports put women's rate of candidacy around 43 per cent in 2021 (Dunham 2021). Scholars also argue that elected officials should mirror the diversity within each social group (Trimble 2008). In terms of race, white women

Table 1.1. Percentage of candidates for the Canadian House of Commons who were white, racialized, or Indigenous between 2008 and 2019, by gender

Election year	Women (n = 1,530)				Men (n = 2,977)			
	Indigenous	Racialized	White	All	Indigenous	Racialized	White	All
2008	2.3%	13.0%	83.6%	30.0%	1.7%	10.5%	87.5%	70.0%
2011	1.3%	13.2%	85.1%	30.3%	1.7%	8.6%	89.7%	69.7%
2015	6.5%	15.7%	77.4%	30.9%	2.6%	14.7%	82.5%	69.1%
2019	5.6%	17.7%	76.4%	41.4%	2.5%	16.6%	80.6%	58.0%

Source: Johnson et al. 2021.
Note: The figures might not add up to 100% in each year because of a small number of individuals whose racial identity was not identified.

Table 1.2. Percentage of elected members of the Canadian House of Commons who were white, racialized, or Indigenous between 2008 and 2019, by gender

Election year	Women				Men			
	Indigenous	Racialized	White	All	Indigenous	Racialized	White	All
2008	1.4%	15.9%	82.6%	22.5%	1.3%	4.6%	94.1%	77.5%
2011	2.7%	18.9%	78.4%	24.1%	1.7%	5.6%	92.7%	75.9%
2015	3.4%	18.4%	78.2%	25.8%	2.8%	12.8%	84.0%	74.2%
2019	3.2%	21.1%	75.8%	28.2%	2.5%	12.8%	84.7%	71.8%

Source: Johnson et al. 2021.
Note: The figures might not add up to 100% in each year because of a small number of individuals whose racial identity was not identified.

comprised the largest share of women candidates between 2008 and 2019, but that is decreasing over time as more racialized and Indigenous women seek a seat in the House of Commons. The same pattern holds for men: more minority men are running for federal office over time, though white men made up four-fifths of men candidates during the 11-year period.

Women experienced an even lower rate of success in federal elections. Table 1.2 shows that women have slowly increased their share of seats in the House of Commons from 22.5 per cent in 2008 to 28.2 per cent in 2019. Equal Voice, an organization dedicated to increasing women's political representation, placed their share around 30 per cent after the 2021 federal election. As with candidacy, Indigenous and racialized women are increasing their proportion of women MPs over time, with racialized women in particular enjoying a large increase since 2008. In contrast, Indigenous and racialized men made up a smaller proportion of men MPs during the same period.

Our ability to assess the descriptive representativeness of Canadian political institutions, especially at the subnational level, is hampered by a lack of (easily accessible) public records on candidates' social identities. Federally, candidates only need to indicate their gender, occupation, partisan affiliation, riding, contact information, and other administrative details on the nomination form submitted to Elections Canada before each election. The inclusion of gender allows feminists to track women's slow, uneven, and incomplete progress towards gender parity at the federal level. But federal nomination forms do not ask candidates to state their race, ethnicity, sexuality, religion, or other characteristics deemed important for monitoring the ability of federal politicians to "stand for" the diversity of the Canadian population. The racial information presented above was only made possible by the hard work of scholars and activists in obtaining details about racial identities from public records, news coverage, and candidates themselves. Data collection is inconsistent at the subnational level, with some provinces providing extensive, archived information about candidates and other provinces posting temporary and/or limited information on ministry websites. To the best of my knowledge, no province monitors the social identities of candidates beyond gender. Meanwhile, a complete list of candidates for municipal elections is almost impossible to obtain in many provinces, let alone details about their social characteristics.

Despite these challenges, advocacy organizations do their best to keep track of the diverse candidates running for office at the federal, provincial, and municipal levels. ProudPolitics, an organization seeking to improve LGBTQ political representation, promotes the campaigns of queer candidates at all three levels through their website and social media accounts, but queer candidates must contact them first. As a result, the number of publicly out LGBTQ candidates in Canada is likely under-reported. In 2021, 41 LGBTQ candidates ran for federal office, with just seven winning for 2.1 per cent of the seats (Bogart 2021). In terms of race, Tracy-Ann Johnson-Myers and Joanna Everitt (2022) note that the number of Black candidates at the federal level doubled from 45 to 70 between 2015 and 2021, while the share of Black MPs rose from 5 (1.5 per cent) to 9 (2.7 per cent), bringing them closer to mirroring their 3.5 per cent share of the Canadian population. Indigenous peoples are also seeing slow improvement in representation at the federal level: 78 Indigenous candidates contested the 2021 election, with 12 winning (3.6 per cent), up from 11 in 2019 (3.3 per cent) (Hobson 2021). Evidence suggests similar advancements are being made by various social groups at the provincial and municipal levels.

Several normative arguments have been made in favour of descriptive representation. First, one of the most important principles of liberal democratic countries, like Canada, is political equality, or the belief that everyone has the right to wield political power (Malcolmson et al. 2016). Equality therefore requires that members of a country's various social groups be represented in legislative bodies at every level of government. Second, descriptive representation is thought to strengthen democratic institutions and their ability to embody democratic ideals (Dovi 2002; Mansbridge 1999). Third, it improves democratic deliberation and political agendas as the presence of more diverse politicians is expected to lead to government policy that reflects a greater range of interests (Celis and Childs 2020). Fourth, citizens are more likely to express greater knowledge, interest, efficacy, and trust in politics if they see people like them in elected office (Atkeson and Carrillo 2007; McAllister 2019; West 2016). Diverse role models might even encourage diverse citizens to get involved in politics (Campbell and Wolbrecht 2006; Stokes-Brown and Dolan 2010).

The traditional impetus behind monitoring descriptive representation, however, is a belief that an increase in the number of diverse politicians will lead to an increase in the substantive representation of diverse Canadians. Pitkin defines substantive representation as "acting for," or when an official deliberately acts on behalf of the needs, demands, and interests of constituents (Tremblay 2010, 4). Because women, Indigenous, racialized, and LGBTQ individuals have life experiences that differ from those of white, heterosexual men, each social group has their own set of demands and issues that need to be addressed by government (Celis and Childs 2020; Newman and White 2006). In this framework, substantive representation is said to have occurred when those interests are reflected in public policy. A cause-and-effect relationship is thus postulated between the presence of diverse politicians and policy outcomes. This raises the problematic issue of defining the interests of a particular social group. The Black feminist theory of intersectionality argues that Black people, for example, share many life experiences related to race and racism, but factors such as gender, sexuality, religion, class, and so on also mean Black people have different life experiences from each other (Crenshaw 1989, 1991). The resulting diversity of needs, priorities, and opinions among Black people cannot necessarily be expressed as a unified set of political goals (Trimble 2008). Instead, we must assume that Black people have interests both in common and in conflict, unless proven otherwise. Black interests then become subjective and specific to a group of organized Black people who have built a solidarity around a particular issue or issues (for this argument in relation to women, see Vickers 2006).

Regardless of how they tackle challenges related to defining a social group's interests, scholars routinely investigate the substantive representation of diverse groups to determine whether the presence of diverse politicians equates to diverse policy outcomes. Part of their research has centred on critical mass theory. Derived from nuclear physics, the term refers to the idea that politicians from a social group can only transform politics once their numbers reach a high enough proportion in a particular legislative body (Dahlerup 2006), with the tipping point usually pegged at 30 per cent. Testing the theory's validity, however, has been hampered by the fact that politicians from different social groups rarely reach that threshold in legislatures and, in some cases, likely won't ever do because of their small share of the general population. Women politicians have come the closest to achieving critical mass, and even gender parity in a few legislatures around the world, but research on their impact has yielded mixed results. Other scholars instead point to the importance of critical actors, or individuals who don't need to be part of a large cohort to act for a social group (Childs and Krook 2006, 2009). Some diverse representatives are highly motivated to pursue policies that favour their social group (Bratton, Haynie, and Reingold 2006; McAndrews et al. 2020; Miruka et al. 2021; Mügge, van der Pas, and van de Wardt 2019), though in some cases more for electoral reasons than ideological ones (Sobolewska, McKee, and Campbell 2018). Suzanne Dovi (2002) argues that diverse politicians need to have deep, mutual ties with disadvantaged communities for effective representation. It is not enough just to descriptively represent a given social group, politicians must act as symbolic and surrogate representatives.

Symbolic representation has gained importance as countries like Canada become incredibly diverse in terms of social identities but their national symbols like politicians do not reflect that diversity. Emanuela Lombardo and Petra Meier define symbolic representation as "the representation of a constituency through a symbol that presents this constituency in a particular way and thus constructs meanings about it" (2019, 234). Although symbols usually refer to flags, statutes, and national anthems, they can include politicians and other government officials (Lombardo and Meier 2019). Changing conceptions of who is the ideal Canadian can be seen in relation to the governor general. The first governor generals were white British aristocrats, but in the mid-twentieth century the decision was made to appoint white Canadian ex-politicians, followed by the move to multiracial Canadian public figures in the early twenty-first century. This evolution expanded the viceregal position's symbolic representation of the nation to include a broader section of the Canadian public. Politicians also serve a symbolic function when they reinforce or challenge societal notions about who can be a politician and, by extension, who is the ideal citizen. Having politicians who primarily come from one social group reinforces historical and marginalized positions in society as well as hampers the ability of various social groups to make claims against the government (Lombardo and Meier 2019). Having politicians who reflect the demographics of the country subverts these asymmetrical power relations and broadens who is considered a legitimate political leader and which issues can be placed on the public agenda.

As symbolic agents, diverse politicians can help change public attitudes towards politics, leadership, and citizenship. But limitations of the electoral system, especially at the federal and provincial levels, mean diverse politicians are also expected to act as surrogate representatives. Mansbridge asserts that surrogate representation "occurs when legislators represent constituents outside their own districts" (2003, 515). This type of representation is necessary in multicultural countries with territorially based electoral systems. Canada uses the single-member plurality system, also known as first-past-the-post, at both the federal and provincial levels. In this system, a polity is split up into a series of distinct ridings with one elected representative for each. A territorial approach to representation makes it difficult for a politician to advocate for the needs of various social groups unless one such group makes up the majority of voters in a riding, as is the case in majority–minority districts in the United States, which are designed specifically for that purpose. Surrogate representation overcomes territorial limitations by facilitating identity-based representation (Tremblay 2022). Celina Caesar-Chavannes (2021) championed the interests of Black Canadians and Black women in particular during her four years as a member of Parliament, even though Black people made up only a small portion of the voters in her Whitby riding (Statistics Canada 2022a). Research has found that other diverse politicians often feel compelled to represent their social group (Bratton, Haynie, and Reingold 2006; Sobolewska, McKee, and Campbell 2018).

Improving the quality of political representation in Canada therefore requires more diverse individuals to become candidates for elected office. This book takes an intersectional approach to investigating the role of people's potentially differing attitudes towards electoral politics in the political candidacy process in Canada. The next section briefly explains the political candidacy process and where this particular study is situated.

Figure 1.1. The political candidacy process

Stages of Political Recruitment

Political candidacy is fraught with pitfalls at every stage of the political lifecycle. Drawing upon Pippa Norris and Joni Lovenduski (1995), Figure 1.1 depicts the political candidacy process from start to finish.

Eligibles are individuals who are legally permitted to hold elected office based on criteria such as age, residency, and citizenship (Tolley 2023). Since these requirements are not overly restrictive, most adult citizens are eligible to become legislators, but the degree to which individuals possess the necessary ambition to pursue that career varies. Most citizens don't want to become politicians. Many individuals, especially young people, are put off by the political polarization, hyper partisanship, and aggressive nature of politics in Western liberal democracies (Carbert 2006, 2009, 2010; Lawless and Fox 2015). Indigenous people often refuse to get involved in Canadian politics because of a larger rejection of the settler colonial state (Green 2000; Green and Peach 2007; Henderson 2002; Ladner and McCrossan 2009). Indigenous people also have lower trust and more negative opinions of Canadian politicians and democracy than non-Indigenous people (Bouchard and Bourgeois 2024). Traditional gender stereotypes in several cultures condition many women to believe that their focus should be on raising children and that their husbands are better suited for politics. One consequence is that women express less confidence in their political abilities than do men, which can depress ambition among those women willing to consider a political career.

Although many citizens don't want to run for elected office, a select few give it serious thought. *Aspirants* are individuals who signal an interest in a political career. This interest can be expressed in different ways, such as approaching party officials or politicians for information about this career option (Dhima 2022, 127), announcing their desire to run for elected office, and seeking a party nomination to actually do so (Tolley 2023, 377–8). But many aspirants don't move beyond this stage of the candidacy process because of personal circumstances. Aspirants of all social backgrounds choose not to run because they want to finish their education, establish a career, raise a family, or care for elderly parents. Many women delay their entry into politics until their children are in school (Beck 2001; Brodie 1985; Wilford et al. 1993), though more and more women aspirants are finding solutions to their caring responsibilities. Individuals in working-class occupations find it difficult to pursue a career in politics because their jobs do not offer the same high salary or flexibility in working hours that lawyers and entrepreneurs often enjoy (Carnes 2018). Class issues help explain why some men wait to run until after they retire.

Candidates are individuals who run successfully or unsuccessfully for elected office at the federal, provincial, or municipal levels. People have various reasons for choosing to run, with the opportunity to have an impact on public policy a major one (Wagner 2022a). But even when people decide to run, they face major challenges. In partisan systems, party recruitment practices influence which aspirants make it to the candidate stage. The left-wing NDP has long required local electoral district associations to make a concerted effort to find women and minority candidates, while the centrist Liberal Party urged the public to nominate potential women candidates as part of its Invite Her to Run campaign in the lead-up to the 2015 federal election. In contrast, the right-wing Conservative Party refuses to engage in such affirmative action (Thomas 2017), often leading to the nomination of fewer women and minority candidates. Again, the electoral system matters (Hinojosa and Franceschet 2012; Tremblay 2007; Trounstine and Valdini 2008). In single-member plurality systems, parties can only select one candidate to represent them in each riding and they might opt for candidates who appeal to the largest number of voters or who have a demonstrated ability to win elections – historically men (Fortin-Rittberger and Eder 2013). Women and minorities' level of representation at the federal and provincial levels are also tied to the electoral fortunes of the main political parties (Black 2008, 2011, 2013).

Voter bias against non-traditional candidates is another factor that can determine who does, and does not, make it to the next stage in the political lifecycle (Black and Erickson 2003; Golebiowska and Thomsen 1999; Philpot and Walton 2007). At the back of voters' minds are traditionally masculine notions of political leadership (Duerst-Lahti 2010; Duerst-Lahti and Kelly 1995). Politicians are expected to possess the agentic traits associated with men and not the communal qualities ascribed to women (Eagly and Carli 2007), leaving women at a potential disadvantage when trying to convince voters to support their candidacies (Dolan 2004, 2010; Sanbonmatsu and Dolan 2009), especially when seeking office at higher levels of government (Huddy and Terkildsen 1993b). However, an extensive literature finds that voters are usually more influenced by partisanship than by candidate gender

(Goodyear-Grant 2010). Making it to the next stage of the candidacy process is thus more challenging for some Canadians than others.

Legislators are those individuals who won election and consequently hold a seat in a federal, provincial, or local governing body. The descriptive representativeness of this group is why activists and advocacy organizations work hard to encourage more diverse people to run for elected office as well as make structural, institutional, and party changes that would make politics more welcoming to them. Empirical research on the substantive representation of diverse interests also focuses on this group. Finally, *former legislators* are individuals who no longer hold elected office at any level of government. Ex-politicians tend to be forgotten once they leave office, but some scholars are investigating their post-politics experiences (cf. Byrne and Theakston 2016).

Although obstacles at each stage of the candidacy process serve to continually winnow the number of women, Indigenous, racialized, and LGBTQ individuals in politics, this book is primarily interested in the first stage of candidacy and why *eligibles* choose not to run for elected office. What is keeping otherwise qualified and interested people from entering politics? In other words, how do perceptions of the barriers to candidacy vary by social, economic, and political background, and how do these differences help us to understand variation in the level of representation among social groups? To answer this question, I interviewed 101 individuals of diverse social backgrounds and political ideologies about their perceptions of the main drawbacks to political candidacy. My primary focus is on eligibles, but I also interviewed a large number of former candidates and elected officials to better understand what is keeping eligibles from taking the next step. Candidates obviously weren't deterred by challenges such as campaign fundraising or party behaviour, but their decision-making process before making the leap into politics can provide insights into the obstacles that everyone must surmount and which ones are specifically tripping up eligibles. Candidate experiences in politics can also reveal how they overcame these obstacles, providing valuable information for eligibles contemplating a future in politics. I opted not to interview losing aspirants, or people who sought a party nomination but did not get selected, because I am more interested in how challenges play out in a general election and not during the nomination process.

Outline of the Book

The next chapter explains the research methodology used for this project as well as the overall and intersectional findings regarding the major drawbacks to political candidacy. The rest of the book explores individual factors in more depth. Chapter 3 takes a nuanced look at an historical factor limiting women's political participation – family responsibilities. Results indicate that women no longer see family as a tall barrier to their electoral ambitions and that men view it as more of an issue than previously acknowledged. Insights from eligibles suggest the family-unfriendly nature of politics and legislatures today is an impediment to the political inclusion of parents. Candidates further reveal that the burden of making family and politics work rests on political spouses.

Campaign fundraising is one of the most cited challenges in candidacy. However, as Chapter 4 explains, money has a far more complicated role in structuring an individual's opportunity and willingness to get involved in electoral politics. Not only do eligibles need to consider how they are going to fund their campaigns, but they also need to find a way to fund their living expenses. Before people can run for office, they need to consider the impact on their current employment and future prospects. Many lower-income individuals cannot afford to take time off from work to run, while some higher-income individuals don't want to take the pay cut that comes with public office. Moreover, jobs could be harder to come by post-candidacy because of employer reluctance to hire individuals whose partisanship is now publicly known.

Chapter 5 explores other aspects of partisanship and its impact on candidacy. It finds that ideological alignment between a party and an eligible is a key, but overlooked, factor in the decision-making process to become a candidate. Because party discipline is intense in federal and provincial politics, individuals say they must agree with at least three-quarters of a party's platform before they are willing to run for that party. This finding suggests many strong potential candidates for elected office in Canada are staying out of partisan politics because they cannot find an ideological home.

While family, campaign fundraising, and party issues are traditional factors that have long shaped candidacy in Canada, research participants identified several other factors that could become barriers in the future. Chapter 6 investigates the downsides of public scrutiny. Eligibles and candidates alike express reservations about submitting themselves to constant public criticism of their political views and actions as well as a potential loss of privacy, both for themselves and family members. But only LGBTQ eligibles cited public scrutiny as a key reason why they won't run for elected office. They are deeply concerned about the moral regulation of non-traditional gender identities and sexual orientations that often underline scrutiny of public figures.

Chapters 7 and 8 explore the specific roles of the news media and social media in public scrutiny. The news media are a common source of public scrutiny of politicians, yet as Chapter 7 demonstrates, eligibles and candidates are not fearful that journalists will cover them in a sexist, racist, homophobic, or otherwise discriminatory way. They are far more concerned about sensationalist or partisan coverage that distorts public perceptions of their campaigns. Worse still, they worry about receiving no news coverage at all. A public profile is vital to a successful election campaign. News media aside, research participants are far more apprehensive about social media. Chapter 8 identifies the digital dangers awaiting would-be candidates related to social media scandals and online harassment. Young people expressed unease about the possibility that opponents could dig through their social media platforms and other digital sources for incriminating information to discredit their candidacy. Their fear is real. Several candidates in recent federal and provincial elections have resigned or been dismissed by their party because of online comments or embarrassing photographs and videos coming to light. Women also dread the possibility of being targeted by sexist trolls during a campaign. Online harassment of women politicians is a growing international phenomenon that reinforces politics as the domain of men. But so far, it is not discouraging Canadian women from running for elected office for the first time.

All of the stresses involved with electoral politics make health issues an additional factor to consider in the political candidacy process. Chapter 9 examines the role that mental and physical health issues play in the willingness of eligibles to run for elected office and candidates to remain in office. Some research participants expressed doubt that voters would support their candidacies if their depression, anxiety, and other mental health challenges were publicly known. Other individuals discussed the importance of strengthening one's mental and physical health before running for office and maintaining it once in politics.

The concluding chapter reviews the book's main conclusions before offering suggestions on how various political actors can address these drawbacks to candidacy. While eligibles can take some steps to resolve these issues, I argue that it is the responsibility of political parties, nonpartisan organizations, legislatures, and governments to make politics a more hospitable environment for more than just white, heterosexual men. We need elected representatives of varying genders, races/ethnicities, sexualities, ages, socio-economic circumstances, and family situations to help generate ideas to address the diverse needs of Canadians.

Chapter Two

The Intersectional Calculations: Approaches to the Study of Political Candidacy

Uncertainty is the greatest drawback [to political candidacy]. Politics is not just about what happens after you're elected, it's mostly about getting elected and there's lots of hurdles along the way. It requires a tremendous amount of dedication to get past all those hurdles, and even then, you can fail. It's that level of uncertainty in your life that makes it challenging.

– A white man eligible

Introduction

Not all individuals perceive or experience political candidacy in the same way. Gender, race/ethnicity, sexuality, class, age, and political ideology are important markers of difference in politics. Yet scholars often conceal differences among individuals by not taking a complex approach to understanding people's perceptions of politics. They either treat research subjects as a unified category, as in "candidates," or only examine two categories, such as those related to gender (women and men candidates). In the process, they leave intact presumptions of whiteness, affluence, and heterosexuality (Trimble 2009). This limited approach results in a limited understanding of political candidacy. Scholars have a general idea about political ambition (cf. Fox and Lawless 2005) and why women as a group are deterred from running (cf. Lawless and Fox 2010; Thomas 2012), but little is known about why different types of women and men choose not to become candidates (for exceptions, see Harell and Panagos 2013; Johnson, Oppenheimer, and Selin 2012; Shames 2015). This book therefore investigates the following research question: *How do Canadians perceive political candidacy, how do these perceptions vary by social location, and what are the implications for the candidacy process?* To answer this question, I interviewed 101 individuals of diverse social and political backgrounds.

The theoretical framework, methodological choices, and empirical analysis of my research on political candidacy in Canada is informed by feminist principles. Feminist scholarship has made significant contributions to our understanding of politics and the power relations that undergird it. It has accomplished this task by foregrounding women in its analysis, challenging the very understanding of politics and the political order to promote a research program that focuses on the societal interactions that create and sustain gender inequality and, in the process, enhances the intellectual rigor of the discipline of political science. But feminist scholarship has its shortcomings, too. Until recently, feminist research has struggled to incorporate an intersectional analysis that recognizes differences among women. Nor has it interrogated the complexities of men as a group as it has those of women, presuming men to be static and uniform as a social category rather than dynamic and diverse. To address these shortcomings, I drew upon the Black feminist theory of intersectionality in two ways: (1) as a methodological practice to recruit diverse research participants and (2) as an analytical practice to make sense of the insights they provided. Black feminism's theory of intersectionality highlights how gender itself is mediated by other descriptive characteristics such as race/ethnicity, class, and sexuality (Crenshaw 1989, 1991; Hancock 2007; Mohanty 2003), and how the alternative positionings and perspectives stemming from intersecting identities influence politics. This chapter outlines the feminist intersectional methodology used in this book before illustrating the insights that this approach can provide about how different social groups view the drawbacks of political candidacy. Subsequent chapters explore each drawback in more depth.

Feminist Intersectionality

Political scientists can better understand the complexities of political candidacy by embracing a feminist intersectional approach. Feminist intersectionality has its origins in Black feminist thought. Kimberlé Crenshaw (1989, 1991) argues that women are differently positioned in society depending on the interaction of gender and race and that these burdens are not additive but combine in unique ways for each group of women to produce yet another burden. Her theory of intersectionality has since been expanded beyond race to include other types of difference (Hancock 2007). Patricia Hill Collins ([1990] 2009) describes intersectionality as a matrix of domination, wherein different axes of identity intersect with each other and with power structures to form intersecting oppressions and result in unique lived experiences. Yet no one is entirely privileged or entirely oppressed; some aspects of our identity give us privilege in society while other aspects disadvantage us. This book therefore rejects the premise that all women face strong obstacles to candidacy and that all men are privileged political actors who face no barriers at all. Instead, it investigates the possibility that some drawbacks to candidacy will be more consequential for some types of people than for others.

This research is also inspired by Cynthia Enloe's call to be curious. Enloe suggests feminist scholars need to widen their gaze to search for the omissions, absences, and silences that have, up to this point, escaped their attention. She dares scholars to develop a new curiosity about settled "truths" to uncover what was previously hidden:

> Every issue has become an issue only because some people stopped taking it for granted, developed a new curiosity about it, and managed to persuade a lot of us who used to be complacent about it to become newly curious, too – and to start finding answers that made them think afresh about citizens' and governments' responsibilities for those dynamics that they had discovered. (Enloe 2007, 10)

Enloe (2004) says scholars can best accomplish this task by listening to the silences, inspecting the margins, and looking to the bottom rungs that prop up the powerful. She argues that this curiosity needs to be accompanied by openness to being surprised – and confused – by what one finds and a willingness to "let go" when one's pre-existing notions are challenged (Enloe 2000, 1025).

One pre-existing notion that I have attempted to challenge in this book is the assumption that men are a stable analytical and social category, with little or no diversity among men across historical, political, economic, or social contexts (Carrigan Connell, and Lee, 1985). Differences among men, and the ramifications of these differences for politics, are often overlooked in feminist research on political candidacy and political behaviour more broadly. Feminist inattention to inequality among men replicates the tendency of mainstream social science to treat men as universal and women as partial, but with a twist. It generally considers men to be universally privileged and it promotes women's specificities as a positive characteristic, not a negative one, for politics.

Adopting an intersectional lens and a willingness to be curious led me to ask a different set of questions than is typical in feminist research on political candidacy. The first step was to explore potential variations among women. How do different types of women perceive barriers to candidacy? Do these barriers affect all women equally or some types of women more than others? An intersectional analysis enabled me to determine that, regardless of social background, women shared a concern about online harassment of women politicians, but they expected the nature and content of that online abuse to vary according to each woman's set of personal characteristics (see Chapter 8 for more details). The next step was to treat men as gendered, sexed, raced, and classed individuals. How do men perceive barriers to candidacy, and do these perceptions vary by men's social locations? An analysis that rejected men-as-norm revealed that some men change or abandon their political ambitions to meet their family responsibilities. Raising their children is more important to them. The small number of men in this research who put family first meant that this finding could not be further analysed by race/ethnicity or sexuality, but this finding calls for further research to explore potential differences amongst the men who prioritize family over politics.

The third step was to integrate gender, race/ethnicity, and sexuality into a fully realized intersectional analysis. How do Canadians perceive the drawbacks of political candidacy, and do these perceptions vary according to a person's social location? A constant comparison of answers within and across categories led to important insights regarding how members of different social groups view family, money, parties, media, and health as potential challenges to candidacy. Individual chapters explore in depth the nuances of each factor from several perspectives. The final step of the analysis was to explore the implications of the research findings for the candidacy process in Canada. The empirical chapters offer some insights, but the concluding chapter explores this issue more fully.

In addition to contemplating new research questions, feminist scholarship on political candidacy needs to become more methodological diverse and to be upfront about methodological choices. The restricted range of research techniques used in studies on political candidacy limits the kind of data that can be collected and, consequently, renders partial and incomplete any conclusions drawn. One of the dilemmas of conducting feminist intersectional research, though, is finding a methodology that enables scholars to empirically capture its complex effects (Jordan-Zachery 2007; McCall 2005). Many scholars use quantitative methods to study political ambition, or the desire to run for elected office (cf. Lawless and Fox 2010). This statistical approach leads scholars to treat gender, race/ethnicity, sexuality, class, and other personal characteristics as distinct variables, leaving women to be compared to men, Black people to white people, and homosexual individuals to heterosexual individuals. Exploring intersectional differences within each group is performed less often, possibly due to the necessity of using more complicated mathematical models (Scott 2010) and the need to recruit a substantially larger number of survey respondents. Another drawback of quantitative methods is that they limit the possibility of identifying new barriers to candidacy, especially those pertaining to groups historically excluded from politics. Survey respondents must select from a pre-determined list of answers when responding to a question, and these answers are often determined by what previous research had uncovered. If a barrier has not been previously identified, it is not likely to be explored in a survey.

Qualitative techniques such as interviews are more ideally suited to reassessing traditional barriers to candidacy like money and family responsibilities, to identifying new or overlooked ones like social media and health, and to exploring the role of gender, race/ethnicity, sexuality, and other aspects of identity within each barrier. The open-ended nature of interviews gives participants an opportunity to raise new topics, issues, or perspectives that enable a more nuanced understanding of political candidacy (Kvale 2007). The conversational nature of interviews allows research participants to voluntarily identify a barrier as well as explain why that issue is such a concern. This approach proved especially fruitful when it came to establishing public scrutiny as a queer barrier to candidacy (see Chapter 6 for more details).

However, an interview-based study that aims to understand candidacy from a variety of perspectives has the problem of numbers. Understanding why members of social groups choose not to run would ideally be based on more than 300 interviews, but this number of one-on-one conversations is simply not feasible within typical financial and labour restraints. As it stands, 101 interviews far exceed the normal 20 to 40 interviews more common in qualitative political science research. This book therefore lives up to the expectations of feminist intersectionality when it comes to diversity among research participants, but it has limitations in terms of data analysis. While every effort was made to focus on intersecting perspectives on candidacy, additional research is needed to fully understand why some barriers are more challenging for specific social groups. One follow-up to this project could be a quantitative survey that draws upon the findings of this book to craft a questionnaire that not only incorporates a greater range of issues but also explores the extent to which they matter in the candidacy calculations of different types of individuals. Other research could examine a specific social group to understand in greater depth how its members view various barriers.

Research Participants: Recruitment

Understanding why different types of Canadians choose not to run for elected office requires talking to a wide range of people about their perspectives on political candidacy. In total, I interviewed 101 people from varying social, political, and economic backgrounds between 2016 and 2017. The book treats candidate status, gender, race/ethnicity, and sexuality as the main categories for recruitment purposes, but it adds class and age as part of the data analysis.

The first recruitment category was candidacy status. *Eligibles* are people identified as strong candidates for elected office but who had not run for office at the time of the interview (Carbert 2006; Lawless and Fox 2010). Eligibles did not need to be individuals who had privately or publicly expressed any ambition for elected office; they only needed to be recognized by third parties as possessing the necessary experience, qualifications, skills, and/or qualities to be strong candidates. *Candidates* are individuals who ran successfully or unsuccessfully for elected office at the federal, provincial, or municipal levels in Canada. Most candidates had run in elections just prior to when interviews began in 2016, but the small number of publicly out queer candidates, especially racialized ones, meant some candidates sought office several years earlier.

Eligibles and candidates were recruited for several reasons. First, the purpose of recruiting *eligibles* is obvious: only they could reveal why they decided not to run for elected office. Through the semi-structured interviews, eligibles had the freedom to identify the reasons why they had not become candidates. Analysis of their answers enabled this book to reassess traditional barriers to candidacy such as money and family responsibilities as well as identify potentially overlooked barriers such as employment and health issues and new ones such as social media. While the drawbacks to candidacy obviously did not deter them from running, *candidates* could shed light on how these challenges played out during their campaign. Did fundraising turn out to be as difficult as they anticipated? How did they deal with the news media? Candidates could further explain how they handled online harassment or what it was like to be at the centre of a social media scandal. Elected politicians, in particular, could indicate how they dealt with family responsibilities while in office. These insights might help legislatures, political parties, advocacy groups, and future candidates take steps to address these challenges.

Second, a comparison of eligibles' and candidates' perceptions of the drawbacks of candidacy could reveal the factors that have an outsized impact on the decision of eligibles to opt out of electoral politics. For example, are eligibles deterred from running because they give greater weight than candidates to the difficulties of combining family responsibilities with politics? If so, governments need to make legislatures more family friendly while political parties and advocacy groups would need to adjust training programs to ensure would-be candidates developed skills on how to achieve work–life balance during the election and in office. By addressing the barriers identified in this book about how they relate to different social groups, recruiters can help interested but reluctant individuals feel more confident in running for elected office.

Third, a comparison of eligible perceptions and candidate experiences could reveal whether eligibles' concerns about various drawbacks are simply an expression of fear or a realistic assessment of the electoral environment. Should eligibles be worried about fundraising? Is it hard to get the party nomination? Comparing eligible expectations with candidate reality proved fruitful when trying to understand why some queer individuals opted not to run because of public scrutiny. Their concerns about being subjected to greater regulation of their gender and/or sexual identities during a campaign were confirmed by queer candidates, who faced pushback from both family members and voters. Candidates could thus reveal what to expect on the campaign trail, giving eligibles a better sense of what they need to prepare for should they ever run.

Fourth, candidates could also identify potential drawbacks to candidacy that occur *after* one has run for or held elected office. Partisanship was the main drawback: candidates discussed the difficulties they faced in getting employment after a stint in politics. They found it hard to get government contracts or private sector jobs because their partisan leanings were now public knowledge. Candidate insights highlighted the hidden challenges that await individuals who make the decision to run for office. Finally, candidates could provide advice on how future candidates might tackle these challenges. What have they learned from their campaigns that they think the next generation of candidates need to know before embarking on their own bid for elected office? In summary, interviewing both eligibles and candidates offered a more nuanced understanding of the various factors that can make candidacy difficult as well as some ideas on how to address them.

Potential research participants were identified through three approaches: electoral, reputational, and positional (Wiltse 2018). The electoral approach was used for candidates. White, racialized, and Indigenous candidates were drawn from electoral lists for federal, provincial, and municipal office. The federal and provincial lists were obtained from the relevant electoral management agencies, while the municipal lists were obtained from provincial departments, provincial municipal associations, and municipalities directly. LGBTQ candidates were drawn from a dataset maintained by Joanna Everitt and Michael Camp (2014) of every publicly out LGBTQ candidate who had run at the federal and provincial levels since 1979. News reports and the online sites of ProudPolitics, an organization dedicated to increasing queer representation in politics, were also consulted. LGBTQ recruitment focused on individuals who were already publicly out to avoid potential harm to research participants, but the sample includes three closeted individuals recruited by other means who identified themselves as LGBTQ to the researcher.

Eligibles were identified through reputational and positional approaches. The reputational approach involved asking informants such as elected officials, former candidates, and party officials to identify up to three people in their networks who would make good candidates for elected office but had not run at that time (Wiltse 2018). This approach assumed that such informants are well-connected in political circles, knowledgeable about what parties look for in a candidate, and involved in recruiting future candidates (Wiltse 2018). These informants are well placed to not only identify white individuals but also racialized and queer people who would make strong candidates. The positional approach involved recruiting individuals involved in organizations from which candidates typically emerge (Wiltse 2018), in this case LGBTQ and cultural organizations.

Each potential participant was sent a recruitment email. Non-respondents received a follow-up email within a few weeks of initial contact. Individuals who agreed to participate were asked to sign a consent form. Participants were assured that their identities would be kept confidential, unless they checked off a statement on the consent form granting permission to be named. In addition to the consent form, research participants filled out an online survey seeking biographical and political information and participated in an interview.

During the interview, participants were asked about their views on political candidacy. This book focuses on their responses to questions about the drawbacks of running for elected office. Interview questions were adapted from Jennifer L. Lawless and Richard L. Fox's (2010) work on political ambition in the United States (see appendix for the interview protocols for both candidates and eligibles). Interviews ranged from half an hour to two and a half hours, with most taking a little over an hour. Eighteen interviews were carried out in person and the rest were done by telephone. Only one interview was not recorded with a digital audio recorder, at the request of the participant. All participants received a transcript of their interview and survey, and any requested amendments made. Following Erin Tolley's (2016) example in her research on racialized politicians, I have chosen to extensively quote research participants in this book not only to illustrate analytical points but also to emphasize the voices of marginalized individuals in political research. Feminist research centres the narratives and lived experiences of the historically excluded to ensure scholarship reflects the full complexity of social and political life (Harding 1998).

Because the opportunity to get involved in politics can vary based on a person's social location, participants were also recruited according to gender, race/ethnicity, and sexuality. The complexity of this approach necessitated the use of quota sampling (Teddlie and Yu 2007), which selects participants who display particular combinations of characteristics. The aim was to recruit an equal number of eligibles and candidates overall, as well as individuals by gender, race/ethnicity, and sexuality. For candidates, an even number of individuals who ran municipally, provincially, or federally were targeted. Research participants at different stages of the lifecycle, from diverse occupational backgrounds, and located across the country were also sought, though no quotas were set. The target for each quota cell was six individuals, ensuring enough people were interviewed within each group to allow themes to emerge, but not so many as to make the interview project unmanageable.

Figure 2.1 shows that the quota target of six individuals was not achieved in some of the racialized categories. These results are because of the small number of racialized individuals who had run in recent federal, provincial, and municipal elections at the time of data collection and agreed to be interviewed. Recruiting racialized men eligibles also proved challenging. Conversely, the quota target was exceeded in several categories, most notably for racialized heterosexual women among both candidates and eligibles. One reason is because of the assistance of a City of Edmonton program that encourages women to run for municipal office, called Opening the Potential. Several attendees responded to a general call about this research project put out by the program coordinator, and I opted to interview them to gain insight into the strengths and weaknesses of this candidate program. These individuals also tended to be racialized and/or queer, hard-to-recruit groups for eligibles. Despite these issues, conscious recruitment efforts resulted in a sample of research participants who were incredibly diverse in terms of gender, race/ethnicity, and sexuality.

Figure 2.1. Distribution of research participants across quota sampling cells

Research Participants: Characteristics

An intersectional approach to recruitment resulted in a group of participants who are unusually diverse for research on political candidacy. Of the 101 individuals, 51 identified as women, 46 as men, and four as non-binary or genderqueer. As for the other analytical categories, 50 individuals were eligibles and 51 were candidates, 48 were racialized individuals and 53 were white, and 50 were queer and 51 were heterosexual. Participants ranged in age from 21 to 68, with the average age around 41. One-third of participants (33.7 per cent) were single at the time of the interview, while 37.6 per cent were married and 15.8 per cent were in a common-law relationship. The remaining 12.9 per cent were separated, divorced, widowed, or in a non-traditional relationship (such as polyamorous). Less than half of the individuals (46.5 per cent) had children. Almost half (48.5 per cent) of the participants identified with a religious faith. In terms of religiosity, 26.7 per cent of participants were somewhat religious, 28.7 per cent considered themselves to be spiritual but not a member of an organized religion, and 6.9 per cent reported to be very religious. Another 36.6 per cent said they were not a religious person, while 1 per cent did not offer any answer.

Most participants had some kind of post-secondary education, with 40.6 per cent holding a bachelor's degree, 35.6 per cent a masters or professional degree, 9.9 per cent a college diploma, and 5.9 per cent a PhD. Only 5.9 per cent listed a high school diploma as their highest level of education. Gross household income ranged widely among participants, but most participants listed it as greater than $40,000 a year, with 15.8 per cent saying it was greater than $180,000 a year. Only 6.9 per cent listed it as less than $20,000 a year. While research participants came from all 10 provinces and two of the three territories, the largest number came from the populous provinces of Alberta (27.7 per cent) and Ontario (24.8 per cent). Three-quarters (78.2 per cent) of the individuals lived in a city, 8.9 per cent in a town, 7.9 per cent in a suburb, and 4 per cent in a rural area, while 1 per cent listed some other kind of community.

The pre-interview survey also asked research participants about their political and volunteer backgrounds. Almost three-quarters (73.3 per cent) of participants had been a member of a federal political party, with 22.8 per cent affiliated with the NDP, 19.8 per cent with the Liberals, 15.8 per cent with the Conservatives, and 3 per cent with the Greens. Another 5.9 per cent indicated that they had been members of several different parties over their lifetimes, while 31.7 per cent had either never been a member of a federal party or declined to give their partisan details. One-quarter of participants (23.8 per cent) had held an appointed or elected position within a federal party at one point. Participants were also heavily involved at the provincial level: three-quarters (75.2 per cent) had been a member of a provincial party. One-quarter (24.8 per cent) had been a member of a provincial Liberal party, 23.8 per cent with the provincial NDP, and 9.9 per cent with a Conservative party, while another 1 per cent had been a member of the right-wing Saskatchewan Party. About one in ten (9.9 per cent) had been members of different provincial parties over their lives. A further one-third (30.7 per cent) were either not members of a provincial party or declined to provide details. Participants were slightly more involved in executive duties, with 26.7 per cent having held an appointed or elected position with a provincial party. The general absence of political parties in territorial politics (Nunavut and Northwest Territories) and in most municipalities in Canada is a major reason why far fewer research participants were involved in partisan politics at these levels. Only 2 per cent of participants had been a member of a territorial party, while 5.9 per cent had held a membership in a municipal party. Few individuals had held appointed or elected party positions at the municipal level and none at the territorial level.

Aside from partisan politics, research participants were active volunteers in their communities. A strong majority (83.2 per cent) indicated they had been involved with professional organizations, community groups, and charities, with service at an overall mean of 14.4 years. Figure 2.2 reveals the diversity of participants' volunteer interests. Approximately one-third were involved with social welfare groups (39.6 per cent), government organizations (34.7 per cent), and educational or school groups (29.7 per cent). Women's, ethnic, and religious organizations were popular but not men's groups. One-fifth of participants (21.8 per cent) also volunteered with other types of groups. This level of volunteerism is not surprising considering it demonstrates a candidate's commitment to the community and its voters.

A Word About Language

Interviewing a cross-section of Canadians provides rich insight into the challenges associated with political candidacy in the early twenty-first century. But it also necessitates a thoughtful use of language. Research participants include non-binary, racialized, and queer individuals who use a variety of terms to describe their social identities. When known, each person's preferred language is respected when referring to them

Figure 2.2. Percentage of research participants who volunteered with different types of professional, community, and charity groups

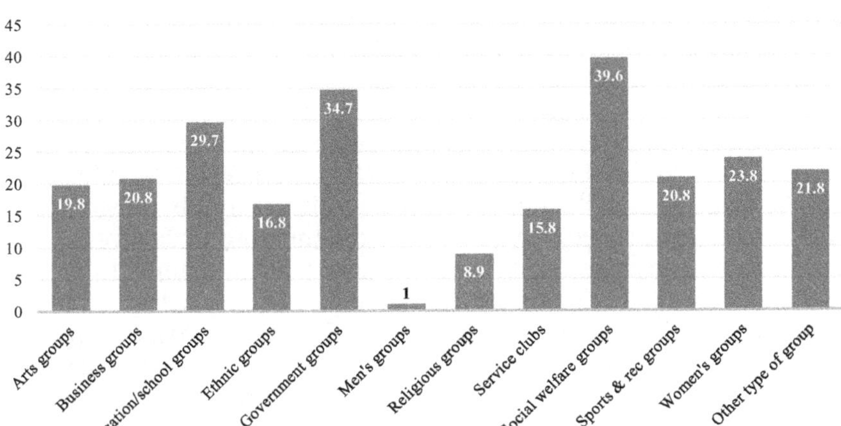

individually, including their choice of pronouns. The pronouns "they" and "them" are used in the plural (to refer to several individuals) and the singular (either in relation to a non-binary individual or when speaking in the generic or about a hypothetical person). Transgender individuals who agreed to be publicly named are identified using their chosen name rather than their birth name (or dead name). Transgender individuals are also included in the gender category with which they identify (i.e., transgender women are in the woman category). For the purposes of this book, the term "queer" is used when referring to research participants who identify as sexual minorities. The term "LGBTQ" is used when referring to both sexual and gender minorities in the data analysis, such as in the chapter on the drawbacks of public scrutiny. LGBTQ is also used when noting previous research on and organizations advocating for both sexual and gender minorities. Capitalization preferences have also been followed. For example, the B in Black has been capitalized in accordance with the wishes of Black Canadians.

These preferences aside, umbrella terms are used for the main analytical categories. The gender category comprises women, men, and non-binary/genderqueer individuals. Transgender individuals have been placed in their chosen gender category. Queer is used to refer to individuals who have identified themselves as sexual minorities, such as gay, lesbian, bisexual, and polyamorous. The term "racialized" is used to refer to all individuals of a non-Caucasian background. Scholarly research has used different terms over the years to describe this group, including visible minorities, but these terms are contested. An easy approach would be to use "non-white," but this term centres whiteness, linguistically annihilating the uniqueness of those individuals who are not white. While also contested, I have opted for the term "racialized" to reflect the social construction of racial/ethnic identities and to acknowledge the power relations inherent in this construction. Ideally, Indigenous people would comprise their own category as they do not see themselves as an ethnic minority. But the limited number of Indigenous participants necessitated putting them in the racialized category for the purposes of analysis. In other words, not enough Indigenous individuals were interviewed to be able to draw conclusions about candidacy specific to this group. Future research should investigate the particular challenges that Indigenous people face when running for elected office, including for Indigenous organizations like the Assembly of First Nations.

Finally, the book refers to social media companies by their original names to recognize and preserve how the research participants understood these communication tools at the time of the interviews. That means the microblogging site X continues to be referred to as Twitter despite its rebranding in July 2023.

Overview of Main Drawbacks to Candidacy

Research participants identified a wide range of drawbacks to running for elected office in Canada. Figure 2.3 presents the descriptive statistics. Because this study is qualitative in nature, percentages in tables and figures are only used to illustrate proportion rather than to explore statistically significant differences among groups. As the literature predicted, the number one drawback to political candidacy was money. Almost one-third (29.7 per cent) of participants expressed doubts about being able to fund a campaign, especially at the federal and provincial levels. But money concerns did not end there. Employer expectations meant some individuals would have to take an unpaid leave of absence or even quit their jobs to run for elected office, a move that many people simply couldn't afford. For their part, high-income individuals were reticent about running because of the pay cut that would come with winning the seat. Financial challenges can continue after a person leaves politics. Some ex-candidates had difficulty finding work after an election because their partisanship was now known, and potential

Figure 2.3. Percentage of research participants who identified a specific drawback as a (potential) reason not to run for elected office, by candidacy status

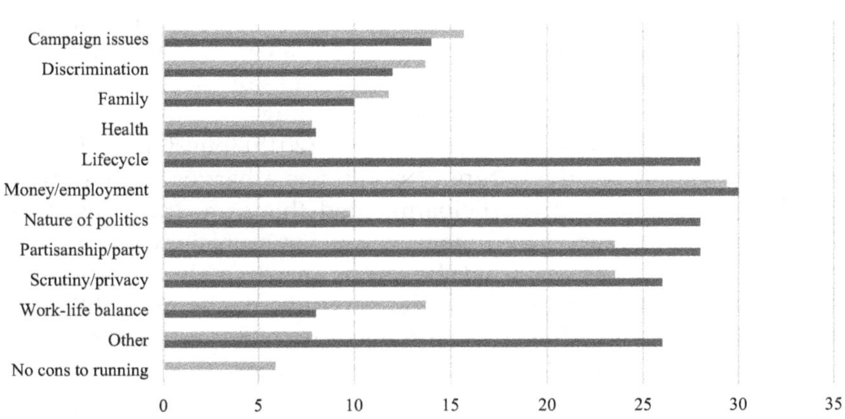

employers wanted to avoid partisan politics. Ex-politicians faced similar challenges, especially if their partisan affiliation differed from the general political bent of their hometown.

Party politics and partisanship were the second most important drawback. One-quarter (25.7 per cent) of research participants identified various aspects of Canada's strong party system as barriers to candidacy. Several individuals indicated that their values didn't align enough with any of the major political parties to feel comfortable submitting themselves to the intense party discipline that is a feature of Canadian politics. Others felt they needed to become (more) involved with a political party, especially its local riding association, to be competitive in any race for a party nomination. Other individuals simply didn't like the intense partisanship of federal and provincial politics. They saw non-partisan municipal politics as more welcoming.

Following close behind financial and party drawbacks was public scrutiny. Almost one-quarter (24.8 per cent) of participants expressed grave doubts about subjecting themselves to the intense public criticism that is directed at politicians today, especially on social media. Participants accept that media scrutiny is a necessary part of the democratic system, but they were dismayed by the online vitriol that politicians must deal with. Women participants were especially alert to the misogynistic nature of social media attacks. Still, participants of all backgrounds were concerned about the potential loss of privacy. Politicians are constantly in the public spotlight. Some individuals didn't want their mistakes or misdeeds becoming fodder for public discussion. Of greater concern was that opponents would dig through social media accounts to find damaging comments or compromising photographs that could be used to discredit them during a campaign. Candidates who had experienced such social media scandals described the experience as emotionally and professional devastating.

As Jennifer L. Lawless and Richard L. Fox (2015) found in the United States, Canadians see the nature of politics as a barrier to candidacy. Overall, 18.8 per cent of participants cited this as a drawback. One woman was encouraged by others to run for municipal politics but refused to do so because of what she saw as an extremely dysfunctional local council. Other individuals don't like the focus on politicking rather than policy. Of almost equal concern was lifecycle: 17.8 per cent of individuals weren't at a place in their life where they felt ready to run. They wanted to finish their education, establish their careers, get married, or start a family before taking on electoral politics. This explanation was common among young participants. Aside from these factors, participants identified other drawbacks such as specific health and legal issues, insufficient political knowledge, self-doubt, fear of losing, unsure of potential contribution to governance, and greater potential impact on society outside of politics. Because a limited number of individuals cited each reason, these answers were aggregated into the Other category for the purpose of producing descriptive statistics.

Overview of Intersectional Findings

An intersectional analysis found that candidacy status and social characteristics can be an important marker of difference in how research participants viewed the drawbacks to candidacy. Figures 2.4 to 2.7 reveals that money and employment, partisanship and political parties, and public scrutiny were not major concerns for all types of eligibles. White women and white men were more likely than their racialized counterparts to see money and employment as a barrier to candidacy, and white women and racialized men cited party/partisanship and public scrutiny more often than did white men and racialized women. Meanwhile, queer women and men were more likely than heterosexual women and men to cite public scrutiny and party/partisanship as major drawbacks to candidacy. Heterosexual women and queer individuals more often saw money and employment issues as barriers compared to their respective counterparts.

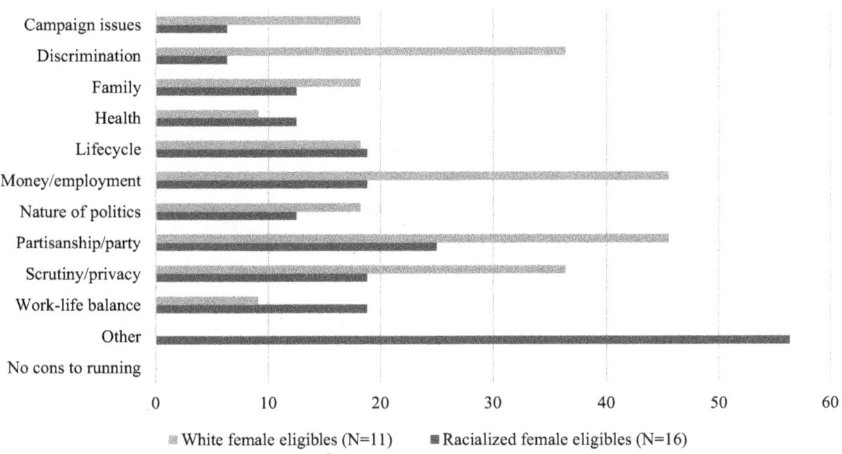

Figure 2.4. Percentage of women eligibles who identified a specific drawback as a (potential) reason not to run for elected office, by race/ethnicity

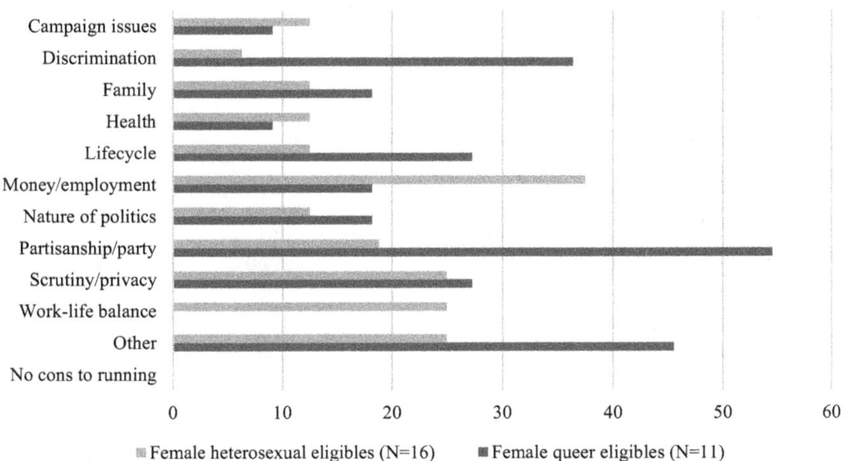

Figure 2.5. Percentage of women eligibles who identified a specific drawback as a (potential) reason not to run for elected office, by sexuality

Figure 2.6. Percentage of men eligibles who identified a specific drawback as a (potential) reason not to run for elected office, by race/ethnicity

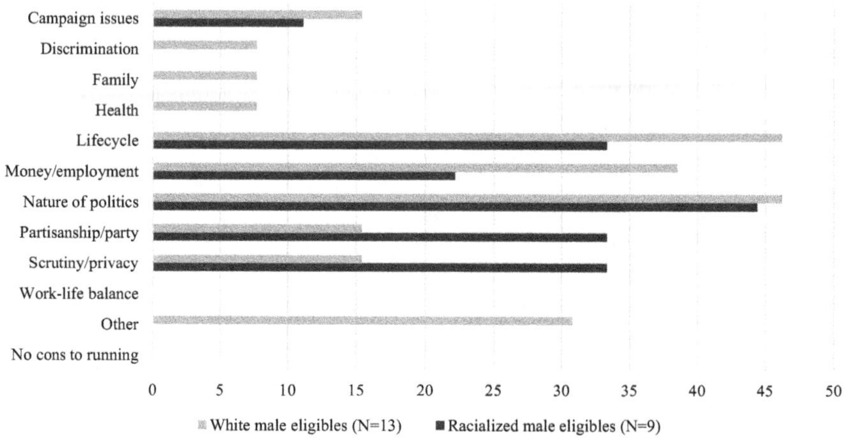

Figure 2.7. Percentage of men eligibles who identified a specific drawback as a (potential) reason not to run for elected office, by sexuality

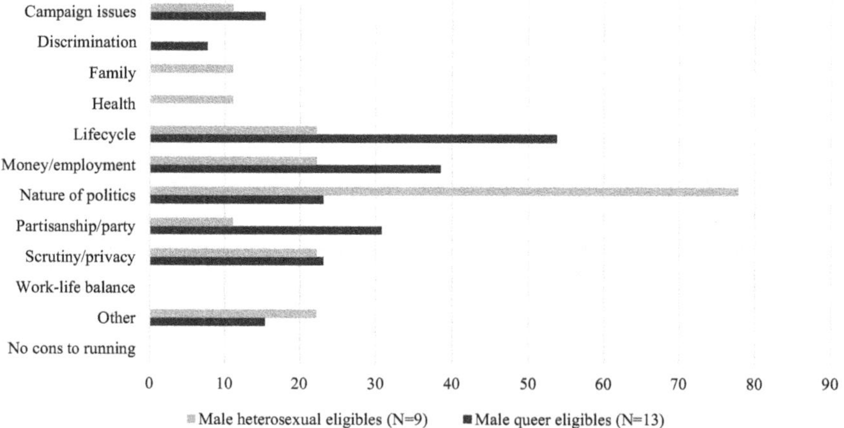

As for lifecycle, white and racialized men eligibles said they would give much greater weight than did their women counterparts to where they were at in their lives as well as the nature of politics when it came to deciding whether or not to run for elected office. Lifecycle was especially important to queer men and somewhat important to queer women, but it mattered less for heterosexual women and men. Regardless of race/ethnicity and sexuality, women eligibles agreed that work–life balance was important to consider before deciding to run, but it did not register as an issue at all for any of the men eligibles. Surprisingly, discrimination was only a major concern for white women eligibles. It was less of an issue for racialized women and white men, and none at all for racialized men. Sexuality followed a more predictable pattern: queer women and men were more likely to cite discrimination as an important drawback to candidacy than their heterosexual counterparts, but queer women cited this factor more often than did queer men. Few heterosexual women said so compared to no heterosexual men.

Candidates expressed sharper differences in opinion by race/ethnicity and sexuality, as Figures 2.8 to 2.11 show. Racialized women and men candidates were more likely than their white counterparts to say money and employment, partisanship and party, and public scrutiny concerns loomed large in their minds as they considered whether or not to run for elected office. Queer women candidates were more concerned about money and employment than were heterosexual women candidates, but both groups were more likely to cite these issues as a drawback than did queer or heterosexual men, who appeared to give it equal weight. Interestingly, heterosexual and queer women gave more thought to party and partisanship issues than did heterosexual men, while queer men gave them none at all. Public scrutiny was the single most important issue for queer men candidates and a major one for heterosexual women and queer women, but a non-issue for heterosexual men.

One of the surprising findings was the low ranking of family considerations. Only one in 10 participants (10.9 per cent) cited family responsibilities as a drawback to running for elected office. The received wisdom in scholarly research is that family is a major barrier to women's participation in electoral politics. But while women research participants (13.7 per cent) were more likely than men research participants (6.5 per cent) to identify family as an overall drawback, more women selected finances, partisanship, and scrutiny as major factors for them – and this was the case regardless of women's candidacy status and social characteristics. Women who want to run for elected office apparently find a way to deal with childcare and household duties (Fox and Lawless 2014).

Figure 2.8. Percentage of women candidates who identified a specific drawback as a (potential) reason not to run for elected office, by race/ethnicity

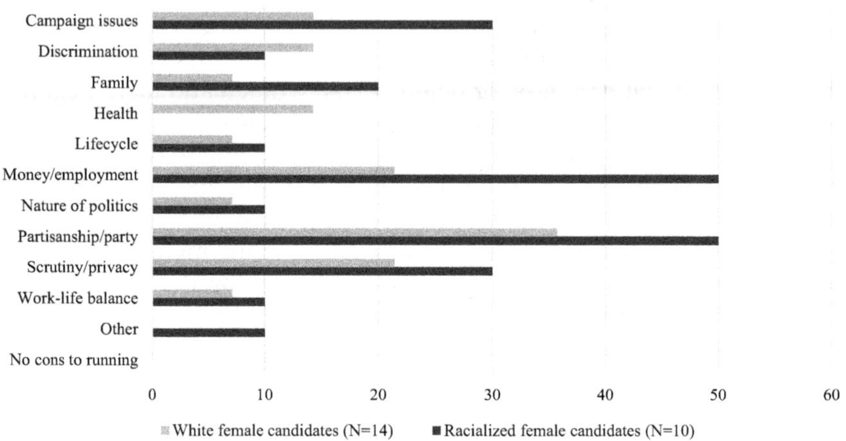

Figure 2.9. Percentage of women candidates who identified a specific drawback as a (potential) reason not to run for elected office, by sexuality

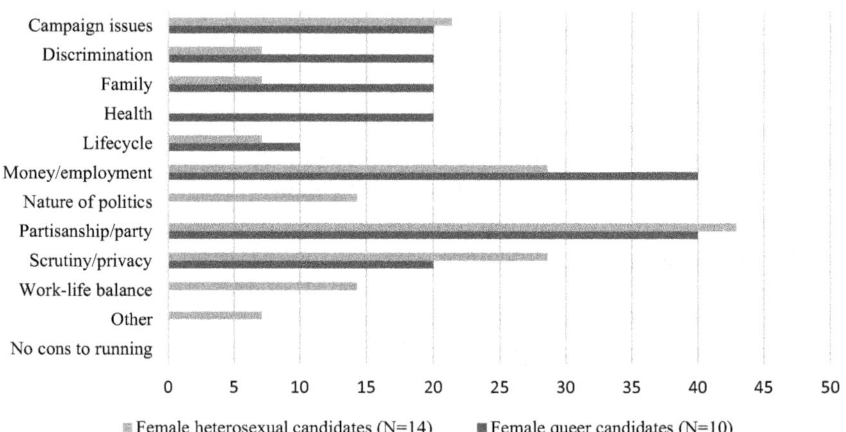

Figure 2.10. Percentage of men candidates who identified a specific drawback as a (potential) reason not to run for elected office, by race/ethnicity

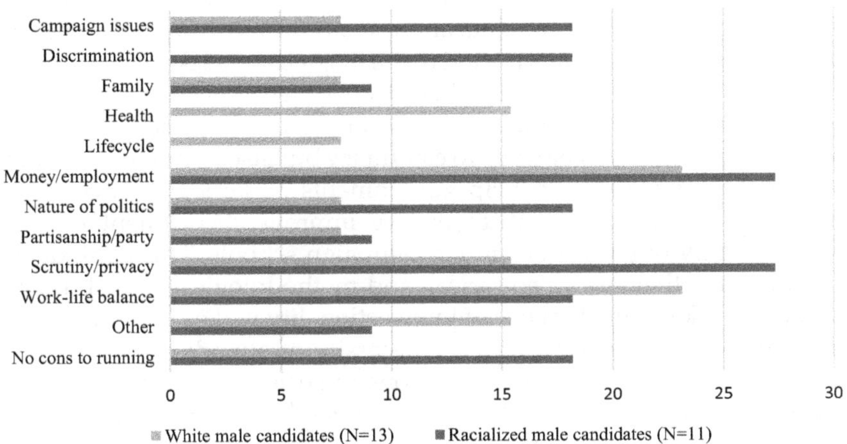

Figure 2.11. Percentage of men candidates who identified a specific drawback as a (potential) reason not to run for elected office, by sexuality

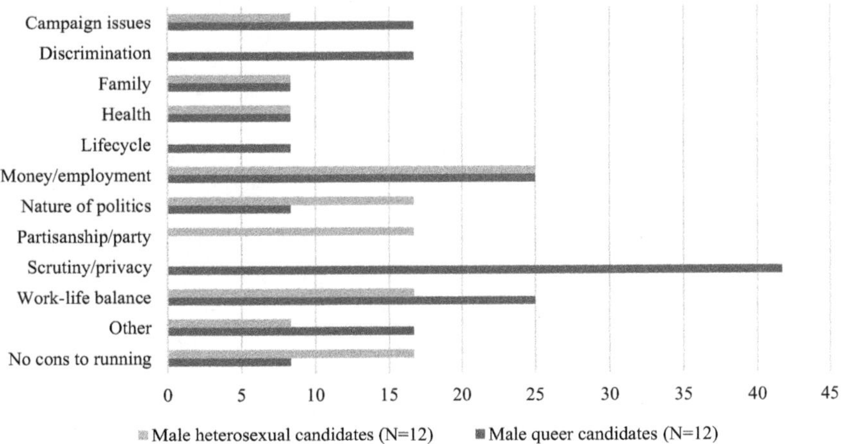

Conclusion

This chapter outlines the book's feminist intersectional approach to participant recruitment and data analysis as well as presents the overall and intersectional findings related to the major drawbacks of candidacy. By deliberately recruiting individuals from diverse social, political, and economic backgrounds, this book not only provides a deeper understanding of traditional barriers to candidacy but also identifies new and overlooked ones that can help governments make legislatures more inclusive workplaces, political parties improve recruitment efforts, and advocacy organizations refine campaign schools. This book demonstrates the theoretical, empirical, and methodological contributions that the Black feminist theory of intersectionality makes to political science research. It demonstrates the necessity of attending to the ways in which asymmetrical power relations in society have material consequences for how individuals are positioned in the political sphere. It thus challenges political scientists to go beyond the generic citizen to explore how Canadians of differing genders, races/ethnicities, and sexualities perceive political candidacy and what that means for political representation and the quality of our democratic system. While this chapter provided a feminist intersectional overview of the main drawbacks to candidacy, subsequent chapters explore many of these factors in greater depth. Let's look at family first.

Chapter Three

The Family Calculation: Burdens of Family Responsibilities and Family-Unfriendly Politics

Elected office is no different than, you know, somebody who's working two jobs in order to get by or somebody who is in a high-stakes position on Bay Street or something. Everybody has their own lives and their own things that are pulling away from certain other aspects of it, right. So everybody has to balance potential things in their life and elected office is no different.

– Bradley Metlin, a white gay man eligible

Introduction

Family is the first factor that comes up in conversation when people offer their thoughts about the reasons why more women don't run for elected office in Canada. Whether I am at a hair salon, doctor's office, or family gathering, people immediately point to women's caregiving duties as the primary reason why women remain under-represented in legislative bodies. Their response is a common one when I reveal that my job involves studying why different types of people choose not to become political candidates. Their statements stem from traditional assumptions that women are primarily responsible for childrearing. Individuals are socialized from an early age to societal gender norms, including stereotypical beliefs about the appropriate roles for women and men.

In Canada, gender stereotypes proclaim men to be aggressive, competitive, ambitious, self-reliant, rational, intelligent, emotionally detached, courageous, independent, and stoic (Coleman 1997; Lafrance 2012; Mara 2012; Nicholas 2012; Rutherdale 2012; Strong-Boag 1991; Whitworth 2005). As fathers, they are called upon to be providers and protectors. Men are thus presumed to be natural leaders. No such assumption exists for women. Women are expected to be gentle, kind, caring, co-operative, subordinate, obedient, meek, mild, and responsive to the needs of others (Barman 2008; Comacchio 1997; Greig 2012; Jubas and Jubas 2006; Lafrance 2012; Mara 2012; Neering 2005; Strong-Boag 1991). A strong belief that women are "naturally" suited to be wives and mothers implies that they are expected to be the primary caregivers for children and to prioritize these roles over any others, including political ones. Many of the traditional gender stereotypes for women are in direct contrast to those of men. Women are assumed to be procreative not productive, dependent not independent, fragile not strong, passive not assertive, and emotional not rational (Lafrance 2012; Loch-Drake 2008; Mara 2012; Wamsley 2006).

Traditional gender stereotypes work to perpetuate a sexual division of labour that has historically slotted women and men into different fields of activity: men in the so-called public realm of politics, business, military, and professional sports and women in the so-called private domain of housework and childrearing. Social changes in recent decades have rendered the border between these public and private spheres more porous, especially for women, but this pattern still holds.

Scholars have long examined the potential role of family responsibilities in limiting women's political participation (Bird 2003; Bristowe 1980; Brodie 1985; Campbell and Childs 2014, 2017; Carroll and Sanbonmatsu 2013a; Fox and Lawless 2014; Hills 1983; Joshi and Goehrung 2021; Lee 1976; O'Neill and Gidengil 2017; Sapiro 1982; Sevä and Öun 2019; Trimble 1995). Descriptive research on the personal circumstances of politicians is limited in Canada and elsewhere, but the general finding is that women politicians are less likely than men politicians to be married, parents, and parents of young children (Bird 2003; Campbell and Childs 2014, 2017). The implication is that married women with young children are less inclined to become politicians. Women without caring duties are in a better position to make politics work. No spouse, no (young) kids, no problems!

Yet childcare is not the only family-related reason why women might opt not to get involved in politics. Research suggests romantic partners and family members can play an outsized role in women's political ambitions. In the 1970s, a majority of American women activists with the Republican and Democratic parties reported having spousal support for their political activities compared to less than half of the men activists (Sapiro 1982). In other words, men were far more willing than women to pursue their political ambitions without family support, a likely result of societal expectations that men are, and should be, autonomous and independent and that their wives and children should accept their ambitions. "Political ambition is costly to both men and women in terms of their family commitments, but by the end it appears that most of the people who can or will pay the price are men" (Sapiro 1982, 274). Decades later, not much had changed. Surveying American mayors, Susan J. Carroll and Kira Sanbonmatsu (2013a) found that spouses, friends, and coworkers played a greater role than party officials and organizations in encouraging women to seek elected office. Women and men were equally discouraged by spouses from running for municipal office but women were far more likely than men to "face resistance from other family members" (Carroll and Sanbonmatsu 2013a, 127). Probing further, the authors found that women mayors rated spousal support and having older children as key to the decision to run for elected office. These findings "suggest that even at the local level where officials do not have to relocate or live apart from their families as state and federal office holders sometimes do, the responsibilities of parenting might often deter women than men from seeking office – at least until their children are older and their parenting responsibilities have diminished" (Carroll and Sanbonmatsu 2013a, 129).

Women's political ambitions are assumed to be affected by family responsibilities in at least four ways. First, childless women might not run because they expect to one day have a family that will need their full attention (Bristowe 1980). Second, women with young children are expected to prioritize childrearing, leaving them without much time to volunteer or pursue high-octane careers that are common pipelines into politics. Third, women with older children can finally get involved in politics but "they will have acquired few of the politically-useful and organisationally-relevant skills which their male contemporaries will have learned (often instinctively and unconsciously) during their working experience" (Bristowe 1980, 86). Moreover, they won't have developed the networks and resources through volunteering that are vital to a future candidacy. Fourth, women who delay entry into elected office will be older, giving them less time to acquire the necessary expertise, experience, and associational links once in politics to move up the political ladder and become a cabinet minister, party leader, or government leader.

Until recently, empirical research confirmed these assumptions: women's traditional responsibility for childrearing led many women to reject, or delay, a career in politics despite having the qualifications necessary to be viewed as credible candidates. But newer studies have discovered that women in Western countries are finding ways to address their childcare needs in ways that allow them to pursue elected office. Surveying Americans in professions that traditionally lead to political candidacy such as law, business, education, and activism,

Richard L. Fox and Jennifer Lawless (2014) found that women were no more likely than men to consider family constraints when pondering a bid for elected office. What mattered more than gender was parental and marital status. Married individuals and parents were more likely than their respective counterparts to cite family-related issues as deterrents to candidacy. A Canadian study also found that family responsibilities do not limit women's political or civic participation, but they can influence the type of activities in which women engage (O'Neill and Gidengil 2017). These findings raise questions about the degree to which family responsibilities depress women's political ambition today. This chapter explores how various types of women and men view family responsibilities as a potential barrier to candidacy.

Personal Circumstances of Research Participants

Despite the role of family responsibilities in political ambition, scholars have not systematically mapped the parental or marital status of different types of women and men politicians at the federal, provincial, or municipal levels in Canada. International research is equally limited. Scholars have focused on the role of family in political self-presentations (Thomas and Lambert 2017; Wagner 2019), media depictions (Auer et al. 2022; Trimble et al. 2013) and voter evaluations (Stalsburg 2010; Stalsburg and Kleinberg 2016). It is therefore difficult to know the percentage of candidates who are married, have kids, and have young kids, as well as how marital and parental status differ by gender, race/ethnicity, sexuality, and level of government. For example, are married women with young children more likely to run for municipal office than for provincial or federal office? We *assume* municipal politics is more amenable to women with families, but we really don't know. We lack data. Knowing the demographics of individuals seeking elected office would give us a starting point from which to identify which social groups might be more, or less, affected by parental responsibilities.

This chapter, unfortunately, cannot provide that descriptive overview. Interviewing 101 individuals offers rich insights into family and politics, but a much larger and more statistically representative sample of Canadians is required to properly describe the personal circumstances of would-be candidates at the federal, provincial, and municipal levels. This chapter instead details the personal circumstances of the individuals involved in this research project. At the time of their respective interviews, more than half of research participants were either married (37.6 per cent) or in a common-law relationship (15.8 per cent), while one-third (33.7 per cent) were single. Another 5 per cent were divorced, 4 per cent were separated, and 1 per cent were widowed, with 3 per cent indicating "other" such as being involved in polyamorous relationships. Less than half (46.5 per cent) of research participants had children, and of those who did, 19.1 per cent had a child under the age of six living at home, while 55.3 per cent had no children living with them. The rest did not indicate either way. Of those who reported not having any children, a roughly equal number said they had plans (33.3 per cent), might have plans (31.5 per cent), or had no plans (31.5 per cent) to start a family. The remaining 3.7 per cent didn't say one way or the other.

Order of government appeared to matter when it came to the personal circumstances of individuals who took formal steps to become candidates at the federal, provincial, and municipal levels. Specifically, the percentage of candidates who were married and had children increased as the level of government changed from federal to provincial to municipal. Let us look at marital status first. Of those participants who took the step of seeking a party nomination to run for federal office, 33.3 per cent were in a common law relationship, 33.3 per cent were single, 13.3 per cent were married, and 6.7 per cent were divorced. Provincial aspirants were more likely to be married (46.2 per cent) or single (30.8 per cent) than divorced (11.5 per cent) or common-law (7.7 per cent). Because the non-partisan nature of municipal politics in most parts of Canada means those individuals interested in municipal office don't need to secure a party nomination before running, no figures for municipal aspirants are available. We can, however, incorporate the municipal level when looking specifically at individuals who did run for office. Almost half of federal candidates (41.2 per cent) were single compared to almost one-third of provincial candidates (31.6 per cent) and one-fifth of municipal candidates (20.8 per cent). In contrast, one-quarter (23.5 per cent) of federal candidates were married compared to almost half of provincial candidates (42.1 per cent) and municipal candidates (45.8 per cent). A similar pattern repeats itself when we look at offspring. Of those participants who took the step of seeking a party nomination to run for elected office, almost half (46.7 per cent) of federal aspirants reported having children compared to 61.5 per cent of provincial aspirants. Differences weren't as drastic when examining individuals who actually ran for elected office. More than half (52.9 per cent) of federal candidates had children compared to three-fifths of provincial candidates (57.9 per cent) and municipal candidates (58.3 per cent).

Figure 3.1 is a visual representation of the marital and parental status of different types of research participants. Candidates (58.8 per cent)

Figure 3.1. Percentage of research participants who are married or in a common-law relationship and who have children by gender, race/ethnicity, sexuality, and candidate status

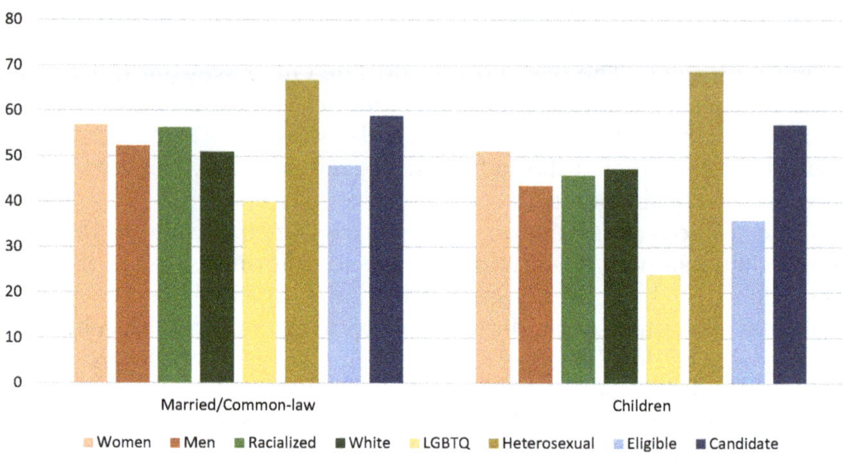

were not only more likely than eligibles (48 per cent) to be either married or in a common-law relationship but also to have children (56.9 per cent to 36 per cent). This is a consequence of efforts to recruit research participants at various stages of life that proved more successful for eligibles than candidates. People in their 20s made up a larger share of eligibles (32 per cent) than candidates (13.7 per cent), but the disparity between the two groups was limited when it came to folks in their 30s or 40s. As for gender, women (56.9 per cent) were only slightly more likely than men (52.2 per cent) to be married or in a common-law relationship, but the spread was greater when it came to children (51 per cent to 43.5 per cent). Non-binary individuals tended to be single and childless. Racialized individuals (56.3 per cent) were slightly more likely than white folks (50.9 per cent) to be married or common-law while the opposite was true when it came to parenthood (45.8 per cent to 47.2 per cent). The most notable difference among social groups related to sexuality: heterosexual individuals were far more likely to be married or in a common-law relationship (66.7 per cent) and to have children (68.6 per cent) than their queer counterparts (40 per cent, 24 per cent). Queer research participants tended to be single and childless. The latter finding suggests marital and parental status do not pose as strong an obstacle to candidacy for queer individuals as it might for heterosexuals. Overall, though, this descriptive picture of research participants' personal circumstances suggests most social groups need to consider the potential impact of political candidacy on their family relationships, a topic to which we now turn.

Family as a Barrier to Candidacy

Each research participant was asked if they thought elected office was compatible with family responsibilities. The question was tailored to indicate the level of government – federal, provincial, or municipal – in which the person was most interested to help them answer the question. For example, did the person believe *federal* office was compatible with family responsibilities? Answers to this question thus depended not only upon the person's personal circumstances but also level of government. I also discovered that the research participants' understanding of family was more expansive than my own. When drafting the interview schedule, I assumed that people would interpret the family questions to mean children, but I quickly learned that they included their parents, siblings, cousins, and extended family members in their calculations and that this was true whether or not they had children. While I do examine differences between parents and non-parents, I also include other family considerations in the analysis. One further caveat: the following results cannot be generalized to the Canadian population as a whole because research participants were not randomly recruited for this project. They were selected to fit a pre-determined set of characteristics. Consequently, the results only reflect the characteristics and views of the 101 participants.

Before exploring variations amongst participants, a brief review of their main responses is in order. Table 3.1 outlines how different categories of individuals answered the question. Overall, research participants were split between viewing family and politics as compatible (23.8 per cent), incompatible (20.8 per cent), or having no clear opinion on the matter (26.7 per cent). Smaller numbers felt the ability to combine the two would be tough (7.9 per cent), depended upon various factors (5.9 per cent), or both possible and impossible (4 per cent). One in ten individuals (10.9 per cent) offered another answer, such as not sure, it would be challenging, or an issue not applicable to their circumstances.

Analysing responses by category, Table 3.1 shows that twice as many candidates (31.4 per cent) as eligibles (16 per cent) felt a work–life balance could be achieved in politics. This result is hardly surprising because the candidates had already made the decision to pursue

Table 3.1. Responses to question about whether elected office is compatible with family responsibilities, by candidate status and personal characteristics.

	No	Yes	Yes/No	Depends	Hard/Tough	Other	No (clear) answer
Overall	21 (20.8%)	24 (23.8%)	4 (4%)	6 (5.9%)	8 (7.9%)	11 (10.9%)	27 (26.7%)
Candidacy status							
Candidate	9 (17.6%)	16 (31.4%)	4 (7.8%)	3 (5.9%)	5 (9.8%)	5 (9.8%)	9 (17.6%)
Eligible	12 (24%)	8 (16%)	0 (0%)	3 (6%)	3 (6%)	6 (12%)	18 (36%)
Gender identity							
Women	18 (35.3%)	10 (19.6%)	2 (3.9%)	3 (5.9%)	5 (9.8%)	2 (3.9%)	11 (21.6%)
Men	2 (4.3%)	12 (26.1%)	1 (2.2%)	3 (6.5%)	3 (6.5%)	9 (19.6%)	16 (34.8%)
Neither group	1 (25%)	2 (50%)	1 (25%)	0 (0%)	0 (0%)	0 (0%)	0 (0%)
Ethnic identity							
White	8 (15.1%)	14 (26.4%)	2 (3.8%)	5 (9.4%)	4 (7.5%)	6 (11.3%)	14 (26.4%)
Racialized	13 (27.1%)	10 (20.8%)	2 (4.2%)	1 (2.1%)	4 (8.3%)	5 (10.4%)	13 (27.1%)
Sexuality							
Heterosexual	12 (23.5%)	9 (17.6%)	3 (5.9%)	3 (5.9%)	2 (3.9%)	5 (9.8%)	17 (33.3%)
Queer	9 (18%)	15 (30%)	1 (2%)	3 (6%)	6 (12%)	6 (12%)	10 (20%)
Marital status							
Married or in common-law relationship	12 (21.8%)	9 (16.4%)	3 (5.5%)	4 (7.3%)	5 (9.1%)	7 (12.7%)	15 (27.3%)
Not married or common-law	8 (18.2%)	15 (34.1%)	1 (2.3%)	2 (4.5%)	3 (6.8%)	4 (9.1%)	11 (25%)
Other circumstances	1 (50%)	0 (0%)	0 (0%)	0 (0%)	0 (0%)	0 (0%)	1 (50%)
Offspring							
Have children	8 (17%)	13 (27.7%)	2 (4.3%)	3 (6.4%)	3 (6.4%)	3 (6.4%)	15 (31.9%)
Childless	13 (24.1%)	11 (20.4%)	2 (3.7%)	3 (5.6%)	5 (9.3%)	8 (14.8%)	12 (22.2%)

Note: The *N* varies according to category. The overall *N*=101. Candidates were asked: "Do you think [federal/provincial/municipal] office is compatible with family responsibilities?" Eligibles were asked: "How compatible do you think elected office is with family responsibilities?"

elected office and likely did so after considering their family circumstances. Eligibles (24 per cent) were more likely than candidates (17.6 per cent) to indicate that politics and family did not mix well, but the gap between the groups was less drastic here. Perceptions of work–life balance did not move in the expected direction when examining responses by level of government. Among those who sought a party nomination, more federal aspirants (33.3 per cent) than provincial aspirants (26.9 per cent) argued that elected officials could meet both their political and family responsibilities. The reverse was true for individuals who actually did run for office. Only one-quarter (23.5 per cent) of federal candidates believed a work–life balance was possible compared to more than one-third (36.8 per cent) of provincial candidates and less than one-third (29.2 per cent) of municipal candidates. The fact that we don't see municipal candidates express the greatest expectation of being able to meet family responsibilities, followed by provincial candidates and then federal ones, raises questions about feminist expectations that municipal politics is more family friendly for aspiring politicians (see Trimble 1995).

Research suggests parents should be more hesitant about entering politics than non-parents, but that is not the case here. More childless individuals (24.1 per cent) than parents (17 per cent) believe work–life balance in politics was *not* possible. In contrast, one-quarter (27.7 per cent) of parents believed such a balance could be attained compared to one-fifth (20.4 per cent) of non-parents, though raw numbers indicate little real disparity between the two groups on this count. The offspring findings might be the result of childless individuals *anticipating* difficulties, while parents already have experience juggling a job and children and, consequently, might be more confident in their ability to make things work. As for marital status, single individuals (38.2 per cent) were more optimistic about combining politics and family than married individuals (23.7 per cent).

In terms of social characteristics, one in three women (35.3 per cent) did not see politics as compatible with family responsibilities compared to one in 20 men (4.3 per cent). The gender gap closed considerably amongst those who felt it was possible to combine politics and family duties, with one-fourth of men (26.1 per cent) and one-fifth of women (19.6 per cent) offering this answer. Table 3.1 shows important racial and sexual differences among research participants. One-quarter of white people (26.4 per cent) and almost one-third of queer folks (30 per cent) indicated a work–life balance could be found in politics while one-quarter of racialized people (27.1 per cent) and heterosexuals (23.5 per cent) felt it could not. The reasons for these two gaps are not clear.

Scholars need to take an intersectional approach to understanding family-related factors in political candidacy, exploring the challenges that politicians from different racial/ethnic groups experience in this area of their lives. What these results do reveal, however, is that different social groups perceive family responsibilities as an important issue when considering a bid for elected office.

Time-Consuming Occupation

The time-consuming nature of politics is the number one reason why eligibles and candidates alike believe that it is challenging to combine political office with family responsibilities. Elected representatives are often expected to work long hours each day, for seven days a week, for 52 weeks of the year. When the legislature is in session, politicians devote themselves to prepping for and participating in parliamentary debates, legislative committee meetings, party-related events, media interviews, and other activities. They also keep in regular contact with constituency staff to resolve the government-related concerns of individual voters. The job is so demanding that they have little time for anything else. "Ottawa life is literally a bubble," explained Alexandra Mendès, a long-time Montreal-area Liberal MP. "We are so into it that anything from the outside is almost an aggression to our concentration." Their schedule eases up a bit when the legislature is not in session, enabling them to focus more attention on their ridings and to spend more time with family, but the hustle remains. Newly elected politicians clue into this reality quickly. "One of the myths you learn right off the bat is the myth about the lazy politician who's just filling a seat," said Cheri DiNovo, a long-time Ontario MLA who retired from politics in 2017. "Ain't nobody like that. I've never met one anywhere. I mean, it's the nature of the job that you're working all the time."

Like federal and provincial politics, city politics can be time consuming. Some big cities have budgets and operations equal in size to that of small provinces. Big-city politicians thus face their own time pressures. However, the part-time nature of small-town municipal councils means most local politicians in Canada don't need to devote as much time to political duties as their big-city, provincial, or federal counterparts. The ability of many small-town municipal politicians to combine paid employment, family responsibilities, and elected office is why one white heterosexual man opted to get involved with local government. "As I was farming and had a young family, I was able to take on [the] level of commitment" associated with municipal office, he said, "but certainly I couldn't have considered the commitment of a full-time MP."

It wasn't until his children were much older that he finally pursued his federal ambitions, running unsuccessfully in the 2015 federal election.

After a week spent in the capital city, elected representatives head back to their constituencies on the weekend to follow-up on individual voter concerns as well as attend a myriad of community events. But Canada's enormous geography creates challenges for federal politicians. Many MPs must travel thousands of kilometres each Thursday or Friday to reach their ridings before retracing their steps Sunday night to be back on Parliament Hill for Monday. The commute is not only physically tiring but also leaves less time for constituency work and family. Time zone changes can eat up additional time. "There's many features because we're such a big country that adds to the burden of federal office," said a former MP who travelled to her Vancouver-area riding every weekend. "Getting on that plane, you're looking at an additional 18 hours [each week] that I'm putting in as an MP from Vancouver as opposed to an MP from Toronto, who can hop on a plane" and be home quickly. Despite the long plane ride, the former MP said her regular routine was to attend two or three community events after touching down Thursday night. She then spent Friday in the constituency office with additional events in the evening while her Saturday was dedicated to attending up to 20 local events. From this perspective, it is easy to see why finding time for family is difficult for so many federal politicians.

Provincial politicians have less ground to cover than many of their federal counterparts, but if they drive, rather than fly, to their constituency, their commute can still be a long one. Then there's the commute within a federal or provincial constituency. City ridings are compact. Politicians can cover two or three events in one hour because each location is only a few minutes apart. Rural ridings are much larger. Politicians can spend an hour or two on the road just to attend two separate events. This additional travel leaves even less time for family.

Municipal politicians have no travel issues – their homes are a short drive from council chambers, and they can move around the municipality quickly – but that additional time isn't always a luxury. Because they live *and* work in the area, municipal politicians are often expected to attend more local events than are the community's provincial and federal representatives. Small-town politicians have been known to manage this workload by dividing events amongst themselves and/ or by taking turns being the deputy mayor (when this position is not an elected one), during which time they assist the mayor with a variety of duties. Another reason why municipal politics is more amenable to maintaining a strong home life is because voters expect local politicians to prioritize family. "The decisions you make, the life you lead, are all about local families," said the white heterosexual man who chose his young family over federal politics.

Politics is an all-encompassing job that only gets more intense as a person moves higher up the political ladder. A cabinet minister has much greater demands on their time than a backbencher, but it is still nowhere near as bad as those that the prime minister faces. "The simple hours that we all put in is phenomenal and the higher up you go, the more hours you put in," said DiNovo. "I sort of say politics is like the Peter's principle: the higher up you go the worse it gets until you become the president of the United States, at which time you fear for your life and might get shot." Eligibles were equally aware of how different political positions have different time requirements.

The time-consuming nature of political life makes family life challenging, but politics is not the only demanding occupation. Other careers are equally challenging. Bradley Metlin, a white gay man who might run one day, argued that many jobs require a lot of energy and attention. As he argued in the quotation that opened this chapter, many people have to work long hours to put food on the table. "Anything you put a lot of energy into is going to take away from [your family]," said Metlin. An Indigenous queer woman was able to make her professional life work because of the involvement of her wife. "When I travel for gigs, she's with me." Even though she had no plans to run, the Indigenous woman said she would have pursued a political career the same way she did her current career. "To me that means you have to have a partner that's willing to do what mine has done in terms of getting on board with this dream and agreeing that we're going to make it happen together." The consensus was that some individuals simply swap one demanding career for another when they enter politics.

Truncated Political Ambitions

How do potential candidates intend to address the issue of mixing politics and family? By not mixing them at all. Several eligibles indicated that they had either delayed, or denied, their political ambitions to focus on raising their children. Women, in particular, identified family as a barrier to running for elected office. Even though she had long been interested in politics, a white heterosexual woman opted not to run for elected office in her 30s because she had two small kids and was getting a divorce. "I don't think I could have just even physically or financially been able to do that with my kids," she said. "I don't know if I could have dedicated myself to the public realm and the private realm that way. It was definitely a factor in my decision not to run early on." Political candidacy is more possible today because her children are older and her ex-husband is active in their lives.

But women are not the only ones who delay their political ambitions. Men do it too. One white heterosexual man waited until his sons were grown before getting involved in provincial politics. He eventually won a seat in the Saskatchewan legislature.

> It was very important for us as a family to do things together and to be quite involved in their lives and supporting them in whatever they did, and they were both very active young men in sports and all other activities. We wanted to make sure we gave them what they needed. So, no, it was very important that they were off on their own before I made this commitment.

Another white heterosexual man opted out of politics altogether because of the time that it would have taken away from his family. "Time is a very precious commodity," he said. "It's a place of potential conflict. You can't just walk away and leave the burden on the other person. It would just lend too much stress for the family." Missing out on school concerts and sports matches would lead to disappointment on the part of the child and deep-seated guilt on the part of the parent. "Time is such an important resource, such an important commodity, especially for the family," said the man. "I don't see how anybody with younger children can do it." He added that the best time for a parent to become a candidate is when the children are in university and able to care for themselves. That some men chose family over politics means scholars need to reassess the assumption that family isn't a masculine barrier to political candidacy. What type of men choose not to get involved in politics because of family? Do these fathers exhibit qualities and policy interests that differ from fathers who do run for, and hold, elected office? Understanding why certain types of men choose not to become candidates because of family can help us better understand how self-selection contributes to the over-representation of certain types of men in our legislatures and what impact that has on policymaking.

Another way that eligibles address the issue of mixing politics and family is by making sure they have the support of their partner and children. Several individuals indicated they probably would not run for office if they didn't have their family's blessings. They knew politics would have a profound impact on individual family members and on family life, and they needed to make sure that family members would be willing to take on that burden. "If I did not have the support of my partner, I wouldn't do it because I know that running for elected office would mean time away from my daughter," said a South Asian lesbian who, if she ran, was most interested in federal and provincial office. "So, if my partner was not supportive, that wouldn't be something that I would want to pursue because I would need her support and flexibility to ensure that I could continue to have a really great relationship with my daughter, because she would be doing more of that day-to-day parenting, I think, on a lot of levels." Like eligibles, several candidates admitted they would not have run for office without their partners or children being on board.

Other research participants, both eligibles and candidates, admitted that family was not a major concern, though for different reasons. People who were single and/or childless didn't have any family responsibilities to manage, while some individuals indicated that parents and/or siblings lived in different cities or countries. The benefit of living far away from family is that candidates don't need to worry about their political activities harming the privacy or business interests of extended family members. Other individuals didn't worry about family support because they planned to be paper candidates, running for a political party in a lost-cause riding. The only major time commitment would be a one- or two-month election campaign. "I really thought my chances of winning were really low," said one candidate. "I said to my partner, 'Hey, I signed the documents to run as a candidate. I'm looking at the chances historically. It's something I'm working towards but it's not likely going to be something that ends up happening.' But I didn't really tell her beforehand." Why bother if one didn't expect to serve a four-year term in office? Yet that is exactly what happened. The candidate ended up winning the election because of voter dissatisfaction with another party and serving one term before declining to run for re-election.

Some folks, however, saw candidacy as an individual decision. Nolan Crouse, a white heterosexual man, didn't consult his wife or children when thinking about running for municipal office in Alberta. "I wasn't going to be influenced by anyone else. This was my decision." Nolan simply informed them of his candidacy. "I think there was a lot of surprise, but I was just going to do what I wanted to do," said Crouse, who was on St. Albert city council from 2004 to 2017, first as councillor and later as mayor. "And I might come across like I was oversimplifying it, but it was privately researched, privately decided, and privately announced. Just me. This was about me." Another man considered the potential impact on his family, but the decision ultimately resided with him. "Whatever decision I make is for me," said Ted Mouradian, a gay man of Armenian descent who tried unsuccessfully to enter municipal and federal politics. "Considering that, I do my best not to harm anybody around me." A white transgender woman welcomed family support for her municipal and federal candidacies, but it wasn't important to her decision: "This is really something that came from me, through me, and I was going to do it regardless of what family or friends thought," said Jennifer McCreath. Steven Kou, an East Asian heterosexual man who ran for the Liberals in the 2015 federal election, was relieved that his wife supported his candidacy, but it wasn't vital to him. Catherine Meade, a Black lesbian who unsuccessfully pursued a career in federal politics, discussed her political ambitions with her then-fiancée, but "if she had said, 'I don't want you to run,' I don't know if that would have changed my decision. Maybe that's why we're not married today. Hard to say."

Other individuals ignore family objections because of the trailblazing nature of their candidacies. A white lesbian, who sought Saskatchewan municipal office in 2000, refused to let her wider family's concerns deter her from running at a time when out queer candidates were still a rarity. "It mattered more to be able to prove that somebody of diversity could run," said Lenore Swystun, "and I didn't want, you know, fears of some family members to impede the ability to do that." Other queer individuals are estranged from family members because of their gender and/or sexual identities and generally have to pursue political goals on their own. "Being a gay male growing up in a not always overly supportive environment, I think I've just adapted," said Jason Kingsley, who has thought about running for office. A lack of family support is therefore not as much of a barrier to candidacy for queer individuals than it might be for other social groups.

Politics as a Family-Unfriendly Workplace

One of the surprising differences between eligibles and candidates was an appreciation for the role that structural factors can play in making it harder to combine politics and family. Many candidates took an individualistic approach, suggesting it was up to individuals, rather than institutions, to make the necessary adjustments to ensure politicians can combine political duties with family responsibilities. "You cannot blame the Parliament of Canada [for] not accommodating you, [for] not being ready for you," said a white heterosexual woman who ran unsuccessfully in the 2015 federal election. "You have to be ready for office. It means that you have the necessary experience and you gave a very sober serious thought when you got engaged in running for public office." Other candidates noted that politicians have some agency over their own schedules and can set aside time for family when needed. "There's always more to do," said Jeane Lassen, a white heterosexual woman who ran unsuccessfully for Yukon territorial office, "so it's being able to find that balance between when do you turn it off and just spend time with your family." Former Alberta municipal politician Paul Harris said politicians should be willing to make their family a priority. "I've seen politicians who don't make it a priority and they suffer, and then others that do make it a priority like Mike Layton [a Toronto city councillor]," said Harris, adding that Layton "changed the way he works" because of his young children.

However, candidate comments made it clear that the individual making the main adjustment would not be the politician so much as the political spouse. Both women and men candidates admitted that their partner needed to take on the lion's share of the family responsibilities, whether it was for the short duration of an election campaign or for the four-year stretch of a legislative term. "You need a supportive partner in terms of the cooking, laundry, and child care," said Cheri DiNovo. Spouses sometimes call upon extended family members to provide additional support. Donovan Martin, a Black heterosexual man who ran for the Manitoba Liberals in the 2016 provincial election, was impressed with his wife's efforts during his campaign. "It was basically all-hands-on-deck on her part, getting the grandparents, the brothers or uncles and aunties to get the kids from school or shuttling them to activities," said Martin. Without strong spousal support, candidates insisted it would be almost impossible for individuals with families to run for, or hold, elected office at the federal and provincial levels. Other candidates say municipal office is more amenable to family life because the politician doesn't need to relocate to another city, but depending upon the size of the municipality, the job can be no less demanding. Candidates generally believe that it is up to individual politicians and their families to find a work–life balance.

Many candidates appeared to give little thought to the structural factors that make politics difficult for individuals with families. While we know legislatures are responsible for debating government policy and passing laws, we tend to overlook the fact that legislatures are also workplaces with their own institutional norms and practices. Like other workplaces, political institutions are highly gendered (MacRae and Weiner 2021; Palmieri 2019). Created at a time when politicians were exclusively men, Western legislatures like Canada's were built on the assumption that the average legislator would be a wealthy white heterosexual man with a stay-at-home wife who took care of the children, freeing him to focus almost exclusively on his political responsibilities.

He could attend committee meetings, debates, and votes at any time during the week and countless community events in his constituency on the weekend. He didn't need to rush home each day to feed his children or set aside time each week to attend their hockey games. Work–life balance was irrelevant.

Politicians have become much more diverse over time, with varying personal and financial circumstances, yet political institutions remain the same in their gendered and classed assumptions about a politician's home life. Feminists in particular have struggled to convince traditionalists to update institutional norms and practices to make legislatures more family friendly (Arneil 2017). British feminists have been at the forefront of such efforts. They have pushed for everything from setting up daycares in parliamentary buildings and establishing paid parental leave to changing parliamentary working hours and abolishing Friday sittings (Childs 2016). Canadian politicians have pursued similar objectives here. Federal politicians have considered allowing breastfeeding in the House of Commons while provincial governments are starting to allow MLAs to bring their babies into the legislative chambers and are looking at implementing paid maternity leave. The effectiveness of parliamentary reforms in Westminster-style legislatures has been mixed (Campbell and Childs 2017). The ultimate goal is to make political institutions more accommodating to enable individuals from diverse backgrounds to run for, and hold, elected office.

It is unclear why many candidates, and especially elected representatives, emphasized individual responses to the strain of combining politics and family. Their experiences working within political institutions should have made them more aware of how organizational rules and practices can contribute to family stresses that politicians often report experiencing (Allen, Cutts, and Winn 2016; Arneil 2017; McKay 2011). Candidates, for the most part, appeared to accept institutional norms as they are. For the eight candidates who did question institutional norms, most of them ran for the NDP and Greens or ran for municipal office. They noted issues such as childcare and unpredictable, long, or evening work hours. Miranda Jimmy, an Indigenous heterosexual woman who ran unsuccessfully for Edmonton city council in 2017, believes that political institutions can become more child friendly. "But I don't think work-life balance is completely dependent upon children or not," she added. "I think every workplace needs to consider that everyone has a life outside of their jobs." Yet, like other candidates, Jimmy noted municipal politicians have control over their schedules, and if elected, she would have made sure that she didn't work 20-hour days, seven days a week.

Compared to candidates in general, eligibles had a more structural understanding of the factors influencing work–life balance. Eligibles argued that political institutions and political parties need to adjust to ensure politicians can find time for their families despite their hectic work schedules. Women were particularly alert to structural factors. They highlighted ways in which women were disadvantaged in political institutions originally built by men, for men. Danielle Parrell, a white heterosexual woman, argued that federal politics was historically intended to be a "man's world" and wasn't "designed to accommodate women's traditional roles and responsibilities." Other women pointed to parliamentary working hours as one example of how this masculine logic plays out. Night sittings are not unusual and can sometimes last until midnight or later. Parties expect their members to attend these legislative sessions so they can pass, or defeat, whatever is being debated. But this institutional norm makes childcare difficult for parent politicians, including fathers active in their children's lives. One woman who worked for a man politician recounted a story of how that politician couldn't get the party's permission to attend his child's graduation because the party deemed that night session to be extremely important. A white queer woman added that politicians are expected to put in long hours each day and "systems that could be in place to support families, you know, like helping with child care or planning things around other schedules a little bit more helpfully, are not really a priority, especially when it comes to caucus organizing."

When parties do lend a hand, parent politicians face public censure over the cost of that support. Former Conservative leader Andrew Scheer was criticized by opponents and supporters alike for the money the party spent to relocate his family to Ottawa and place his children in private schools. One eligible suggested parent politicians can face criticism simply for taking time out of their day to pick up their kids from school and bring them to work. Politicians therefore face a catch-22 situation when it comes to parenthood: voters want politicians to be parents in spirit but not in practice (Stalsburg 2010). In other words, voters want politicians to understand the needs of everyday families, but they don't want the needs of politicians' own families to get in the way of government business. Voters are especially harsh towards women politicians: they evaluate the competencies of women with young children more negatively than men with young children (Stalsburg 2010). But father politicians don't escape judgment either. Men with children are seen as less capable than childless men (Stalsburg 2010). In short, politicians face a parent penalty with gendered implications.

Unlike women eligibles, men eligibles rarely discussed structural factors in politics that can make work–life balance hard and tended to share an individualistic understanding of how to find it. In fact, they echoed many of the same arguments that candidates in general put forward. But some men were certainly aware that women face greater challenges in reconciling family and politics. Felipe Del Campo-Donoso acknowledged that, as a man, he has "a point of privilege" in this regard. "If I were to be elected there's more possibilities for me to stay in office rather than if I were to be a woman and I were to have kids. I wouldn't breastfeed in the House or in the Senate just because it's not allowed," said Del Campo-Donoso, a Hispanic gay man who might run one day. "Depending how child care policies might affect me, I might also not be able to run. I would have to wait for my kids to get older. Because I'm a guy, I see that there's not so many constraints against me." Del Campo-Donoso's comments subtly raise another issue that makes politics easier for some and harder for others: the traditional nuclear family.

Nuclear Families Work Best

Both eligibles and candidates recognized the value of a nuclear family in politics. Their discussion of achieving work–life balance suggests the ideal family circumstance for a politician is to have a supportive spouse who takes on all domestic responsibilities, children who are old enough to care for themselves, and a family who understands the politician must put political duties first. In essence, everyone in the family is not only willing but also able to make sacrifices so one member can pursue a career in politics. Any individual with a different family situation faces stiffer challenges in combining politics and family. People with unsupportive spouses are less likely to pursue candidacy because of the obvious tensions that going ahead with such an all-encompassing activity would produce within a relationship. Parents of young children, especially single parents, anticipate struggling with childcare. A white heterosexual woman, who was a long-time municipal and provincial politician, argues that "family today looks a lot different than when I got married" decades earlier:

There [aren't] the strong partnerships and supports that … I've experienced my whole married life. I have two daughters who are single parents. Neither one of them could get involved in politics because of that, because they are the mom and the dad and they work to bring in the money as well.

Only childless, unpartnered research participants expected an easier time in politics than individuals with adult children and/or supportive partners.

Heterosexual men of any racial or ethnic background benefit most from a traditional nuclear family because of the gendered expectation that the man is the head of the household whose paid employment financially supports the family and the woman is the helpmate who takes care of domestic matters. If she has any paid employment, it is secondary to her family responsibilities. She, and not the man, must organize her life around her spouse and children. The man's life is about his career. This traditional family form is designed to facilitate heterosexual men's involvement in politics, among other activities.

Societal expectations that women must prioritize motherhood means women who pursue elected office cannot focus exclusively on politics. Women politicians are expected to put in a double shift each day, first at the legislature and then at home. They must take care of their political duties *and* their families. This gendered assumption is why journalists routinely ask women politicians about their children and who is caring for them, the kind of questioning that men politicians escape because journalists assume they have a wife at home taking care of the kids (cf. Van Zoonen 1998). Men politicians with heterosexual nuclear families are seen by journalists as more likeable, solid, and suitable for office. No such benefit accrues to women politicians in similar circumstances (Auer et al. 2022). Racialized men are less likely to be accepted by journalists as a family man because of racialized stereotypes of the ideal family as white (Burge, Hodges, and Rinaldi 2020), but they still benefit from societal notions that men are political actors and women are political helpmates. Family is thus a political and personal resource for men in ways that it is not for women (Trimble 2017). Women who place equal, or greater, priority on their political duties are seen as selfish.

The extent to which family forms might pose a challenge for queer politicians is largely unknown because of their small presence in legislatures and limited research on their experiences in politics. It wouldn't be a stretch, though, to suggest they don't benefit from the nuclear norm either. The family circumstances of sexual minorities can upend conventional norms and even defy them altogether. A lesbian politician in a same-sex marriage is similar to a heterosexual man in that they might have a spouse who can take care of any children, freeing them to become involved in politics, but because their relationship doesn't meet heterosexual expectations, they are still subjected to intense questioning over their domestic arrangements. Kathleen Wynne is a case in point. Wynne was divorced from the father of her grown children and married to her long-time woman partner when she became premier of Ontario. Her domestic arrangements closely mimicked the nuclear family. Yet the news media still struggled to make sense of her family background (Auer et al. 2022; McLean 2019; Lalancette and Tremblay 2019).

Family as a Support to Candidacy

This chapter has, so far, focused on how family responsibilities and family responses to political ambitions act as barriers to candidacy. Yet research participants also indicated that close and extended family members can make it easier for individuals to pursue elected office. First, they provide moral support. Some family members actively encourage individuals to seek elected office, while others repeatedly quiz them about their future plans. One white heterosexual man, who was waiting for the right opportunity before running, had to fend off his family's inquiries over Christmas one year. Other family members simply accepted the inevitable. They knew the individual was deeply interested in politics and would likely run for office one day. Why fight it? "They know it's something I'm passionate about and would give my all to," said Patrick Schertzer, a white gay man who expected to one day run for office, "so I think that they would be very supportive of it." Positive reactions from family members embolden individuals to pursue their dreams of becoming an elected official.

Second, family members provide mental support. They can help candidates unwind from a stressful day of campaigning. "I need to go home and I need not for it to be political," said Joanne Bernard, who was a Nova Scotia cabinet minister at the time of our interview but has since left elected office. "I need to have those conversations with my partner about how I'm feeling and about what we're having for supper, and I don't want to talk about my work even if it's on TV and we're watching an interview I'm doing. That's not our priority when we're in our home." Mental health issues in politics are explored in more detail in Chapter 8.

Third, family members provide material support. Donations to the campaign coffers are always a big help but not always expected. Parents, siblings, and extended family might not be in a position to donate money, but they can often donate time. Candidates noted that they relied on close relatives to volunteer on their campaigns, doing things such as putting up lawn signs, distributing pamphlets, recruiting additional volunteers, raising money, and managing social media sites. Oftentimes the best support a partner can give is just taking care of the candidate's daily needs. "It's what he jokingly calls care and feeding of the candidate," Edmonton school board trustee Bridget Sterling said of her husband. "It's somebody who makes sure that you have clean clothes and something to eat and tells you to go to bed and does those things. I think that's incredibly valuable." The campaign contributions that family members can make are so important that would-be candidates are advised to start there when recruiting volunteers for their campaign.

Conclusion

Scholars and citizens alike have long assumed that family responsibilities are a gendered barrier to political candidacy. Traditional gender stereotypes position men as leaders and women as caregivers, making it difficult for many women to not only see themselves as having the qualities necessary for political leadership but also as having the time to pursue it. Women are expected to prioritize their children, especially when the children are young. As political spouses, women are expected to take on the burden of domestic life while their husbands engage in all-consuming political life. But insights from 101 individuals from diverse social backgrounds reveal a more nuanced picture of the role of family in political candidacy.

First, in terms of candidacy status, eligibles were less inclined than candidates to believe it possible to combine family responsibilities with politics. Eligibles – and especially women eligibles – were attuned to the structural and institutional factors that make it difficult to achieve a work–life balance, such as the time-consuming nature of politics and the lack of party or legislative support for parent politicians. In contrast, candidates believed it falls upon individual politicians and, more likely, their (women) spouses to make politics and family work. Differences of opinion thus revolve around who is responsible for change: eligibles believe the system must adapt to politicians while candidates believe politicians must adapt to the system. Without structural and institutional reforms, this finding suggests individuals who take an individualistic view of politics will likely dominate the candidate pool.

In terms of gender, men continue to have a structural and institutional advantage because legislatures were historically built on the assumption that elected representatives are wealthy white heterosexual men with wives at home to take care of the children, and this favouritism makes it easier for them to find work–life balance in politics. But interviews reveal that not all men fit that mould. Some men participants prioritized their children, downgrading or setting aside their political ambitions to make sure they had the time to be active fathers when their children were young. This finding raises the possibility that family is also a barrier for men – not in the sense of preventing men in general from running but from discouraging *certain kinds* of men from doing so. The political absence of these men could have implications for public policy, especially in relation to families.

Meanwhile, queer eligibles expected to face greater difficulty in politics because of other types of family issues. Supportive families are an important resource for politicians. Extended family members often donate money, time, and other resources to the person's campaign. Regardless of social background, research participants viewed spousal support as vital to political candidacy because they know most of the domestic burden will fall on their partner. Queer participants were less likely than their heterosexual counterparts to be married or in a common-law relationship and to have children, making spousal support or childcare less of a necessity. But family resistance to their gender and/or sexual identities means queer research participants cannot expect the same emotional or material support from extended family members that heterosexual candidates can. The absence of a supportive family can make candidacy, and politics, harder for everyone but especially for queer individuals.

Finally, this chapter reveals that men are not the only ones who don't give family much consideration when making the decision to run for political office. People of varying gender, ethnicities, and sexualities have their own reasons for not giving much credence to family concerns. In short, this chapter demonstrates that family might not be the strong barrier it once was to women's candidacy, it could play a stronger role in men's decision not to run than previously thought, and it is a complicated factor for queer folks. What matters to everyone, however, are the financial challenges of political candidacy. The next chapter explores the complex role that money plays in the decision to run for elected office.

Chapter Four

The Financial Calculation: Challenges of Fundraising and Post-Politics Employment

I think fundraising is very important. It's unbelievably important. If you don't have the money there's no shot, and you need the money to build the support, to market yourself.

> – Gurpreet Kaur Sodhi, South
> Asian heterosexual woman eligible

Introduction

All candidates need money to seek elected office, whether it is a hundred bucks to produce a home-made brochure for a village campaign or millions of dollars to launch a competitive bid for the leadership of a national political party. For larger campaigns, money makes it possible to "build a campaign organization, to mobilize one's network of supporters, and to build name recognition through advertisements" (Farrar-Meyers and Boyea 2013, 211). Money is also a metric by which journalists, political insiders, donors, volunteers, and voters assess the electoral viability of candidates (Kitchens and Swers 2016; Thomsen and Swers 2017; Wagner et al. 2017). Candidates who can raise large amounts of cash from many people have a much greater base of support than those who cannot or who are largely self-funded. The extent to which campaign financing shapes the electoral environment depends on numerous factors. For example, the level of government and type of office sought often determine the amount of financial resources needed. Partisans running in winnable ridings at the federal or provincial levels, or candidates in big cities, need to raise more cash than individuals vying for a seat on town council. The same is true for big-city mayoral contestants and party leadership hopefuls in comparison to candidates for a regular council or legislative seat. Personal financial circumstances and professional backgrounds might also influence a person's ability to solicit donations from others and to contribute to their own campaigns, even with donation limits.

Despite the importance of money in electoral politics, research on the challenges involved in raising money for a Canadian election campaign is limited. Scholars typically analyse the regulatory aspects of fundraising, such as changes in federal or provincial laws around public financing of political parties, or who is or is not permitted to contribute to candidates (cf. Jansen and Lambert 2013; Young and Jansen 2011). Scant attention has been paid to the role of gender, race/ethnicity, sexuality, or class in determining which Canadians can acquire the financial resources necessary to make a competitive bid for elected office (for exceptions, see Besco and Tolley 2022; Tolley, Besco, and Sevi 2022). A rare Canadian study found that, in the 2015 federal election, racialized donors typically gave money to candidates at lower rates than white donors did, with South Asian donors a notable exception (Besco and Tolley 2022). South Asian donors were not only highly active contributors, but they also gave a significant portion of their money to South Asian candidates, which likely explained why South Asian candidates received the majority of their campaign contributions from South Asian donors (Besco and Tolley 2022).

Research in other national contexts is scarce on all but gender. Race is an important cleavage in American politics, yet US scholars have rarely examined differences in the fundraising abilities of, and sources of donor support for, white and racialized candidates (for exceptions, see Arrington and Ingalls 1984; King 2009; Smith 1988; Wilson 2018). The only clarity is that racialized candidates in the US generally raise less money than white candidates. To my knowledge, fundraising challenges faced by queer candidates have not been studied at all.

Regarding gender, most of what we know about campaign fundraising largely comes from the American context. A series of studies on the US House of Representatives found that women were every bit as successful as men in raising money for their campaigns and that this has been the case since at least the 1980s (Burrell 1985, 1996, 2005, 2014). Gender gaps in financing might be more because of candidate status (challenger versus incumbent) or lack of need than differences in fundraising ability (Burrell 1985). Donors tend to support incumbents, likely winners, and candidates in close races (Uhlaner and Schlozman 1986). Other studies examining different aspects of campaign fundraising (Crespin and Deitz 2010) and candidates running at other levels of government (Adams and Schreiber 2011) also found few gender differences. But research on the role of partisanship in campaign financing has found sharp variations in funding sources between Democratic and

Republican women candidates (Day and Hadley 2002; Francia 2001; Kitchens and Swers 2016; Thomsen and Swers 2017). While women's political action committees such as EMILY's List and WISH List have provided valuable funds to women candidates, these resources disproportionately go to Democrats (Crowder-Meyer and Cooperman 2018; Francia 2001; Thomsen and Swers 2017). Women are also more likely than men to accept public financing for their campaigns (Werner and Mayer 2007). It is unclear, however, whether men (Herrick 1996) or women (Green 2003) received more value for their fundraising dollar in terms of votes. A rare Canadian study found that men were far more likely to donate, and to donate larger amounts, to federal candidates between 1993 and 2018 than were women (Tolley, Besco, and Sevi 2022). Women donors preferred to contribute directly to federal political parties – especially left-wing parties – than to federal candidates, but when they did support candidates, women candidates tended to get more of their money (Tolley, Besco, and Sevi 2022).

Despite evidence that women candidates are successful fundraisers, many individuals continue to perceive money as an important barrier to elected office for women. An American survey of state-level candidates found most Democratic women and a sizeable minority of Republican women believe fundraising remains an issue for women because they do not have the same networks or are not as comfortable asking for money as men. Women are also less likely than men to donate and, when they do, it is typically in smaller amounts (Carroll and Sanbonmatsu 2013b). Another state survey found that women perceived fundraising to be more challenging than men did and that they needed to use more sources and techniques to achieve their fundraising goals (Jenkins 2007). While she acknowledged the importance of women's political action committees (PACs) to women's advancement in politics, Shannon Jenkins wondered if "their mantra that women must focus on fundraising may discourage potential female candidates from entering into the electoral arena" (2007, 237). Whatever the empirical reality, perceptions of women's fundraising ability can influence parties' receptiveness to their candidacies. Carole Jean Uhlaner and Kay Lehman Schlozman argue that "[i]f political influentials believe that women cannot raise money, they will be reluctant to encourage women to become candidates. If potential women contenders believe that they will have trouble filling their campaign coffers, they will hesitate to run" (1986, 46). Campaign fundraising can thus be a gendered barrier to candidacy.

Scholars have focused far less attention to the way in which money shapes other aspects of political candidacy. Occupation has been the main subject of interest. Studies have explored whether women candidates share the same professional backgrounds as men candidates (Adams and Schreiber 2011; Trimble and Tremblay 2003) or whether they mainly come from the traditional pipeline professions of business and law or use other routes to get into politics (Carroll and Sanbonmatsu 2013b). Among those in the pipeline professions, women tend to be less confident in their abilities and less likely to want to seek elected office (Lawless and Fox 2010). Political ambition is also depressed among working-class individuals but not for the same reasons. They don't lack interest so much as money. A 2014 American survey found that blue-collar workers were far more likely than professionals to be worried about covering personal expenses, but both groups were equally concerned about raising enough cash for a campaign (Carnes 2018, 84). "Everyone hates fundraising. The concerns that are *unique* to workers seem to be more basic concerns about paying the bills and taking care of things at home" (Carnes 2018, 84; italics in the original). Workers generally earn less money, making it difficult to build up savings to cover their living expenses during the election period. They often cannot afford to take time off from work to campaign either. Moreover, campaign finance laws in Canada generally don't allow candidates to use campaign funds to cover personal expenses.

Professional norms and employer expectations also shape a person's willingness to become a political candidate. The professional cultures of law and business might make it possible for people in those fields to pursue political office while continuing to earn a living. Different orientations towards politics in other fields, however, might discourage employees from doing the same. Civil servants were legally barred from getting involved in politics until the passage of the Charter of Rights and Freedoms in 1982. But while governments have since dropped this ban, Louise Carbert asserts that the motivation behind it remains: "[T]he legal prohibitions were merely formal manifestations of a much more broadly applied and widely held principle of staying above politics and that this principle persists to varying degrees throughout the public sector" (2006, 99). The Public Service Commission, for example, has extensive rules governing the political activities of federal bureaucrats to protect the impartiality of the civil service. Civil servants can now seek elected office, but they must first obtain the commission's permission. The principle of impartiality might depress women's involvement in electoral politics because many women work in the public sector (Carbert 2006, 100).

Government bureaucracies are not the only organizations that place a priority on non-partisanship. In an era of increasing political polarization, companies might emphasize non-partisanship to maintain favourable business links with federal or provincial governments regardless of the political party in power. Some women in Atlantic Canada have opted not to run for elected office because of partisan divisions within their communities and how customer responses to their political activities might harm their family's business interests (Carbert 2006, 105–12).

Partisanship is typically not an issue at the municipal level, as political parties do not contest local elections in most parts of Canada. The part-time nature of municipal council in many communities also makes it possible for individuals to hold paid employment and an elected position at the same time. Still, taking time off from their day jobs to attend daytime council meetings or events might be difficult for those in working-class occupations, those who want to advance in their careers, or those who cannot afford the lost wages (Hills 1983). While official policies and personal considerations apply to everyone, Jill Hills suggests these effects might be gendered because of the potentially different socio-economic circumstances of women and men: "[A] woman seeking to establish herself after returning to work or seeking to establish a career is under additional pressure not to take time away from paid employment" (1983, 46–47). Immigrants and racialized individuals, who typically earn less than native-born and white Canadians, probably face challenges of their own when it comes to combining full-time paid employment with part-time municipal office.

Often overlooked when calculating the financial costs of politics is the impact of candidacy on future job prospects. Most politicians in parliamentary systems like Canada's don't walk into lucrative jobs soon after leaving politics, whether their departure was voluntary or forced. Politicians who don't seek re-election fare slightly better, especially in terms of salary (Docherty 2001), but that is because they have time to plan the next stage of their careers before becoming unemployed. Politicians who lose an election are abruptly thrown out of work. In either case, it can take months to find paid employment (Byrne and Theakston 2016; Roberts 2017). One reason is that the knowledge, skills, and experience that individuals gain as backbenchers are not fully understood or valued by employers (Roberts 2017). As a consequence, former prime ministers, premiers, and cabinet ministers in key portfolios such as finance and trade have the most realistic chance of securing plum jobs with excellent salaries (Theakston 2012; Würfel 2018). The US is the exception to this pattern. One study found that almost half of the country's federal senators secured corporate directorships upon leaving office (Palmer and Schneer 2015). Many jurisdictions offer pensions to former elected representatives, but restrictions mean this money might not be (immediately) available to everyone. For example, Canadian MPs must hold office for six years before they qualify for this pension, and if they have this service, they must be at least 55 years old before they can start receiving at least partial pension benefits (Canada 2021). Former MPs with less than six years of service do not receive this pension. These challenges make it important to explore the role of employment-related factors, both before and after candidacy, in the decision to run for elected office.

The Public Costs of Political Candidacy

As the introductory chapter discussed, money was a major reason why eligibles hesitated to run for elected office and a major consideration for the candidates who eventually took the plunge. Few variations existed among social groups. For example, slightly more women (31.4 per cent) than men (28.3 per cent) cited money-related factors as a drawback to candidacy. A similar pattern emerged for eligibles (30 per cent) and candidates (29.4 per cent), queer individuals (30 per cent) and heterosexuals (29.4 per cent), and whites (30.2 per cent) and racialized individuals (29.2 per cent). These figures indicate that everyone, regardless of their social background, saw financial considerations as a reason to give sober second thought to running for elected office at any level of government. But *why* they saw money as a factor was an open question.

If research participants didn't voluntarily mention money when asked about the major drawbacks to candidacy during the interview, a follow-up question was posed about what they thought the challenges might be in raising money for a campaign. The following analysis draws on participant responses to the initial drawback question and subsequent fundraising question, but also includes discussion about campaign finances that occurred at other points of the interview. The aim is to understand the various factors that make campaign fundraising a barrier for individuals considering a bid for public office. People who had not run for office identified five interconnected challenges to financing a campaign: fundraising inexperience, limited networks, ethical concerns, psychological barriers, and political context.

Campaign fundraising is a mystery for many eligibles, especially women. Many eligibles have little prior experience raising money for anything, whether it be for a business venture, non-profit organization, community group, or someone else's political campaign. They simply don't know who to ask, how to ask, or when to ask for financial support. Several questions go through their minds: How much money would they need to field a campaign? Could they raise that amount of money from their network of family members, friends, associates, and supporters? If they ran provincially or federally, would they get any help from the political party or riding association? These questions were especially pertinent for those individuals who did not want to go into debt to run for elected office. Eligibles who expressed confidence in their ability to raise money for a campaign included those who had prior fundraising experience. These eligibles knew to approach people in their professional and personal networks early in the electoral cycle when donors are less likely to have hit the maximum contributions allowed under campaign finance laws. Waiting too long makes it harder to leverage one's networks for funding.

Many eligibles admitted to fears that they did not have the confidence or skills to be successful fundraisers. In line with previous studies (Carroll and Sanbonmatsu 2013b; Jenkins 2007), more women than men expressed doubts about their fundraising abilities. "It's not a skillset of mine," said Cindy de Bruijn, a white heterosexual woman who is interested in one day running. "Could I do it? Yes. But I would struggle to ask." A communications professional echoed this sentiment: "I think just doing that ask for money is always something that's a little bit difficult," said the white heterosexual woman. "Putting yourself out there that way and basically selling yourself as someone that people should give their hard-earned money to." Self-assured women tended to be those who had learned how to fundraise through their jobs or volunteer activity. "The fear of failure is less of a thing when you've been an entrepreneur," said Hannah Bell, a white woman who worked for a non-governmental organization at the time of the interview. "I think that's a really valuable crossover skillset that balances out some of the other risks. ... I know how to fundraise. I know how to do the fiscal piece." A South Asian woman who planned to run municipally (and later did) said her "ability to raise the money needed to run a campaign is strengthened by the fact that I've done it for the past seven years" for other candidates.

Another reason why some women eligibles are reluctant to ask is because they fear it will jeopardize relationships, regardless of whether they win or lose. Cindy de Bruijn outlined the conundrum: If she were victorious, donors might expect to exert influence over her policy priorities and decisions as compensation for that campaign support, and if she were defeated, donors might feel that they wasted their money. "I don't want to risk those friendships," she said. Another woman shared de Bruijn's concern that family and friends would feel let down if they contributed to her campaign and she didn't end up winning. This fear was heightened for a South Asian heterosexual woman because her network includes highly educated immigrants who had to work low-income jobs to make a life for themselves and their children in Canada. She was uncomfortable taking money from these immigrants "and then maybe losing it and not getting the return that they want. For me, in my heart, that sits really poorly." She would rather self-fund and approach wealthier businesspeople for financial support.

Whatever concerns they might have had, many women eligibles understood that they needed to overcome their discomfort, learn new skills, and assemble a strong team to field a strong fundraising effort. Men eligibles and candidates were equally aware of the importance of money to a successful campaign, but they were far less likely to voice any apprehensions about their ability to generate donations. As with political ambition in general (Lawless and Fox 2010), more men than women expressed confidence in their fundraising prowess. "I really like fundraising. I'm good at it and I like it," said George Smitherman, a former provincial politician in Ontario and former Toronto mayoral candidate. The white gay man later added: "I enjoy the process, I enjoy the logistics, and I enjoy the power that comes from achieving it. If you're going to be in politics, it's really good to be good at fundraising." Other men acknowledged that it is difficult work. A white heterosexual man, who once thought about running for federal or provincial office but has since decided against it, would have been willing to approach others for money but he didn't relish the idea.

> I don't know of anyone who really likes to do it – calling and spending hours on the phone and talking to people, trying to get them engaged or trying to convince them. It's not something that brings a lot of joy to one's heart. It's a function that has to be done. It's like doing the laundry – you just have to do it. There's no joy in it.

More men than women claimed that they did not, or did not expect to, encounter any difficulties in raising what they needed for their campaigns. "I didn't really lose sleep over it," said Shazad Shah, a West Indian queer man who ran unsuccessfully for municipal office. Subsequent comments indicate that some of these men did not need much money because they ran for municipal office in smaller communities or preferred low-cost campaign techniques such as door-knocking.

Candidates identified three main sources of fundraising assistance during an election campaign: (1) one's own network of family, friends, colleagues, and supporters; (2) campaign staff; (3) and the riding association and/or political party. Gendered and class elements were apparent in research participant evaluations of the relative strength of their networks in comparison to other candidates in their community or riding. Women noted that their personal finances made it difficult for them to self-fund and that their networks were comprised of less affluent people who simply could not afford to write big cheques. Two women eligibles argued that men candidates could easily raise money from their wealthy friends or foot the whole bill themselves:

> It is a very male-dominated space, and it's dominated by, frankly, old white guys with money. That's a particular kind of face. These are people who are in the Masons, Rotary Club, they golf together, and their wives all know each other, and they're affluent. I'm not in that space. I don't golf. I'm not rich. I'm not married. So socially, the social piece of it is hugely, hugely important and if you're not travelling in that social space or you travel there uncomfortably or as a third wheel or a fifth wheel or whatever, (laughs) that can be a problem. (Hannah Bell, a white woman from Prince Edward Island)

> [I]f an individual already is of a certain wealth they have a lot less concerns than an individual who was born into generational poverty like myself. It would be a lot more difficult for me to engage in fundraising efforts than somebody who already has that money in the bank, to pull on that kind of sponsorship. But I'm an optimist, and I do have experience in fundraising. It's not enough to stop me. I think it would be a challenge, but I do think it is something that I can navigate. (Danielle Parrell, a white woman from Newfoundland and Labrador)

That women have not achieved economic parity with men might explain the class-based assessment offered by women research participants. The racial or queer dimensions of campaign fundraising were rarely raised, but the lower average household income of immigrants and racial minorities[1] vis-à-vis the general population suggests racialized candidates would face more obstacles raising money from social networks that likely contain less affluent individuals. Statistics Canada (2022b) figures revealing economic diversity within the queer community suggest not all queer candidates will face the same challenges fundraising. On average, gay men have the highest before-tax income

---

1 Canada's 2016 census found that non-immigrants made an average of $36,300 per year while immigrants earned an average of $29,770 (Rocha and Loewen 2017). Looking at one racialized group, Statistics Canada found a wage gap between Black people and other Canadians, with the largest gap observed between Black men and non-Black men (Houle 2020, 25–7).

followed, in order, by lesbians, bisexual men, and bisexual women; meanwhile, bisexual women and men are far less likely than gays or lesbians to have a job (Statistics Canada 2022b).

The composition of a candidate's campaign team is as important to fundraising success as is the composition of their personal and professional networks. Many research participants argued that would-be candidates need to assemble a strong campaign team early on, identifying individuals capable of spearheading their fundraising efforts so they could devote themselves to campaigning. The candidate should do little more than hand over a list of prospective donors, make some phone calls, and attend events. The bulk of the fundraising should be handled by members of the campaign team. But this practice is far from routine. Comments by several candidates suggested they were heavily involved or entirely responsible for their own fundraising, especially if they ran for municipal office where fewer resources might be needed.

Although gendered differences were observed in women's and men's perceptions of personal fundraising prowess, such disparities were not apparent when it came to perceptions of political parties and electoral district associations (EDAs) as potential sources of financial assistance. Both women and men candidates identified challenges in leveraging resources from party and EDA executives. Candidate experiences were directly tied to their party's level of competitiveness in the riding. Individuals who were expected to simply carry the party banner in an unwinnable riding could expect little, if any, funding from party headquarters. A Green Party candidate in the 2015 federal election was frustrated at his party's decision to put most of its money behind a few star candidates.

Other candidates encountered resistance from their EDAs, but for different reasons. Discrimination was one factor. Some local party executives were uncomfortable with the selection of a racialized or sexual minority candidate and did not throw their full backing behind the campaign. Catherine Meade, a Black lesbian who ran for the federal Liberals in Halifax in 2008, was left wondering what role race might have played in the fact that party members did not donate as heavily to her campaign as they did to the white men candidates who ran before and after her in that riding:

> The elections before, there seemed to be more money in the pot than there was with my particular election. Again, is it because people didn't want to contribute? It can't be that they didn't want to support a losing candidate because we were always going against [a strong incumbent], so you kind

of knew where that was going to go beforehand. That can't be it. But why
it is that people didn't give at the same levels that they did in the past? I
don't know.

The challenges that other racialized and/or queer candidates encountered with their local EDAs were related to the fact that many of them
ran for the NDP or Greens, parties that are not electorally viable in
many ridings across the country. These EDAs tended to be bare-bone
operations with few volunteers and not much money in the bank.

In some cases, the candidate and local party officials had very different interpretations of the NDP's viability in the riding. Perceiving
a shift in public opinion, candidates believed the party had a real shot
at taking the seat for the first time and wanted to make a big push. But
local party officials either continued to believe that it was a lost-cause
riding or that the public mood was not favourable enough for this to
be the election in which the party broke through. One man had the
additional burden of running in a newly created riding, which legally
prevented the EDA from raising any money until it officially came into
existence on the day the election writ was issued. Once everything was
in place, the East Asian gay man wanted to fund a competitive campaign but local EDA executives preferred to fundraise for the future:

> The impression I got was that they wanted to conserve money, they wan-
> ted to use this election cycle to fundraise with a good candidate, not spend
> much money on the actual campaign knowing that that money will run
> over into their bank [account] and will be used for the next election. Then
> they'll do the same thing again and again until they feel it's the right
> moment to put all the money into one candidate because it's winnable
> at that point. But their opinion at that time was that we need one or two
> elections to just focus on fundraising and not spending much money on
> the candidate just to build up the association until it's at the point where it
> is winnable. So, I guess the provincial party was playing more of a strategy
> game – this party can win – and they [the local riding association] were
> playing more of a money game, saying we don't have the money to win
> regardless of the person.

Not surprisingly, high-profile candidates in winnable ridings were
treated like champions by their parties, receiving considerable financial
resources to fund their campaigns. This was the case for Cheri DiNovo,
a white lesbian who held the Toronto seat of Parkdale–High Park for
the Ontario NDP for 11 years before retiring from provincial politics in
2017. "I was running in a riding they thought they could win and as the

candidate they thought could win it for them. All parties will make it a lot easier when that's the case." Her management team did most of the fundraising for her. Aside from calling a few potential donors, DiNovo was able to concentrate on campaigning.

The Personal Costs of Political Candidacy

The challenges of raising money for campaign expenses is only half of the money equation. Would-be candidates also need to think about the personal financial implications of running for elected office. To be in a competitive position when the writ is dropped, individuals often need to spend months – and, in some cases, years – building the donor and volunteer networks, media profile, and name recognition that are crucial to electoral victory. That means attending countless community events, signing up scores of new party members (if relevant), and knocking on endless doors. "These all take time away from your job sometimes, from your career, from your business if you're running a business," said an East Asian heterosexual woman who ran for federal office. Time spent promoting one's political ambitions is time not spent developing one's career. But lost career opportunities pale in comparison to lost wages from voluntary or forced sabbaticals. Many candidates take a leave of absence from their jobs, usually when the formal election period arrives. With no money coming in, candidates find it difficult to pay their own bills, never mind their campaign bills. "There's never a good time to go without salary for five, six weeks," said Catherine Meade. "It's never a good time for that. Even though your campaign can make money, it can fundraise, it's never to compensate you for what you've lost." A former provincial politician noted that "you have to be in a very specific position in your life to be able to do that." This financial burden is made harder when individuals are forced by their employers to take a leave of absence as soon as they publicly express *interest* in running. Provincial medical officer Monika Dutt delayed announcing her intentions for as long as possible to soften the economic blow, but the lost time made it even more difficult for the South Asian heterosexual woman to assemble the financial and human resources necessary to mount a competitive bid for federal office.

Would-be candidates used several tactics to cover their bills while campaigning. Some individuals built up their savings account over a period of several months, but this only works for those who know well in advance when they will run and/or are in a financial position to put money aside for such an eventuality. This option was not available to those who waited until closer to the election to decide or who were under-employed. Many candidates chose to continue working, even if it was only part-time, rather than forgo their (full) salary while campaigning. A long-time municipal politician who tried to enter federal politics got by on his family's farm income, while Cheri DiNovo used vacation time to campaign for provincial office. The political party also covered some of her personal expenses, though its support was likely motivated by the fact that she was widely expected to win her seat. Her experience in this regard was unique among the research participants who had run for elected office. Some candidates expressed a desire for such support from their parties or for election rules to allow campaign funds to cover at least a portion of candidates' personal expenses.

The personal financial costs of running for elected office is a serious drawback for many prospective candidates. Several eligibles listed financial issues, both personal and campaign-related, as a top issue holding them back from running. While it was not the main reason that she had resisted recruitment efforts so far, one white heterosexual woman admitted to being concerned about how a campaign might affect her family's financial well-being, including her ability to send her children to university. "Would it be worth it to put my family in a more difficult financial situation, which being a single parent anyway is pretty difficult," she said. Meanwhile, Hannah Bell wondered if she would have a job to return to once the election was over:

> I would have to take a leave of absence prior to announcing and during the entire campaign … The odds are for a non-profit to lose its [executive director], they wouldn't be able to hold that job for me indefinitely. So, there's a financial risk of how do you get to the point where you've got enough money to cover yourself. If you're not coming from an affluent background, not everybody's got the luxury of being able to take a leave of absence and be paid. I don't work for a company that would say, "Yes, of course you can and we'll pay you while you're doing that." It's not going to happen.

While many individuals can take a leave of absence from their jobs, others would have to quit to pursue public office. Journalists are a case in point. "Every employer I've ever had has pretty much had the requirement that if you're going to be a journalist for them you cannot be active politically, not in terms of being involved in a political party," said a white heterosexual man who works in newspapers. "The only way you can do it is if you actually quit journalism, and some people do it." An Indigenous woman decided against a political career because she could not afford to quit her job on the off chance that she might win.

Nor did she have the connections to find a new job after an election or time in office:

> I think those of us who don't come from that kind of blue blood background, yeah, I can't just quit a job and know, oh, my connections are going to hook me up with some kind of a swank consultant's position after this is over. I might be standing at the Walmart after this is over asking for a cashier's job. ... I've never been in a position where I could just walk away from what I do to earn money in order to run. That would be scary beyond belief. I hadn't actually thought about that until now! Now I'm absolutely sure!

The personal financial challenges of running for elected office were viewed as a key reason why wealthier individuals tend to dominate politics. "That made me realize – and this is a generalization on my part – well, no wonder rich people can run for politics because they can afford to," said Lewis Cardinal, an Indigenous heterosexual man who ran municipally and federally. "They don't have to worry about paying the bills because they'll have the bills paid. They can focus totally on being a candidate." He was not in the position to do the same.

The Personal Costs of Elected Office

While less affluent eligibles focused on pre-election wage loss, more affluent eligibles raised the issue of post-election wage cuts (see also Carnes 2018). Remuneration for officeholders varies from one government to the next, with federal, provincial, and big-city politicians earning around $100,000 a year or more. By way of comparison, members of Parliament received a base salary of $178,100 in 2024, while members of provincial legislatures got $106,603 in Manitoba, $116,550 in Ontario, and $119,532.72 in British Columbia. Edmonton city councillors received $122,363, while their Toronto counterparts got $133,776.24. For lesser affluent eligibles, these salaries are higher than what they earned. But such compensation rates represented a pay cut for more affluent individuals. "I can't live on that," said George Smitherman, who spent most of his professional career in politics but was earning an excellent living in the private sector at the time of our interview. Keen to get back into politics, he was considering a bid for school board. "School board pays $30,000 and doesn't create the expectation that you'll do anything other than it as a part-time job. ... So, for me it's like a client. If I think about the way I compartmentalize my life these days, it's a client. I'm going to take that $30,000 and that's going to pay for all my child care. I could justify it on that basis." Other individuals would take a pay cut for the opportunity to affect government policy, but only after carefully considering the implications to themselves and their families. One Indigenous heterosexual man, who was a struggling entrepreneur, blamed public perceptions of politicians for what he saw as low pay:

> There's the joke "You never see a T-shirt that says Future Prime Minister of Canada on a baby." It's because we don't value the politicians and what they do. … The people that are there right now in the Liberal government give up multimillion-dollar businesses to be politicians. They would be getting paid more and their families would be benefiting more if they never went into politics. There's this funny thing that when we look at a corporation and say, "Well if you want anything run by people that are sensible and good at their job, you've got to pay them a lot of money." But when we look at politicians, people think "Well, they're just a waste of money."

Not all politicians earn six-figure salaries, however. Municipal politicians outside the big cities earn far less than that, which can pose challenges for many people across the socio-economic spectrum. The salary can seem small considering the demands that even a part-time elected position places on a person's time. "I think our local [councillors] get $17,000 a year. That's nothing," said Ted Mouradian, a gay man of Armenian descent who ran for federal and municipal office. "You're working for 50 cents an hour." While men's perspectives were highlighted here to illustrate this issue, remuneration was also an issue raised by women eligibles. Some women didn't want to jeopardize their family's financial security or quality of life because of their political ambitions.

The Professional Costs of Political Candidacy

Remuneration was far less important to research participants than other employment-related issues such as organizational rules, employer relations, career attachments, and future job prospects. The experiences of several candidates demonstrate the challenges of overt partisanship for future and former politicians in governmental and corporate contexts. In line with Carbert's (2009) research in Atlantic Canada, some women research participants in this study had to confront public sector rules regarding political activities. It took months for one South Asian heterosexual woman to get permission from her public service commission to run because the rules were not clear. An East Asian lesbian opted to run for school board not only because she believes in education but also because it posed fewer conflict-of-interest problems for herself and her employer. A different South Asian heterosexual woman who moved into the public sector a few years before our interview had her employer's needs in mind as she prepared to run for the first time:

> [Since] I took on this position with the university, I've been aware of the optics as well as the regulations. It indicates very clearly in the university guidelines that you can run for office but you can't do any kind of campaigning or anything that is perceived as campaigning during your office hours. Afterwards you're able to do whatever you want. But that's a fine line. I would want to make sure that my dean understands my intention, and we can have a very frank conversation about whether he would want me to step away and take a leave, whether I would have to quit, or whether he's comfortable with me staying in my role until after the election time.

The nature of employer–employee relationships shapes how individuals are able to navigate organizational rules and expectations. Although she was expected to take a leave of absence, an Indigenous heterosexual woman working for a First Nations organization had the moral support of her bosses. They also made adjustments at work to facilitate her candidacy. But not everyone had a positive experience. "They didn't want me to be involved," said Cyrille Giraud, a racialized gay man who worked in the financial sector. "They considered that if I was dedicating that much time to politics, I wouldn't dedicate enough time to be efficient to my work. I find it's a very twisted way of seeing the political involvement of citizens." He believes he lost a job because of his various election bids.

Aversion to overt partisanship was a reoccurring theme in candidate stories about the negative repercussions for their careers. Since most provincial and federal candidates run under a party banner, people who seek office at those levels of government make their partisan affiliation a matter of public record. They are now Conservative, Liberal, or NDP politicians, regardless of the outcome of the election. "For the rest of their lives that's all they'll be known as," said Jasmine Leicester, a white transgender woman who sought both a provincial and municipal seat. The implications to one's career prospects only truly become apparent once the election or time in office is over. "I think maybe it might have entered my mind [before running], but I didn't take it as a serious threat because I thought that I had really good, strong relationships with a lot of people in the provincial government," said Lewis Cardinal. "But politics being what it is, it's not thicker than political blood, I guess you could say." He lost out on government contract work, especially after his federal run, because he was not from the same political party as many provincial bureaucrats. "What I've learned about people in government roles is that even [though] they're supposed to be impartial and fair, they wear their colours prominently." A change in the governing party can also affect a person's ability to find work when they leave elected office. A former right-wing politician could not resume her consulting career after leaving office because she lived in a left-leaning city. "[R]unning your own consulting firm, you had to be non-partisan. I cannot go back to running my consulting firm because which level of government is going to hire me when they know I'm not non-partisan? So not only did I give up my job [to run] but I gave up my future earning potential." She urged people to think about what might happen post-politics when deciding whether to become a candidate.

The negative consequences of partisanship on future job prospects were not the main issue for everyone. Some research participants simply loved their current careers too much to leave them. Marni Panas, a white transgender woman who worked in the Alberta health care sector at the time of our interview, knows she would have the support of her immediate bosses if she were to run but derived immense satisfaction from her work improving the lives of other transgender individuals. Other research participants expressed concerns about the impact of an extended absence from their careers while they held elected office. Cheri DiNovo explains:

> Imagine you're taking seven to 10 years out of your most productive earning years, out of your career. Well, try to go back into your career after that. That's really difficult. So if you were a lawyer and you had a practice, forget your practice. You have to start all over again. If you're in business, ditto. If you're in any other profession, you've taken 10 years out and everything that means in trying to get a job again. So, again, it's really not for personal gain that people come into this place in any way shape or form.

An undercurrent in many interviews with candidates was the perception that politics is a public service rather than a profession. They did not seek elected office to have a job but to change the country for the better, however they approached that. Politics therefore was seen as a disruption to their normal professional activities, something that took them away from their actual career rather than being a career in its own right.

Conclusion

Money remains an important barrier to elected office in the minds of individuals with a deep interest in politics. Both eligibles and candidates identified financial concerns among their top drawbacks to political candidacy, but they didn't see this issue in the same ways. Eligibles mainly focused on the financial challenges of campaigning, both in terms of raising enough money for their electoral bid and covering their personal bills when they had to take time off from work to campaign. Many eligibles lacked prior experience in fundraising and thus questioned their own ability to raise what they needed. Occupational norms and employer expectations also meant many eligibles knew they would have to take a leave of absence or even quit their jobs to seek elected office, but election laws prevented campaign funds from being used to cover those lost wages. Less affluent eligibles weren't sure if they could afford to campaign for office. In contrast, more affluent eligibles hesitated to run because politicians' salaries were (much) lower than their own.

This chapter also confirmed important gender differences in how eligibles viewed campaign fundraising, in line with American research (Carroll and Sanbonmatsu 2013b; Jenkins 2007). More women than men expressed doubts about their fundraising skills; men more often conveyed confidence. One reason might be differences in their respective personal and professional networks: women suggested they would have a harder time raising money from their connections. Women might also be less comfortable asking others to donate to their campaigns, in part because doing so might change the dynamic of personal relationships. Friends might regret donating in the event of a loss or try to exert undue pressure on policymaking in the event of a win. Men eligibles did not raise these relationship or ethical issues. This study also found that people were simply reluctant to leave their careers, deriving more satisfaction from their current jobs than they expected to find as a politician.

Like eligibles, candidates identified campaign fundraising as a drawback, but they revealed that money in politics can be more complicated than that. Candidates noted challenges related to assembling strong campaign teams and receiving financial assistance from their political party or local riding associations. Some racialized and LGBTQ candidates wondered whether their fundraising struggles were because of resistance to their candidacies on the part of local party officials and supporters. Candidates were also alert to how political candidacy in general, and overt partisanship in particular, could affect current careers or future job prospects. Similar to Carbert's (2006) findings in her study of Atlantic Canada, this chapter found that occupational norms, organizational rules, and employer attitudes can make it difficult for candidates to find employment once the election or term in office is over. Employer and client aversion to overt partisanship was a reoccurring theme in candidate stories about the negative repercussions to their careers. Finally, both eligibles and candidates tended to view elected office as a form of public service rather than as a career, potentially heightening perceptions of the financial and professional risks involved with becoming a candidate. The next chapter delves more deeply into the partisan factors shaping candidacy in the early twenty-first century.

Chapter Five

The Partisan Calculation: Reticence Towards Party Discipline and Ideological Misalignment

I don't feel that my values align identically to any of the parties. I wouldn't feel compelled to saddle myself to any one of them in particular, at least given their current platforms. I feel I would have to fiercely believe in what the party stood for in order to run as a candidate, and that hasn't yet happened.

– Jesse Hitchcock, a white heterosexual woman eligible

Introduction

Political parties are the most important conduit to elected office at the federal and provincial levels in Canada. It is rare for an independent candidate to win because voters know political parties control those legislatures. Constitutional conventions allocate governmental power to the party able to command the confidence of the legislature, which is essentially the party with enough seats on its own or with the help of one or two other parties to survive any non-confidence vote that could lead to their defeat as a government. Parties therefore put a lot of effort into winning every seat they can during an election. Major parties like the Liberals and Conservatives compete to win a majority of seats so they can form government and pass their legislative agenda. Meanwhile, small parties like the Greens want enough seats to achieve official party status so they can get additional resources from the government to influence its agenda. Parties also control the spoils of legislative life. One plum assignment is a cabinet post. The leader of the governing party (the federal prime minister or provincial premier) picks their cabinet from among the party's elected representatives. Not only is the job prestigious but cabinet ministers also play an important role in shaping government policy. Consequently, individuals who aspire to federal or provincial office, and eventually a cabinet post, must run under a party banner and preferably a party with an excellent shot at forming government.

A desire to see government policy reflect the needs, interests, experiences, and perspectives of a diverse group of Canadians is why scholars monitor the extent to which political parties field a representative slate of candidates. Women comprise 50 per cent of Canadians, but are they 50 per cent of the candidates? Indigenous people make up 4 per cent of the Canadian population, but are they 4 per cent of the candidates? For now, the answer is no. The problem is that parties have erected several obstacles to federal and provincial office, which hinder the candidacy of women, Indigenous people, racialized folks, and LGBTQ individuals. An extensive literature explores how gendered and racialized recruitment practices reinforce the notion that white heterosexual men are the ideal candidates (Ashe and Stewart 2012; Cheng and Tavits 2011; Crowder-Meyer 2013; Tolley 2019, 2023). Candidate nomination processes only deepen this social group's structural advantage (Cross and Pruysers 2019; Thomas and Bodet 2013). These are just two reasons why our legislatures are over-populated by white men.

As the introductory chapter showed, political parties were the second most cited drawback to candidacy. One-quarter (25.7 per cent) of research participants identified various aspects of Canada's strong party system as barriers to candidacy at the federal and provincial levels. Differences of opinion were starkest along gender lines. Keeping in mind the small number of interviewees, women (37.3 per cent) were twice more likely than men (15.2 per cent) to select parties as a drawback while no gender-neutral individual did so. Variations within other categories were more limited but in the expected direction. Eligibles (28 per cent) were slightly more likely than candidates (23.5 per cent) to see political parties as obstacles to a career in politics. The same was true for racialized people (27.1 per cent) versus white individuals (24.5 per cent) and queer folks (28 per cent) versus heterosexuals (23.5 per cent). These results show that people who have traditionally been involved in Canadian party politics – men, heterosexuals, and white people – don't see parties as major barriers to their candidacies in comparison to those who have traditionally been marginalized in parties. What these figures cannot reveal is *why* some people are put off by parties.

Interviews with 101 individuals from diverse social backgrounds indicate that party recruitment practices and candidate nomination processes are just two components of the partisan calculation. Individuals thinking about running for elected office at the federal and provincial levels also assess a party's ideology, leadership, message discipline, electoral competitiveness, candidate expectations, and internal politics before deciding. This chapter explores the reasons why research participants identified these factors as key party-related challenges to federal and provincial candidacy in Canada. Before we begin, though, it is important to note that such party calculations are not usually necessary at the municipal level. With the current exception of parts of Quebec and British Columbia, municipal politics is non-partisan. Some candidates might have partisan affiliations at the federal or provincial levels, but they run as independents when seeking seats on municipal councils or school boards. We also cannot underestimate the impact that a lack of familiarity with party politics can have on candidacy calculations. Eligibles know that they need to join the partisan fray to run, but they didn't know much about how parties operate or how to get involved with them. The following sections present assessments of the challenges of partisan politics.

Party Ideology as General Barrier

Ideological alignment is an important barrier to candidacy but one not quite explored in prior research. To be willing to run for a political party, candidates need to believe in the party, its ideology, and its platform (Marland and Wagner 2020). Not surprisingly, this wasn't a problem for the federal and provincial candidates interviewed for this book. They expressed little disagreement with their party's platform, but when they did, they often looked at the bigger picture in terms of what was best for the province or country as a whole. "Provincially, when you make policy, it affects the whole province. So, while it might not be your favourite thing, if the majority of the province is going to benefit then that's the process, right," said a white heterosexual woman who had been an MLA in British Columbia. "Certainly, while there may have been things I didn't 100 per cent like, you do them for the greater good, for the majority."

Strong ideological alignment is important if a candidate is to defend party policies with which they do not agree. Many of the eligibles simply weren't there yet. They felt that all of the major parties put forward some good policy ideas and, as a result, they couldn't decide which party to join. In a few cases, individuals had figured out which party they absolutely *could not* support but were left struggling to decide which one of the remaining parties could work. Other eligibles knew which party most closely aligns with their values but that party wasn't competitive in their area. "I probably philosophically align myself most with the Liberals but they're so ridiculously unhealthy and unsuccessful as a party" in Alberta, said Cindy de Bruijn, a white heterosexual woman eligible.

The inability to choose a political party was a key reason why some individuals had yet to take the plunge despite being acutely interested in political affairs. A Hispanic heterosexual woman eligible argued that she would need to support at least 75 per cent of a party's platform before she would run for provincial or federal office: "You really have to believe what you're going to be advocating later on. It speaks to the whole being true to your word, true to yourself." That candidates generally expressed stronger ideological alignment with a political party than did eligibles indicates how important ideological alignment between party and individual is in the decision to become a candidate in Canada.

Party Ideology as LGBTQ Barrier

Although party ideology matters to all prospective candidates, it has particular ramifications for conservative-leaning LGBTQ individuals. To outsiders, it can appear that members of the LGBTQ community share many of the same values. Studies indicate that LGBTQ individuals are more likely to be liberal (Lewis, Rogers, and Sherrill 2011; Worthen 2020) and vote for left-wing politicians and political parties (Lewis, Rogers, and Sherrill 2011; Perrella, Brown, and Kay 2012; Swank 2018a, 2018b; Turnbull-Dugarte 2020). A survey of American college students, however, found meaningful differences in liberal values among LGBTQ individuals, with bisexual women more liberal than other sexual minorities while gay men were more liberal than lesbians (Worthen 2020). These findings remind us not to assume that LGBTQ individuals are monolithic in their political outlook or behaviours. LGBTQ voting patterns, for example, might be the result of left-wing parties being more responsive than right-wing parties to LGBTQ interests rather than a simple expression of ideological preferences (Boily and Robidoux-Descary 2019; Chaney 2013; DeGagne 2019; Jeffrey 2019). In Canada, the federal NDP has long supported LGBTQ issues while the Liberals have played an instrumental role in passing LGBTQ-friendly legislation since the 1960s. The Conservatives, however, have often rejected LGBTQ goals. Party ideology could explain why many queer candidates in this study ran for the left-wing NDP or the centrist Liberals over the right-wing Conservatives, and why many of the queer eligibles followed suit in their partisan affiliations.

Yet, despite the general liberal bent of the community, eight LGBTQ research participants of varying ethnicities and genders indicated they were staunchly conservative. Patrick Schertzer, a white gay man eligible who is active in party politics, has met many gays who want "smaller government, lower taxes, and believe in the free market, which aligns more with the Conservatives in general on economic policy." A white queer woman eligible indicated that she is a member of the Conservative Party of Canada because of a strong belief in fiscal responsibility and couldn't see herself switching to the NDP, Liberals, or another party because of their economic platforms.

But LGBTQ participants' views differed on the degree to which conservative parties are receptive to LGBTQ candidates. Some eligibles were acutely aware of the influence, and biases, of these parties' socially conservative base. Felipe Del Campo-Donoso believes he has three things working against a potential candidacy with the party: he is young, queer, and of Spanish descent. "Those three will conflict probably with the Conservative party, in my opinion." The white queer woman also expects the party base to have a hard time accepting her candidacy if she were ever to seek the Conservative nomination. The same would be true for voters in a general election, who would be confused by a candidate who doesn't match the stereotype of a typical Conservative.

> Part of me wishes that we could do this interview in person because then you could see me. I have coloured hair, I have facial piercings, I have quite a few tattoos, but I belong to the Conservative Party of Canada. A lot of people see those things and they don't mesh for them. And I definitely would never fit, if there was a mold – which there kind of is – for someone to run for politics under those parties. I definitely don't fit that mold.

She knows she would find greater social acceptance with the NDP and Liberals, but she would have a hard time fitting in there because of her policy preferences. That is why she has ruled out switching to another party. "I would still feel like I would be fitting someone else's mold."

A gay Black man eligible believes the mold doesn't matter as much to partisans as the electoral outcome. Even if some Conservative supporters don't like a person's sexuality, Christopher Matthews argued that they will still fundraise and vote for a LGBTQ candidate if that person is competitive in a riding. Winning seats and forming government are what matter most. Other gay Conservatives insisted that the federal party is actually becoming more welcoming. Former party leaders Stephen Harper and Andrew Scheer refused during their tenures to reopen debates on contentious issues such as abortion, even in the face of strong pressure from social conservatives within the party.

Prominent Conservative politicians, including former interim leader Rona Ambrose, have also made public comments in support of LGBTQ people. It is for these reasons that Schertzer believes the party had changed in recent years.

Why do some Conservatives welcome LGBTQ candidates and others reject them? The difficulties that some LGBTQ members report experiencing in conservative parties derive from an uneasy tension between two types of right-wing ideology: neoliberalism and conservativism (Boily and Robidoux-Descary 2019, 158–60). Both ideologies advocate for limited government, low taxes, and free markets, but they differ in terms of who they perceive to be the primary unit in society. Neoliberalism considers it to be the individual. Because they believe nothing should stand in the way of individual freedoms, neoliberal actors tend to be more supportive of LGBTQ rights. Conservativism, on the other hand, considers the family to be the primary unit. Conservative actors thus see "the protection of social traditions and mores, such as the nuclear family, as central to its political agenda" (Boily and Robidoux-Descary 2019, 159) and often use the state to accomplish these goals, such as trying to make abortion illegal or regulating public bathrooms.

Conflicting views on the basic building block of society within right-wing parties have important implications. First, they explain why we see mixed messages from Conservative politicians regarding social issues. Some conservatives support individual freedoms, others try to regulate them. Second, and most importantly for our purposes, these conflicting views explain why some LGBTQ individuals are members of conservative parties but struggle to be fully accepted. They are attracted to fiscal policies that strive for balanced budgets, low taxes, limited government, and free markets, but they typically reject social policies that infringe on their personal freedoms. Neoliberal actors are their natural allies because these actors try to make conservative parties more welcoming to LGBTQ folks. The Conservative Party of Canada's decision in 2016 to drop its opposition to same-sex marriage could be seen in this light. The move suggested the party was more accepting of LGBTQ individuals. Social conservative actors, however, reject LGBTQ inclusion (Boily and Robidoux-Descary 2019; Rogers and Lott 1997; Hirczy de Mino and Kergosien 1997).

This tension between right-wing ideologies affects gay conservatives the most, and they have to learn how to navigate it if they want to be Conservative candidates. "The party's a big tent and people are more than welcome, but it means you have to support both sides of the tent," explained Schertzer. "People who believe more right-wing social conservative values are part of the party, and people who believe more socially liberal values are part of the party." The degree to which social conservatives are a problem for gay conservatives depends on their strength within a party at a given point in time. This is where party leadership evaluations come in.

Party Leadership as Hindrance

Party leaders are important political actors in Canadian politics. After any given election, one of them will become the country's prime minister or a province's premier. The power they wield is why party leaders are constantly evaluated for their views on social and economic issues as well as for their character and competence. The main question on everyone's mind is this: How would they govern? Party leadership is especially important to partisans (Bittner 2014). Evaluations of party leaders and the direction in which they are taking the party can influence partisans' level of involvement in the party. Some partisans even decide to leave the party because of it. This leads to another question: What role do party leader evaluations have on an individual's willingness to become a candidate? We simply don't know. Research on leader evaluations typically focus on the perspectives of journalists and voters and what impact their evaluations of party leaders have on electoral outcomes (Bittner 2010, 2018; Gidengil and Blais 2007; Takens et al. 2013).

Scholars rarely question the commitment of party members. They are assumed to be diehard loyalists who always vote for the party, even though recent research shows this isn't necessarily the case (Polk and Kölln 2018; de Vet, Poletti, and Wauters 2019). Negative impressions of the party leader are one reason why a small, but influential, number of party members cast a ballot for another party (Polk and Kölln 2018; de Vet, Poletti, and Wauters 2019). Likewise, shifts in a party's platform or ideology are scrutinized for their effect on voters but not on party members (cf. Adams and Somer-Topcu 2009). Again, partisans' loyalty is presumed. But it shouldn't be. An Austrian study demonstrates that individuals are more likely to tear up their membership card when the ideological distance between their views and the party's views becomes too great, regardless of the reasons why (Wagner 2017).

Fewer assumptions are made about party members when selecting a new leader because of the immense power that party members hold in deciding who gets the job. The increasing democratization of leadership selection processes in Canada over the last half century means all party members now have an opportunity to choose the next party leader (Cross and Blais 2012). Delegate conventions, where a small number of party faithful pick the leader, have given way to leadership elections, where each card-carrying member gets a vote. In this situation, the importance of member evaluations is clear and thus studied (cf. Loewen and Rubenson 2011). But what about in other situations?

My interviews with both eligibles and candidates indicate that party leader evaluations are one of several partisan factors shaping a party's potential candidate pool. Party ideology matters most to eligibles because it provides a clear benchmark to assess the party's (future) approach to public policy. Conservatives advocate for fiscal responsibility, small government, and low taxes. New Democrats believe in social justice and prefer a strong social safety net. As with candidates, leaders are constrained by party values. Their vision for the party, and especially its platform, must fall within the acceptable range of positions for that party. A Conservative leader, for example, cannot call for higher taxes without losing significant member support – and probably their job.

As long as the leader conforms to party ideology, some eligibles don't care who the leader is. Darius Maze, a white man who has been involved with different parties over the years, said that his willingness to run for a party would primarily depend upon "the platform and the values that a party represents." Even if some eligibles don't care who the leader is, they know that voters do. Their association with a particular leader could thus be just as damaging to their reputation or electoral prospects as their association with a particular party. As a result, they feel compelled to place greater emphasis on the party leader when deciding to run than they otherwise would.

Eligibles who do give serious weight to party leaders in their candidacy calculation base their evaluations, in part, on how well the leader's values align with their own. "They are the person who ultimately sets the agenda. In the end, they have final sign-off on things," said a white queer woman. "If their vision doesn't match with yours, then it would be difficult to kind of row in the same direction as that person." The degree of alignment between partisan and leader can shift over time. Party leaders might have to operate within certain ideological confines, but they still have a lot of room to manoeuvre. "Because of the political party system," said an Indigenous gay man active in partisan politics, "the party sways with what the leader is doing and wants."

A change in party leadership can therefore mean a change in party direction, and that shift can inspire some individuals to come forward. Cindy de Bruijn gave serious thought to running for provincial office after Alison Redford became leader of the Progressive Conservatives and, by extension, premier of Alberta in 2011. The white heterosexual woman felt Redford put the progressive back into Progressive Conservative:

> For me, that was the first time that I was optimistic that at the provincial level of politics we would have a balance of conservative values that are really important to most Albertans but also be able to recognize some of the social benefits and the contributions that can and should be made to have good quality of life for the majority of people.

Running in the 2012 provincial election, however, would have been difficult for de Bruijn because it followed just months after Redford's elevation to the premiership. But if de Bruijn was thinking about running in the next election, those thoughts started to dissipate as Redford's term in office became mired in controversy, leading to her ouster in 2014. It also became apparent that a local businessman had a lock on the party nomination in de Bruijn's preferred riding. A new leader can also encourage individuals to step away from the party. Felipe Del Campo-Donoso let his membership lapse after the federal Conservatives elected the socially conservative Andrew Scheer as leader in 2017. In short, party leadership evaluations are one means by which eligibles can assess their ideological alignment with a given party.

Despite the importance of ideology, candidates who identified party leadership as a key determinant in their eventual decision to run also cared about the person's character and leadership style. The leader made all the difference to one West Asian heterosexual woman, who unsuccessfully ran for the federal Liberals. "I think just the fact that Justin Trudeau was the leader of the Liberal party made me more interested in running because I felt like I could trust him, whereas if it had been Paul Martin or somebody I didn't feel cared about youth issues or cared about immigrants and things like that, I probably would have been like, 'Yeah, no way.'" A white heterosexual woman who used to be a member of another party changed her opinion of Stephen Harper after meeting the then-leader of the Conservative Party:

> He didn't appear to me as somebody mean, pompous, snob. He was kind of the 9-to-5 guy, dad who takes his kids to hockey and he goes to their school recitals and he'll do anything for his family to keep it safe. But at the same time an individual with a lot of dignity and self-respect. He was calm. He was more normal than any small or big politicians. Trust me, I met them all.

She wasn't a member of the Conservative Party at the time of the meeting, but eventually became one and even ran for the party in one federal election because of her perceptions of Harper's integrity.

The positive assessments that can come out of these one-on-one connections is likely why party leaders, despite their busy schedules, make sure to spend time with would-be candidates. A former BC politician decided to make the leap from municipal to provincial politics after being personally recruited by then-Liberal leader Christy Clark. The white heterosexual woman was impressed with Clark's humility after plans to connect one night kept being delayed. "The fact that she phoned and apologized to me, I thought that was pretty good." Would-be candidates need to have confidence in the party leader because the latter sets the tone within the party organization. A strong leader keeps the party together. A weak leader drags the party down. "[People] don't leave a bad job, they leave a bad boss," said a South Asian gay man. An unpopular party leader can make life difficult for candidates on the campaign trail. Paul Harris, a white gay man who ran for the federal NDP in 2015, was happy to see Liberal leader Justin Trudeau become prime minister after that election rather than NDP leader Tom Mulcair:

> I don't think Tom Mulcair would have been a great prime minister after working with him. That was a hard conversation to have at the doorsteps because you had to support him and defend him all the way. I shouldn't have to defend the leader of the party, because people did not like Tom Mulcair. Even the NDP didn't like Tom Mulcair.

Still, Harris believed Mulcair was the right individual to lead the NDP when it was the Official Opposition in the House of Commons from 2011 to 2015. Then prime minister Stephen Harper "was so domineering about everything. They needed somebody to keep at him all the time. I don't think anybody else could have done that as well." The party simply needed a different kind of leader to go from opposition to government.

That parties regularly change leaders to find the right person for their needs makes it difficult for eligibles to fully assess what impact the party leadership might have on their experiences in electoral politics. All they can do is evaluate the current leader and hope for the best. "I understand that once you get into the job, that leaders change and things happen and that's a little bit different," said a South Asian lesbian eligible. "But I think that initial decision to run, I would want to support whoever it was who was the leader there."

Party leadership matters because of the high degree of party discipline in the Canadian political system. Because they are expected to fall in step behind the party leader, eligibles want to make sure that the leader is worthy of their fidelity. Before one white queer woman decides to run for the NDP in Manitoba down the road, she wants to know whether the party leader is assertive or autocratic: "I would have to get a sense of how he was going to operate on a lot of the issues, like how tight a ship he was going to run or if he was going to develop some kind of cohesive strategy or plan and then potentially punish anyone who [does] not deviate from that but offers anything in the way of public criticism of it." Her comment speaks to the important role of party leaders in party discipline in Canada. Leaders enforce party loyalty through a series of carrots (e.g., assigning plum cabinet posts) and sticks (e.g., refusing to sign candidate nomination papers, thereby preventing the person from running under the party banner).

Party Discipline as Constraint

Eligibles and candidates alike expressed reservations about the strict message discipline expected by Canadian political parties at the federal and provincial levels. A white gay man who ran in the 2015 federal election was told by his party that "if I was asked a question [about issues where I deviated from the party], I was not to answer with anything but the party line, and if I couldn't do that, I wasn't to answer at all." Some candidates opted to go into municipal politics because its non-partisan nature offered more opportunities for independent voices:[1] "When you're getting into parties, specifically at the provincial and federal levels, you have to toe the party line, and that's an expectation that you're going along with the ideas and ideologies of the party, whether you agree or not," said Tash Taylor, a white heterosexual woman who ran for city council in Alberta.

Strict message discipline not only limits what politicians can say in public but also stymies efforts to promote their policy agenda within the party. Susan Rose, an Indigenous lesbian who had no immediate plans to run for office, recalled the exasperation of political friends who found their room for manoeuvre extremely limited once they were in office. Other research participants noted that candidates and parliamentarians

---

1 Canadian municipal government is non-partisan, with the exception of parts of Quebec and British Columbia. In May 2024, the Alberta government passed legislation to permit municipal political parties in Edmonton and Calgary.

who dare to express dissenting viewpoints can see their political careers stalled or shortened. Nominations are denied, plum committee assignments withdrawn, cabinet positions never materialize.

Strict message discipline gives some prospective candidates sober second thoughts about entering party politics. Several eligibles conveyed doubts about their ability to toe the party line. "I don't want to say I think outside the box, but I walk to the beat of my own drum," said Gurpreet Kaur Sodhi, a South Asian heterosexual woman who has decided not to run for a number of reasons. "I'm not sure that I could vocalize things that I don't believe in." A white queer woman noted that new politicians have to hold their tongue until they work their way up the political ladder: "I think that would be a challenge for me because I have my principles and I'm loathe to part with them." An Indigenous queer woman who had no plans to run believes party discipline is part of what's wrong with Canadian politics today: "I think if the Conservatives have a good idea, I should be allowed to say, 'You know what, that's a good idea, and in terms of the people who voted for me, it's what's best for them so I am going to vote with them on this,' and I don't think my party should have the right to tell me that I can't do that." Sharp conflict between personal opinion and official policy makes it nearly impossible for some individuals to be effective candidates for their party. They simply do not believe enough in the party platform to publicly support it.

Many racial and sexual minorities struggle to believe in parties they view as too narrow in focus. Minority eligibles were concerned that their candidacies would be little more than a symbolic attempt by parties to descriptively, but not substantively, represent the diversity of Canada. Political parties, in their view, are preoccupied with candidates who tick off all the identity boxes in terms of gender, race, sexuality, and disability, but they display far less interest in incorporating into the party platform the perspectives, values, and interests of these candidates or the social groups they represent. Jessica Quan, an East Asian woman who used to be a political staffer, said the "perfect NDP candidate is a lesbian woman who is not white and has some sort of physical disability." A white queer woman declined one party's request to become a candidate because of concerns that she would be little more than window dressing:

I'm not a big fan of that, but I also felt like I didn't really have enough experience or confidence in myself at that point where I would have been able to even call them out on being like, "Yeah, I'll run for you, but I think if you want to have me in as a queer person, I actually want us to talk about queer issues and I don't want to just be someone you can add on your list of candidate sort of things."

Racial and sexual minorities who did run were reluctant to become candidates for a political party they felt was not responsive to the interests of their respective communities. "Maybe the way we do things needs to change rather than just putting somebody in a dress and painting somebody's face a different colour," said El-Farouk Khaki, who ran unsuccessfully for the federal NDP in a 2008 by-election in Toronto.

A one-size-fits all approach to party messaging creates additional difficulties for minority candidates who run in ethnically diverse ridings. In these cases, it is not just about tailoring the party message to suit the candidate's own personal brand but also to highlight those aspects of the candidate's background that might appeal to different voters and downplaying those that do not. For example, racialized LGBTQ candidates know that different aspects of their identities can be problematic depending on the neighbourhood. Khaki, a gay Muslim man of African descent, was frustrated by his party-produced campaign literature. "There's not [a] tactful way of saying this. There's a sense of oblivion on putting gay activist on my campaign materials for me to take into Regent Park," he said about the conservative Toronto neighbourhood. "It doesn't work. It shouldn't take the candidate to say, 'Excuse me, but do you understand there's an issue here?'" Minority candidates want to adapt party messaging to reflect who they are as political actors and to speak to the interests of the voters they are canvassing. For these candidates, authenticity means reflecting their sexual and/or racialized identities in their campaign communications, even if their messages do not strictly reflect the party's more generic messaging. The need for parties to maintain message control, however, severely limits an individual's opportunity for individual expression and, in some cases, their willingness to become a candidate.

Party Competitiveness as Deterrent

If party discipline doesn't deter someone from running for office, electoral challenges certainly could. The ability to win an election is an issue that all would-be candidates must take into consideration when making the decision to run. But competitiveness, also known as winnability, is a multi-faceted concept in partisan politics. First, individuals with aspirations of influencing public policy need to run for a political party that has formed government and might do so again. Only a couple of political parties fit that bill at the federal level (Conservatives and

Liberals) and in most provinces. Other parties are relegated to opposition status or struggle to get any seats at all. But choosing to run for a competitive party might not be an option for those individuals who reject that party's ideological stance. "If you really want your chances to be high [in Alberta], you would run Conservative, but I would never in my life consider running Conservative because it is not my values," said a former provincial politician.

Second, individuals need to consider whether their preferred party is competitive in their preferred riding. Many ridings stick with the same party despite general shifts in voting preferences in the province or country. Even parties that dominate the electoral map in a given area don't take every seat. For example, the Conservatives typically take the lion's share of federal seats in Alberta, but the NDP has held Edmonton Strathcona since 2008 while a few other urban seats appear to be on the path to becoming swing ridings that alternate between the Conservatives and either the Liberals or NDP.

Another wrinkle is that perceptions of party competitiveness in a given riding can vary dramatically between the party's candidate and local riding executives. This was the case for one East Asian gay man. The candidate wanted the local riding association to increase its financial contributions to his campaign because he believed the party had a good shot at flipping the riding in the provincial election, but local party executives disagreed. The candidate believed they wanted to focus on filling the association's coffers and preferred a different type of candidate to help them do it. Flipping the riding was for another time. But another explanation could be what scholars call strategic discrimination. Party recruiters might be open to diverse candidates but select candidates based on assumptions about the biases of local voters (Bateson 2020). Electability is key here. Parties not only want candidates who can do the job but who can also win the seat. If recruiters believe voters will not support diverse candidates, they will go with traditional candidates. This strategic discrimination makes it more difficult for women, Indigenous, LGBTQ, and racialized people to "establish themselves as real contenders" (Bateson 2020, 1069). Together, this man's experience and previous research demonstrates the importance of candidates and local party executives being on the same page regarding the candidate's and party's electability in a riding. Without that agreement, a candidate will find it difficult to get the supports necessary to field a competitive campaign.

Finally, individuals need to assess other aspects of their competitiveness in the party. Can they defeat other aspirants for the party's nomination? In ridings that consistently send representatives from the same party to the legislature, the candidate nomination process is where the real election is contested. Whoever wins the party nomination will go on to win the general election. In more competitive ridings, individuals must have the requisite name recognition, good public reputation, qualifications, and resources to field a viable campaign. A candidate's partisan affiliation guides many vote choices (Goodyear-Grant 2010), but it is not the only factor. Some politicians build up enough of a personal vote (voters who support them rather than the party) to hold on to their seats despite dramatic shifts in the public mood towards their party.

Party Nomination as Obstacle

The issue of party competitiveness also arose when research participants were asked about the challenges they might (or did) face when seeking a party nomination. Eligibles who did not anticipate major problems indicated that their party was not competitive in their area. Consequently, they expected to be acclaimed as the party's candidate. For eligibles who preferred to eventually run in competitive ridings, they expressed an intent to develop strong networks and name recognition within the party as well as sell memberships and raise money for the party. The goal was to demonstrate their value to the party and increase their chances of getting nominated. Candidates who had already been through the nomination process tended to talk about organizational issues such as scheduling. At least two individuals were frustrated with the amount of time it took for their local electoral district association (EDA) to hold the nomination meeting. In both cases, the EDA wanted to find a different candidate, someone they believed would be more appealing to local voters.

It shouldn't have been that way for Alexandra Mendès. Liberal riding officials approached her to become the party's candidate in Brossard-La Prairie (Quebec) after the incumbent Liberal MP retired. She agreed to do so in January 2007 but was still waiting for the EDA to hold the nomination meeting a year later. Party officials explained the delay by saying "they wanted to have a star candidate in the riding because it was a winnable riding." That prompted her to withdraw her candidacy. Seven months later, the EDA came calling again. "They had done a poll in the riding on name recognition, and of all the people they had sort of thrown around, I came up always as the most well known." Turns out Mendès was the star candidate they were looking for all along. She was named the Liberal candidate just one day before the 2008 federal election was called.[2]

Some years later, a white lesbian seeking the NDP nomination in a federal riding long held by the Conservatives faced a lot of opposition from an EDA that was less keen than the national party on selecting a non-traditional candidate. "They worked really hard to try to find other people to run against me in terms of the initial nomination," the woman recalled of the selection process. Not only did they not like the fact that she didn't live in the riding but they also preferred a white Christian man. "I was a little bit too different from the people I was trying to appeal to – in their view." EDA resistance to a candidate can even continue after the person has secured the nomination. Racialized candidates noted the difficulty they had in getting moral or financial support from local party officials during an election campaign. "I think quite a few of the [local riding] executive felt that I, as a person, didn't properly represent the area because I was young and I was gay and I was an Asian," said one man candidate who ran unsuccessfully. "Too many minority cards there or something. I'm not sure."

Party Expectations as Funnel

Notions of what constitutes an ideal candidate emerged repeatedly as both eligibles and candidates identified challenges related to securing a party nomination. Individuals who fit the white, middle-aged, heterosexual male norm of Canadian politics knew these personal characteristics were assets in the eyes of many party executives and voters. "Being a white, heterosexual male doesn't really cause you a lot of problems if there are people with bigoted issues, that kind of thing," said one man. Individuals who didn't fit the norm thought about the degree to which they diverge from it and what impact that might have on their desirability as a candidate. One white queer woman didn't expect too much difficulty because her difference wasn't immediately apparent: "I identify as queer, but I still present really straight, so it's not very threatening. I get along well with lots of different people. It wouldn't be a write-off for people who didn't want to vote for a queer candidate." Age is a factor that weighs on the mind of younger individuals contemplating a future in politics. Felipe Del Campo-Donoso was not only concerned

---

2 Mendès went on to win the riding in the 2008 federal election but lost in 2011. In 2015, she was elected as the member of Parliament for the new riding of Brossard – Saint-Lambert. She was re-elected in 2019 and 2021.

with how his race/ethnicity, sexuality, and immigrant status would be perceived by the Conservatives but also his relative youth. "The way I see it is that the party does not like young people to run because they don't have the experience an older person might have." Another eligible, however, was reluctant to seek a party nomination because of strong anti-LGBTQ sentiment from the general public. A South Asian gay man who has travelled extensively around Ontario was surprised at the venom directed at Kathleen Wynne, a white lesbian, when she was premier of Ontario. "As an LGBT individual, I would want to be in a place that's safe but so do a lot of other people." The most welcoming seats for LGBTQ individuals tend to be in the larger urban centres such as Toronto, making the nomination process in those ridings even more competitive. "So that's one big obstacle," he said. In short, the more a person deviated from the straight white male norm of politics, the more they saw their social characteristics as a barrier to getting the party nomination.

Yet growing demand for politicians from diverse social backgrounds has opened up space for non-traditional candidates and made it a bit more difficult for traditional ones. Some parties make a concerted push to find candidates from all walks of life. "I tick a lot of boxes," said a South Asian lesbian, "and that's often appealing." Having diverse candidates allows parties to look like they reflect Canada, even if their policies don't. Here the issue of tokenism reemerges. One candidate recalls how she was treated as a prop:

> INTERVIEWER: What did you, or what did others perhaps, think made you a good candidate for federal office?
>
> RESPONDENT: I was young, Muslim, female.
>
> INTERVIEWER: Why were those things considered strengths?
>
> RESPONDENT: Because they didn't have anybody like that. I was the youngest candidate across all of the parties for that election. They could use me as an example. If I went to an event or something, they would bring that up just to make the party seem like it was really diverse and it had everybody included, a plethora of different Canadians from all walks of life and everything like that. So, they could say, "We have our hijabis, we have our young candidates, we have our old candidates, etcetera."

Party efforts to recruit diverse candidates is especially pronounced in ridings with large minority populations. The desire to appeal to these racialized voters means a large portion of racialized candidates for the major parties run in urban ridings, especially in British Columbia,

Ontario, and Quebec (Black 2008; Griffith 2015). The same is even true for ridings with a large white population from a particular ethnic background. "It used to be in my riding that it was preferable to have a Polish person with a Polish last name running," explained Cheri DiNovo, a white lesbian who was Ontario's Parkdale–High Park MLA from 2006 to 2017.

The quest for diverse candidates has created ethical and practical issues for the straight white male. Many of them are interested in getting involved in electoral politics but know their demographic is over-represented among current politicians. Should they run anyways, or step aside to let another type of individual run? Darius Maze struggles with this question. "I've got this privilege to be able to run for the position but I'd love to see more diversity in our House of Commons and our local legislature." Public pressure for candidate diversity can have harmful consequences. Maze pointed to the case of Gerry Taft, who was forced to publicly reveal his bisexuality after securing the NDP nomination in Columbia River-Revelstoke in the lead-up to the 2017 British Columbia election (McElroy 2016). "He wasn't happy having to out that aspect of himself" to meet public expectations, Maze recalled. "He just wanted to be a representative."[3] Efforts to recruit diverse candidates run the risk of being little more than tokenism.

Party Politics as Minefield

Overall, eligibles identified several party-related factors that have made them reluctant to enter partisan politics at the federal and provincial levels. While candidates also gave some thought to ideological alignment, leadership assessments, party discipline, electoral competitiveness, and candidate ideals when making the decision to run, their experiences working within the party system led them to identify another factor that was often under-estimated by eligibles: internal party politics.

Eligibles, of course, know they have to get involved with a political party to run successfully for federal or provincial office. The party is unlikely to pick an unknown person to be its candidate in a winnable riding. Getting involved in party politics is necessary to develop the networks and name recognition needed to secure the nomination. Once selected, they expected the party to provide at least some resources

---

3 Taft went on to lose the 2017 provincial election to Doug Clovechok of the BC Liberal Party.

(information, human, or financial) to support their campaign. For those individuals thinking about running for office one day, they planned to begin the candidacy process by getting involved with their preferred party.

But candidate stories about their campaigns, both successful and unsuccessful, reveal that party involvement is not so straightforward. Party politics is about more than just networking. Would-be candidates need to understand how people and processes work within their preferred party to increase their chances of success. A long-time Liberal operative with aspirations to sit in the Ontario legislature, George Smitherman used his knowledge of party rules to thwart another man's candidacy and secure a party nomination in the late 1990s:

> SMITHERMAN: At that time, for some odd reason, the Ontario Medical
> Association had determined that they were going to be backing
> candidates in particular ridings. For some stupid reason, they'd come
> to lend support [in my riding] to a guy whose father was a doctor …
> I had to utilize a tactic which is no longer available to political riding
> associations to snuff the life out of the gentleman's candidacy.
> INTERVIEWER: That's an interesting turn of phrase. (Laughs)
> SMITHERMAN: Yes, do you want to know what I did?
> INTERVIEWER: What did you do?
> SMITHERMAN: Well, I sold a lot of memberships. The membership price was
> $10, so I handed in my memberships – 1,400 members – and I brought in
> my $14,000. I had already gained control of the riding association, which
> is a tactic of usually reasonably inconsequential effect but having some
> influence over the control of the nomination meeting, date, etcetera.
> The riding association at that time had the liberty of establishing the
> membership price. So, once we had 1,400 memberships sold, we raised
> the membership price to $25.
> INTERVIEWER: Oh, interesting.
> SMITHERMAN: [The other man] was sitting on a whole bunch of
> memberships that he now needed to pay $25 for instead of $10, so
> he quit. So, I was not contested. Now the Liberal party establishes a
> membership fee uniquely across the province or something.

The formal rules around membership fees might have changed, but would-be candidates who know the party terrain can likely find other ways to work the system to their advantage. Lacking this knowledge, however, can result in a person being on the receiving end of such manoeuvres. A racialized heterosexual woman found it difficult to get her party's nomination because of the machinations of regional party officials looking for the "right" candidate. Once she did get the nod, she felt some officials gave her bad advice to sabotage her campaign because she wasn't the candidate they wanted.

These two experiences demonstrate the importance of capturing the EDA before a nomination run. Smitherman downplayed the value of controlling the EDA, but it is unlikely he would have been able to raise the membership fee when needed if EDA executives weren't his allies. Moreover, if the racialized woman had stacked the EDA executive with her supporters, local party officials would have been invested in her electoral success rather than in pursuing their own agendas. Being in control of the EDA is especially important in those instances where the candidate and local party executives might not agree on strategy. Failed candidates noted that some of their biggest challenges came from within their own party, not their opponents. Ambitious candidates were dragged down by pessimistic party officials who didn't believe success was possible and didn't want to put any real time, money, or effort into the campaign. Other candidates didn't have a choice when it came to controlling the EDA. They were expected to set up the EDA when new parties established themselves or new ridings were created. These expectations placed additional burdens on candidates who already had a lot of work to do in organizing their election campaign.

Conclusion

Political parties play an important role in recruiting individuals to become elected representatives. Research typically focuses on party recruitment and nomination practices to find out why most politicians remain white, heterosexual men despite decades of activism to encourage the selection of a wider range of candidates. My interviews, however, identify additional party-related factors shaping candidacy at the federal and provincial levels.

One of the most important factors for eligibles was ideological alignment between individual and party. Because political parties control the House of Commons, all provincial legislatures, and the territorial legislature in Yukon, individuals who want to get elected in these party-based systems need to pick a party. Independents rarely get elected. But it can be difficult to pick a team when no political party, especially a competitive one, offers a platform that an eligible is willing to publicly support. Concerned about tokenism, racialized and LGBTQ eligibles especially needed the party platform to address the interests of their respective communities. Canadian politics is notable for its intense party discipline. Politicians who cannot practise strict message discipline and publicly support most of their party's platform will find their time in office extremely unpleasant, unproductive, and unrewarding. Awareness of these facts gave some eligibles pause about a future candidacy.

The issue of ideological alignment also emerged in relation to other aspects of political parties that eligibles saw as challenges to candidacy. The party leader matters to many eligibles because of the control that person has over the policy direction of the party. A change in leader likely means a shift in policy – and not always in the desired direction. Likewise, eligibles felt that a strong understanding of how a political party and the people already within it operates is necessary to better navigate the internal party politics that has thwarted or sabotaged the candidacies of other individuals. Eligibles also pay close attention to electoral competitiveness. Do they have what it takes to win the party nomination in their desired riding? Has the party ever elected a candidate from that riding? Can the party form government? Interviews suggest ambitious individuals need a yes to at least the first two questions before putting themselves forward as candidates.

Although these issues crossed their minds before running, candidates drew attention to the difficulties posed by local riding associations. Non-traditional candidates in particular expressed frustration over the continuing preference for white, heterosexual men candidates in many parties and the degree to which local party officials remain resistant to new entrants to the political system. Even the left-wing NDP, which has made the most effort to recruit more diverse candidates, did not escape this criticism. Racialized and LGBTQ candidates expected riding executives to be more supportive of their campaigns. They did not want to be treated as tokens.

In short, this chapter reveals that political parties aren't the only ones making assessments regarding suitability during the candidacy process. Prospective candidates evaluate multiple facets of partisan life when deciding if electoral politics is for them. A related drawback to candidacy is reputational factors, including ones related to partisanship. The next chapter explores the role of public scrutiny in the candidacy process.

Chapter Six

The Reputational Calculation: Regulation of Personal Lives and Public Personas

Most people … have anonymity. They move about the city and go about their way and don't have to put too much thought into what others think of their activity and to be put on the spot for anything. Whereas someone running for public office, you are always on. Whether you are out having dinner at the end of the night, or whether you are commuting on the subway to something or actually out canvassing, you have to be prepared for interactions with the public who rightfully want to talk to those aspiring to hold public office and represent them in the legislature.

– White gay man, former provincial candidate

I am not asking to be Pope, so you shouldn't be asking me to not have a past or that I have to answer for every mistake I've ever made in my life because mistakes are part of life.

– Indigenous queer woman eligible

Introduction[1]

Public scrutiny is a double-edged sword in politics. On the one hand, it is an important means by which citizens can hold elected officials accountable for their actions. Citizens can evaluate a politician's effectiveness in office by monitoring their voting records, public comments, and other activities related to a range of policy issues. In the case of aspiring politicians, citizens can assess their potential as legislators by examining their campaign promises and policy statements as well as their professional backgrounds, volunteer histories, and political

---

1 Parts of this chapter are adapted from Wagner 2021, 502–18.

activities. Journalists have historically performed this monitoring function in a democratic system (Kuhn and Neveu 2002), but the advent of digital media has provided citizens with the tools to do this themselves. Many citizens not only use online platforms to keep track of what politicians say and do but also to publicly reflect on or attack political performances (Burroughs 2013; Summers 2012). Digital media has thus multiplied the sources of accountability in a democratic system. Whether it is journalists or citizens who hold politicians accountable, public scrutiny serves to remind them of public expectations.

On the other hand, public scrutiny often goes beyond issues related to governance to include matters such as character, physical appearance, sexual orientation, family circumstances, and private conduct (Langer 2007, 2010). Politicians find their personal attributes and activities subjected to intense evaluation (Benoit and McHale 2004; Langer 2007), even when the subject matter has no direct bearing on how they might conduct themselves as legislators. Regardless of news content, Daniel Sutter (2006) argues that the news media's intense vetting of political candidates can reduce the quality of elected officials because self-interested individuals are more willing than publicly minded individuals to bear the privacy and reputational costs of politics. He calls this the media scrutiny paradox.

Journalists are not alone in scrutinizing politicians. Opponents, partisans, activists, and citizens also evaluate politicians' personal attributes and behaviours, and they often use social media to launch both political and personal attacks (Azari and Stewart 2015; Burroughs 2013; Summers 2012). But accountability and public scrutiny are not the same (Tetlock 1985). Robert Sutton and Charles Galunic (1996, 203) define scrutiny as "an intensive and obtrusive form of attention from others" that is comprised of sustained attention, monitoring and evaluation, frequent interruptions, and relentless questions about what they have done, are doing, and will do in the future. They argue that public scrutiny is most likely to occur when "there is something sufficiently novel, interesting, or important about the leader or organization to attract close attention and interference from observers and exchange partners" (Sutton and Galunic 1996, 205). The means by which scrutiny happens varies, including through in-person or online interactions.

Public Scrutiny as Problem

When research participants were asked what they considered to be the major drawbacks to running for elected office, 25 people raised the issue of public scrutiny. One-quarter (26 per cent) of eligibles singled out public scrutiny as an important drawback, but they varied on whether it was enough to keep them out of electoral politics. One-sixth (16 per cent) of eligibles cited public scrutiny as a key reason why they were refusing or hesitating to run for office. Another 10 per cent saw public scrutiny as a drawback but said it was not sufficient reason to stay out of politics, a sentiment shared by 12 candidates. While other individuals did not count public scrutiny as a barrier, many touched upon the issue when asked about other matters such as news coverage and family-related concerns.

That one out of every four eligibles identified public scrutiny as a potential barrier to political candidacy is striking for two reasons. First, research participants *volunteered* this information. The interview schedule did not contain a question asking people for their thoughts regarding public scrutiny because it was not identified as a leading barrier in the political candidacy literature. Second, public scrutiny was only established as a major concern in the late stages of data collection, when the bulk of the queer eligibles were interviewed because of challenges in identifying and recruiting members of this hidden population. Of the eight eligibles who identified public scrutiny as a barrier, all come from traditionally under-represented groups in politics: six are sexual minorities, five are members of racialized groups, and five are women. This finding indicates that fear of public scrutiny is a key factor limiting the political ambition of traditionally under-represented groups in politics, thereby reducing the pool of high-quality candidates necessary to ensure the best possible political representation (Shames 2017, 18).

Eligibles and candidates alike offered several explanations for why public scrutiny was a drawback to candidacy. Politicians are under a constant spotlight, even if all they are doing is their grocery shopping. This raises concerns about privacy. Is any part of their life off limits? Research participants were also concerned about the potential for the spotlight to shine on their family. For their part, LGBTQ eligibles were hesitant to subject themselves to the moral regulation of sexual behaviour and gender identities that often underlines public scrutiny of elected officials. While the first three issues weren't enough to keep many research participants from running for office, LGBTQ responses indicate that the last one constitutes an important barrier to political candidacy for this under-represented group in Canadian politics. It is for that reason that moral regulation will be discussed in depth later in this chapter. The next section will review the general concerns about public scrutiny voiced by research participants.

Constant Spotlight on Politicians and Their Families

Canadians are well aware that politicians face an unrelenting public spotlight, with everything they say and do constantly evaluated by opponents, journalists, and voters. "Everything you do goes under a microscope for [the] public to see and assess," said a white gay man who ran unsuccessfully for provincial office, "and for some people, that is not something that they're open to." Part of the risk of public scrutiny is being evaluated by other people on a larger scale than what one is used to. Candidates have little to no control over how they are evaluated by others and on what basis. Voters might judge them on substantive matters like their policy stances all the way to trivial matters such as what food they buy at the grocery store. Unlike in everyday life, the people passing judgment have likely never met the candidate and don't know them on a personal level. Although one white heterosexual woman was mainly hesitant about seeking an elected position because of the low remuneration in comparison to her private sector employment, she was equally put off by the public shaming that politicians often have to endure. "At the end of the day, am I willing to [take a pay cut], especially coupled with the amount of public scrutiny that our public officials now have to endure?" asked Cindy de Bruijn. "It just doesn't seem like it's good value for [the] dollar." Other people who do not want to be in the public spotlight indicated that they might get involved behind the scenes as campaign workers or political staffers.

Eligibles, in particular, mentioned the need to be resilient in the face of public criticism. Their comments suggest a person can possess that fortitude in one of two ways: innate personality or past experience. Some individuals did not put much stock in what other people thought of them or were comfortable with criticism, suggesting they had the necessary personality traits to withstand scrutiny. Christopher Matthews, a Black gay man who might one day run provincially, insisted that anyone who wants to pursue a political career needs to develop a certain degree of emotional distance from the job:

> I think every politician gets attacked in some way and I think it's part of being a politician. If you don't have that backbone, then you're in the wrong job because regardless of what you do or how you do it or even if you think you're doing it for the best, somebody is going to disagree with you, and if you can't handle that criticism or even that wild comment, it would be a difficult job for you as a politician.

Other eligibles admit that such resiliency does not come easily to them. "I don't think I have the fortitude or the temperament to be able to deal with things like that on a day-to-day basis," said a South Asian gay man. But it is possible to grow a thicker skin. Jeane Lassen was a competitive weightlifter, competing for Canada in the 2008 Olympics in Beijing. The white heterosexual woman faced constant criticism of her sports performance throughout her athletic career and thus wasn't surprised by what she encountered as a Liberal candidate in the 2016 Yukon territorial elections. Bradley Metlin, a white gay man, was often targeted for items he wrote during his five years as a student journalist at an Ontario university. Because of their previous experiences, both individuals are better skilled at dealing with critics and criticism.

What weighed more heavily on the minds of many research participants was the potential for the public spotlight to shine on family members. Eligibles discussed this issue more than candidates, indicating it might be of greater concern to those who have not yet run for elected office. That family members might face public scrutiny is why many candidates and eligibles considered family support to be necessary before pursuing one's political ambitions. Even then, women and racialized men were especially attuned to the potential for family members to be drawn into politics. While it might not be enough to deter them from becoming candidates, they would consider the ways in which family members might be affected by their political ambitions before making a decision. Concerns revolved around three key issues: their family's privacy, psychological well-being, and physical safety.

Research participants were concerned that family members, and especially their children, would see their own lives subjected to public scrutiny because of their association with the candidate. The general expectation was that only the person putting themselves forward for elected office – the actual candidate – should be evaluated by the public in any way. Family members should remain private individuals who are free to live their lives as they see fit without those decisions or actions being discussed in the news media, online forums, or around the water cooler. This expectation was even more pronounced in relation to their children. Adult partners were generally expected to take care of themselves, but children should be protected from such intrusion. Two individuals noted that family members often get dragged into the public spotlight because of a general expectation that they accompany the candidate to events and/or appear in campaign materials.

Another major concern was the psychological or emotional distress it causes family members to see the candidate subjected to intense public scrutiny. Family members experience frustration, anxiety, and anger when watching the politician being attacked by opponents, journalists, and members of the general public for things said or done in the past, during an election campaign, or while in elected office. Their frustration is heightened by a sense of helplessness at being unable to defend the candidate from these attacks. Although not overtly stated, the underlying assumption by some research participants is that family members should stay out of the political fray and not engage in verbal sparring matches with opponents. Such actions would presumably increase the possibility that family members would come under public scrutiny as well, with harm to themselves and to the candidate's campaign the likely outcome. Joanne Bernard, a former Nova Scotia cabinet minister, noted that her son would become anxious whenever they were out in public together during her time in office. When someone approached her, his body would become tense as he awaited a potential confrontation over some policy matter put forward by his mother or her government. She was grateful that such confrontations were rare – most people respected their privacy as they went to the movies or spent time together – but it highlights the constant emotional and physical stress that family members must live with as their loved ones pursue and hold elected office.

Two women candidates also discussed the possibility of physical attacks and their impact on family members. A racialized lesbian candidate was deeply concerned that her wife would be assaulted at her socially conservative workplace, even though the woman was out regarding her sexuality. That is why the candidate made the decision to limit public exposure of her family during the election, opting not to include photographs of her wife in any campaign material. Bernard, a white lesbian, said a homophobic man kept coming to her campaign office in an increasingly aggressive manner, leading her to call the police to address the issue. She expressed concern that her family would become the focus of public aggression.

The need to protect their families is of paramount importance to participants, but they also expressed a strong desire to maintain a private life within the political fishbowl. Eligibles talked about this issue at length, illustrating that privacy is of far greater concern to those thinking about running for elected office than those who have already done so. Maintaining some degree of privacy was important because of what it allows individuals to do. Politicians work long days, attending not only legislative sessions and committee meetings during the week but also community events on the weekend. Carving out some private time for themselves and their families was necessary to achieve a work–life balance and maintain their mental and physical health. Some research participants wanted a clear demarcation between their political activities and their private life. They don't want to give everything to the job. Others were keen to prevent every misdeed, secret, or personal struggle from becoming public knowledge. Some people feared that they would be negatively judged for having a stigmatized mental health issue, such as addiction or depression. Health-related issues are discussed in more depth in Chapter 8.

Moral Regulation and LGBTQ Individuals

While all candidates face potentially intrusive public scrutiny, it can be especially problematic for sexual- and gender-minority individuals because moral regulation of non-traditional lifestyles and identities are often embedded in public evaluations of politicians. Research has found several examples of women being judged harshly for supposedly neglecting their responsibilities as wives and mothers to pursue public office (Atkins-Sayre 2009; Loke, Harp, and Bachmann 2011; Van Zoonen 1998, 2000). In this instance, moral regulation of women politicians' domestic arrangements reflects anxieties about changes in women's status in society and their increasing involvement in historically male-dominated activities, such as politics. But political women are not the only targets of moral regulation. Allan Hunt defines moral regulation as a "significant form of politics in which some people act to problematize the conduct, values or cultures of others and seek to impose regulation upon them" (1999, 1). These moral enterprises are ongoing processes of reformation, designed to change the identities and/or behaviours of the targeted individual or social group to reflect the desired ideal (Hier 2011; Ruonavaara 1997). While efforts at social control are coercive in nature, moral regulation is persuasive insofar as it encourages subjects to engage in self-formation or self-regulation (Hunt 1999; Ruonavaara 1997). Moral entrepreneurs – the ones doing the regulating – can be state actors such as government agencies or judicial institutions, but they are more often non-state actors such as parents, teachers, and activists. Hunt notes that the middle classes are a common source of regulatory movements. Regulatory subjects – the ones being regulated – are as varied as moral entrepreneurs in terms of social, political, and economic location (Hier 2011; Hunt 1999). Politicians are often the targets of moralizing discourses.

Hunt (1999, 8) raises the important point, though, that subjects do not necessarily internalize these discourses and can contest attempts to govern their identities and/or behaviours. The problem for efforts to achieve descriptive representation in legislative bodies is that some

LGBTQ individuals chose not to get involved in politics to avoid experiencing the more intensive form of moral regulation that public scrutiny brings. A key reason is that sexuality, in all its complexities, has long been the focus of moral regulatory projects. Hunt argues that "the 'moral' element in moral regulation involves any normative judgement that some conduct is intrinsically bad, wrong or immoral" (1999, 7). While Hunt discusses sexuality more broadly, such as efforts to achieve (hetero)sexual purity and combat sexual exploitation, religious discourses have long held non-heterosexual practices as deviant. This has led to moral panics around public expressions of homosexuality (Catungal and McCann 2010) and global LGBTQ activism (Tettey 2016). Attitudes towards LGBTQ individuals have improved over time in the United States and Canada (Andersen and Fetner 2008), but mainstream acceptance is uneven across each society. LGBTQ individuals continue to face harassment and discrimination (NPR, Robert Wood Johnson Foundation, and Harvard T.H. Chan School of Public Health 2018). The moral regulation of sexual behaviour and identities, amplified by the intense public scrutiny directed at politicians and candidates, has the potential to dampen the political ambitions of LGBTQ individuals, reinforcing the white, heterosexual boundaries of electoral office.

Like other research participants, LGBTQ people talked about public scrutiny in general terms, noting the potential for loss of privacy and exposure to public criticism. But as they elaborated on their views, it became apparent that LGBTQ people had additional concerns about public scrutiny that many heterosexual individuals did not. Interview data revealed that it was the potential for moral regulation, or negative judgement of their sexual and/or gender identities, that made fear of public scrutiny a major barrier to candidacy for LGBTQ individuals. They believed that candidates who do not fit the white, heterosexist norms of politics face an additional level of scrutiny based on personal characteristics, identities, and/or lifestyles. Extensive experience with discrimination led them to expect this evaluation to be moralizing, judgmental, and dismissive. Their concerns about moral regulation centred on two distinct but related themes: sexuality and physical appearance.

Sexual orientation has long been the target of moral regulation. Homosexuality and alternative sexualities pose a fundamental challenge to the expectation that society should be composed of heterosexual nuclear families with the man at the head. This heterosexist notion has lost some of its power in recent decades, but it continues to hold sway among socially conservative voters. Yet even progressive voters might have a hard time accepting some aspects of LGBTQ culture. "I like the leather scene sometimes," said Ralph Carl Wushke, a white gay man who will not run because of public scrutiny. "These are things that I'm not ashamed of, but I think the Canadian public is a bit skittish about some of the – how do you say – fringe cultural practices of the gay community." LGBTQ eligibles opt out of politics because they do not want their self-worth challenged by voters and opponents who reject their lifestyles. "I'm a proud gay man," added Wushke. "I don't want my sense of who I am to be sullied by nasty attacks by homophobes or people who might think my life is not respectable as a gay man." A white queer woman who also refuses to run expressed a similar sentiment: "[A] lot of us have only found peace and happiness in rejecting the pressure to conform and in finding our own paths. So, the idea of getting onto this path that's, like, so proscribed ... [w]ould actually be very painful to contemplate."

While not all LGBTQ eligibles ruled out a run for public office, they know their sexuality could make them a target if they did. The white queer woman argued that the negative campaigning already taking place during elections could be even more intense for LGBTQ individuals as opponents attacked a presumed weakness. She expected the attacks to be less successful, however, if the LGBTQ candidate otherwise fit the heterosexist expectations of a nuclear family, such as having a partner and "cute kids." It also would not hurt if the person was a gay man:

> I think probably there is more distrust of queer women than there is of gay men in particular and especially white gay men because queer women's deviation from heteronormative structures and a perceived rejection of men is more abhorrent than gay men who sexually reject women.

Her comment suggests moral regulation of sexual identities is not experienced equally by all members of the LGBTQ community. Individuals could be subjected to more or less regulation depending on their particular mix of characteristics (see also Auer et al. 2022). The closer a candidate is to exemplifying the heterosexist norms of society in their mannerisms, dress, and home life, the more the person will be seen as a model minority. Individuals who deviate the most from the norm will likely face the most intense regulation of their sexual identities.

The electoral experiences of LGBTQ candidates confirm the legitimacy of these concerns. As eligibles expected, some candidates noted being the target of homophobic comments during their campaigns. Joanne Bernard was shocked at the level of homophobia directed at her during her first election campaign. One incident that stood out was a handwritten letter from a voter:

> [I]t talked about how, you know, she had such hope in me and knew my
> work from the community and then she said, "Till I read that sentence on
> your bio where you were married to a woman." And then she just went
> off and said I was disgusting, should never have put my name on a ballot,
> wrote the word "hate" all around the edge of the letter.

Bernard was devastated, but she later tweeted that she would represent all of her constituents regardless of their views on her sexual orientation. The tweet went viral and earned extensive media attention, enabling her to challenge public attitudes towards sexual minorities.

Candidates also relayed stories of other individuals, including family members, trying to regulate the open expression of their sexuality. Two racialized candidates discussed the difficulties they encountered within their own ethnic communities. An East Asian lesbian, who lost her campaign, noted that her mother and other community members expressed concern that she would face a voter backlash if she publicly noted her sexuality. A Black Muslim gay man could not arrange meetings with Muslim community leaders during his unsuccessful federal campaign because he felt they could not accept his homosexuality despite demonstrating acceptance of white LGBTQ candidates.

Both candidates and eligibles expressed concerns about how photographs depicting them in LGBTQ-related circumstances – such as attending Pride parades – might be used by opponents to publicly embarrass them. Wushke's involvement in the leather scene dates back to the 1980s and 1990s, and thus pre-dates Instagram, but he still does not "want a picture of me in a leather harness being dredged up." Photographs not only act as symbols of perceived sexual deviancy in the eyes of moral regulators but are also tools used by them to police the heterosexist boundaries of political life. Photographs are offered up as proof that the individual in question is not morally suitable to be an elected official.

Visual representations of difference were a common theme when research participants discussed the moral regulation of physical appearance. Aside from sexuality, candidates and eligibles mentioned different concerns when it came to expectations regarding how politicians look. What these issues had in common was that they exhibited some deviation from European ideals: white skin, straight hair, no tattoos or piercings, and feminine (or masculine) attire (Hardin 1999; Oyedemi 2016; Reddy-Best 2018). LGBTQ candidates felt pressure to as closely resemble this ideal as their bodies would allow but eligibles rejected this expectation. No straight white man reported facing pressure to change his appearance to live up to the gendered, racialized, and heterosexual norms of political leadership.

For eligibles, the main concern was body modifications. A white queer woman cited her tattoos and piercings as one more way in which she deviates from the norm of politics. Gender is implicated in public aversion to people with body modifications. While individuals with tattoos are generally rated lower in terms of competence, character, and sociability (Seiter and Hatch 2005), tattooed women are especially thought to be less intelligent, less honest, less attractive, less motivated, and less generous than women without tattoos (Degelman and Price 2002). Consequently, women with body modifications are believed to have fewer of the qualities desired in a political leader. Awareness of this negative evaluation is one reason why the queer woman refuses to run for elected office: "[The public] just have preconceived notions about what that means, and I don't feel like I would want to change the way that I am so that other people could be more comfortable." Moral regulation can be influenced by partisan affiliation. Non-conforming individuals might find it more difficult to build support within right-wing political parties and their socially conservative base because they do not conform to traditional gender and sexual norms.

Candidate experiences once again reveal the extent to which minority politicians face moral regulation of their gender and/or sexual identities. El-Farouk Khaki, a Black gay man, faced hostility while door-knocking during his federal campaign because he wears earrings. Derrick Biso, a white genderqueer individual who unsuccessfully ran for provincial office, faced family pressure to dress like a heterosexual man: "I had expressed a little bit of my queerness throughout the summer with some family, just putting on a dress and showing up for dinner. It kind of created a bit of a rift because it was unexpected, and so my father questioned my capacity to be a politician or be involved in politics due to such decisions and such sort of genderqueer expressions, which I answered … that's why I'm involved." Despite a strong sense of self, Biso endured personal discomfort and wore only suits during the election to make voters feel more comfortable.

Racialized heterosexual candidates also faced regulatory pressure to dress in accordance with the European norms of their (presumed) gender. Rana Bokhari, a South Asian heterosexual woman, was compelled to straighten her curly hair and wear more feminine attire such as dresses and high heels after she decided to run for the leadership of her political party: "Within days of me talking about it I had a lot of people kind of in my ear being like, 'Well, you know, Rana, you can't just be you. You've got to be pretend that you're these guys.' So that became a con very quickly for me because I'm very comfortable with who I am and what I'm about," said Bokhari, who went on to win the leadership contest. "So, I kind of struggled with pretending to be somebody who I wasn't." These comments indicate that the regulation of politicians' bodies reflect a desire to maintain the gender binary on which Western societies have long been based (Colebrook 2004). Despite growing acceptance of diversity in society, attempts to move towards a greater expression of gender, sexual, and racial identities continue to encounter strong resistance (Dash 2006; Miller et al. 2017; Somani and Hopkinson 2019).

LGBTQ individuals were not the only ones who expressed concerns about their personal behaviour being judged as transgressing moral norms. Eleven people noted the potential for real or perceived misdeeds to come to public attention and the effect they might have on public evaluations of candidates. These misdeeds involved some sort of moral transgression, such as extramarital affairs, bad relationships, or drinking. As with sexuality and appearance, minority individuals voiced much of these concerns. A Black heterosexual man who won't run for office admitted to not behaving in the most moral manner in his relationships. He viewed his misdeeds as private matters that should not be the subject of public disapproval: "I don't need to have thousands of other people or millions of other people looking at me and making judgments about my decisions, my ethics, my morality as I have performed it, so to speak, in my private life." An Indigenous queer woman said she would have expected public criticism for having dated a man with a criminal record if she had run for office. Drinking was the issue for other research participants. Several eligibles and candidates reported being concerned about and/or scrubbing photographs from their social media sites that showed them drinking. As with sexuality, alcohol has long been the subject of moral regulation in Western societies (Blocker 1985; Törrönen, Simonen, and Tigerstedt 2015). That politicians and candidates do not want to be seen with a glass of alcohol in their hand demonstrates that even social drinking is viewed as a moral transgression.

Mistakes Make the Politician

Some individuals expressed frustration with the public expectation that Canadian politicians must be perfect in their personal and professional conduct, including in the years or decades before a bid for elected office. An Indigenous queer woman argued that making mistakes enables individuals to develop empathy for other people and what they are going through in life. People who grow up in political families or develop political ambitions early in life are extra careful in how they behave so they can withstand public scrutiny later on. But that self-regulation leads to a narrowly lived experience that makes it harder for these individuals to effectively represent other groups of people. Despite the value of mistakes, the Indigenous woman believed that members of the general public have unrealistic expectations that politicians be squeaky clean individuals.

> I didn't work the kind of jobs that would be acceptable in politics. (Laughs) I think all of that is part of what makes me such a great person now because I have empathy for people at all levels and I've had a lot of rough times, so it makes me really enjoy the good times. But when you run for politics, they don't want you to be a real human being that has tested yourself on the rocks of life. They want you to be this plastic perfect person with no past and everything shiny and bright…

Derrick Biso also sees mistakes as a natural part of life. The former candidate was not only open to making mistakes but also to having them pointed out. The genderqueer individual wasn't interested in a "clean-looking life path or registry." Perfectionism gets in the way of becoming a better person and politician.

Conclusion

Public scrutiny is fundamental to democracy, especially when it is designed to keep elected officials accountable and transparent for their *political* decisions. But public scrutiny can work against efforts to recruit more diverse individuals to run for elected office because not all social groups experience the same type of scrutiny. Racialized eligibles viewed public judgment of past mistakes unfair while racialized candidates discussed the pressure that they faced to change their appearance to conform to European standards of beauty as much as possible. However, the unexpected discovery of this research is that public scrutiny is a major barrier to elected office for LGBTQ individuals. Although eligibles of all backgrounds expressed reluctance to enter electoral politics because of the potential loss of privacy and constant criticism, LGBTQ eligibles were also cognizant of the ways in which their sexuality and gender identities have always been the subject of moral regulation and how their stigmatized identities can make them appear to be less-than-ideal political leaders. Some LGBTQ eligibles did not want their sexuality to be publicly debated or evaluated, in part to protect their sense of self-worth and the privacy of loved ones. The campaign experiences of LGBTQ candidates revealed that eligibles' concerns about the negative aspects of public scrutiny are well founded. Candidates reported encountering criticism of their clothing, piercings, and other aspects of their physical appearance. But LGBTQ candidates did not let public scrutiny scuttle their political ambitions because of prior experience in the public eye or refusal to let other people's attitudes get in their way.

The decision by some LGBTQ eligibles to not run for office to avoid public scrutiny – and the moral regulation that can accompany it – has troubling implications for the candidacy process. The most important repercussion is that fear of public scrutiny depresses political ambition in an already under-represented group in electoral politics. Micro-aggressions such as criticism of a genderqueer candidate's clothing express the heterosexist boundaries of acceptable behaviour and discipline aspiring politicians who do not conform to those norms. More aggressive behaviours, including death threats, are attempts to scare minorities from entering, or remaining in, politics. That some sexual minorities refuse to enter politics because of public scrutiny suggests these strategies are partially effective in maintaining politics as a domain mainly reserved for straight white men. Efforts to recruit more LGBTQ people to run for office must therefore include training on how to address public scrutiny and, more specifically, the moral regulation of non-traditional candidates. The professional norms of journalism, as well as strong public pressure on journalists to avoid stereotypical coverage, mean non-traditional candidates don't have to worry as much about the news media when it comes to moral regulation. But that doesn't mean the news media don't cause problems. The next chapter explores how research participants view the news media.

Chapter Seven

The Media Calculation: Management of Media Expectations and Biases

You have to actively manage the media. They will do what they want if you don't carefully manage what they do. You can't manage it all the time, but you can certainly set some ground rules.

> – Hannah Bell, a white woman eligible

Introduction

The news media play a crucial role in the Canadian political system. Their primary democratic function is to provide citizens with accurate information about the workings of public institutions and the individuals who populate them. Ditto for other political actors with the potential to influence public policy, including corporations, business associations, activist groups, and social movements. Such fact-based reporting is expected to help citizens make informed decisions when voting for politicians or interacting with government. The news media typically perform their democratic duty by reporting on the daily machinations of institutions like the legislature, bureaucracy, and judiciary. They also monitor routine political events such as general elections, with coverage typically focusing on party leaders or mayoral candidates and occasionally on individual races when something interesting happens. The ideal practice is for the news media to act as watchdogs. Under this approach, journalists thoroughly investigate issues of public importance, such as police behaviour or deaths in foster care, to ensure that governing institutions operate in accordance with public expectations. Election coverage is ideally substantive, featuring a fair but critical assessment of all candidate platforms. However, the degree to which the Canadian news media consistently live up to any of these standards has long been debated.

Three issues are of particular interest for a discussion of how the news media shape political candidacy today: professional norms, commercial interests, and media bias. While space doesn't permit a detailed review of the debates surrounding each issue, I offer a brief overview here to provide some background before presenting research participants' perspectives of and experiences with the Canadian news media.

Professional norms are widely held values, practices, and routines that have guided journalistic behaviour since the late nineteenth century (Nerone 2013). Objectivity is one of the most well-known norms of journalism. American broadcaster Walter Cronkite once said: "Objectivity is the reporting of reality, of facts, as nearly as they can be obtained without the injection of prejudice and personal opinion" (cited in Maras 2013, 7). Many journalists continue to believe in this norm, despite valid criticism that objectivity is difficult to achieve (Cook 1998; Steiner 1998). Critics argue that journalists who claim to be objective are simply ignoring the ways in which their personal views already shape who and what they consider to be newsworthy (Cook 1998). A common alternative to objective journalism is interpretive journalism, which focuses on understanding *why* something happened rather than *what* happened (Salgado and Strömbäck 2012). Analysis is mixed in with facts. Today's journalism features fact-based stories and opinion pieces as well as analytical reporting that combines both approaches. The result is that journalists will either faithfully reproduce a candidate's campaign platform, zero in on only one part of it, focus on a completely different issue, or ignore the candidate altogether. It depends on the type of journalism that individual reporters or their news organization practice.

Political reporting is further shaped by the news media's commercial interests. The traditional emphasis on journalism's democratic function obscures the fact that most news organizations are corporate entities that need to make money for owners and shareholders. Profits are achieved through low production costs and high advertising revenue. One consequence is that, while citizens are the focus of civic-based journalism, advertisers are the focus of profit-based journalism. Attracting news audiences is really about attracting advertisers. But news audiences are dwindling, a trend exacerbated by the Internet and social media (Public Policy Forum 2017; Taras 2015). An increasing number of Canadians get their news from online sources, and advertisers have followed them to the Internet. To retain audiences and advertisers, the news media constantly re-evaluate how they present the news. One long-time trend that has become more pronounced in the digital age is tabloidization, which involves taking a sensationalist approach to covering people and current events (Franklin and Murphy 1998). The news media make politics entertaining by treating elections like games and politicians like celebrities (Aalberg, Strömbäck, and de Vreese 2012; Neveu 2002). A politician's comments or behaviour can be dramatized to make them appear controversial. Because of the media's profit motive, candidates can find it difficult to get a fair hearing from a news outlet that is more interested in a titillating story to drive up its ratings or circulation numbers. This type of media bias has the potential to harm an individual's reputation long after a career in politics has ended.

Other forms of media bias are independent of journalism's professional norms and commercial interests and instead stem from societal attitudes. Regardless of their approach to journalism, journalists and news organizations are no less a product of the societies in which they operate than the politicians and institutions they cover (Goodyear-Grant 2013; Wagner and Everitt 2019b). They can be sexist, racist, and homophobic. They can express these views intentionally or unintentionally and to varying degrees. In this context, media bias is understood as "a *pervasive* pattern [of prejudice] in a *significant portion* of overall news coverage" (Lawrence and Rose 2010, 15; italics in the original). Partisan bias fits within this definition. Individual news organizations can take political sides, but they do not all share the same political ideology. It shifts from left to right depending on the outlet or journalist. Far more pervasive is the news media's tendency to treat women and minorities in stereotypical ways. Studies show that media depictions of politicians often reflect cultural assumptions related to gender, race/ethnicity, sexuality, class, and age (Tolley 2016; Trimble et al. 2015; Wagner and Everitt 2019a). Candidates of all partisan stripes can, and do, experience such coverage.

The news media, whether knowingly or not, defend the traditionally white heterosexist character of Canadian legislatures by depicting as odd or out of place any candidate who does not fit the traditional model of a political leader – a white heterosexual man. Journalists raise questions about women's suitability for politics by paying excessive attention to personal matters such as their physical appearance, fashion choices, and family situation (Beail and Longworth 2013; Devitt 1999; Falk 2008; Fowler and Lawless 2009; Goodyear-Grant 2013; Ibroscheva and Raicheva-Stover 2009; Trimble and Everitt 2010; Trimble et al. 2013) and by downplaying more substantive matters such as their leadership qualities and policy priorities (Bystrom 2005; Hinojosa 2010; Kahn 1994; Manning-Miller 1996; Serini, Powers, and Johnson 1998). Journalists also position racialized individuals outside the political norm by repeatedly drawing attention to their race, ethnocultural characteristics, and religion (Caliendo and McIlwain 2006; Jeffries 2002; Major and Coleman 2008; McIlwain 2011; Terkildsen and Damore 1999; Tolley 2016, 2019; Wehrkamp and Jeffries 2014), as well as by associating them with racialized issues like immigration (Tolley 2016). A similar pattern repeats itself for LGBTQ politicians. Journalists emphasize their sexuality and views on LGBTQ-related issues and ignore their positions on the economy and other widespread concerns (Everitt and Camp 2009a, 2009b; McLean 2019; Mundy 2013). Media depictions of politics get even more complicated when examining gender, race/ethnicity, and sexuality together. Research has found differences in how racialized women politicians are depicted in relation to each other and to men politicians (Gerrits and Besco 2019; Gershon 2013; Tolley 2016, 2019; Ward 2016a, 2016b).

This concise review of the strengths and weaknesses of the news media points to an important question that potential candidates must answer before making the decision to run for elected office: Do I want to subject myself to media scrutiny? On the one hand, individuals can use campaign coverage to promote their political ideas and policy proposals to a wider audience. Even if they lose the election, they can contribute to public debate. On the other hand, individuals risk their reputations and emotional well-being when entering the media spotlight. News coverage might be inaccurate, sensationalized, partisan, or discriminatory, and candidates have little opportunity to correct misperceptions. Candidates might also face a public backlash spurred on, in part, by negative press. These factors are why scholars are concerned that sexist, racist, or homophobic reporting might discourage women, racialized minorities, and LGBTQ individuals from becoming candidates (cf. Falk 2008). In other words, media behaviour could reduce the rate of candidacy of already under-represented groups in Canadian politics. The rest of this chapter explores how candidates and eligibles view media behaviour and the role it plays in the decision to seek elected office.

Media Scrutiny Not a Potential Barrier

To assess perceptions of media behaviour, research participants were asked if they had any concerns regarding how the news media might cover their candidacies. As shown in Table 7.1, approximately half of candidates and eligibles professed *not* to be bothered by how journalists would treat them during an election while one-third admitted they were. Some eligibles were unsure, while several people in both groups did not provide a clear or direct answer to the question. Gender, race,

Table 7.1. Research participants' responses to question about any concerns regarding the news media, by per cent and number.

	Yes	No	Maybe	No Answer	Not Asked
Overall	33.7% (34)	49.5% (50)	4% (4)	10.9% (11)	2% (2)
Candidate status					
Eligible	34% (17)	48% (24)	8% (4)	10% (5)	0% (0)
Candidate	33.3% (17)	51% (26)	0% (0)	11.8% (6)	3.9% (2)
Gender					
Women	32.7% (16)	46.9% (23)	4.1% (2)	16.3% (8)	0% (0)
Men	30.4% (14)	54.3% (25)	4.3% (2)	6.5% (3)	4.3% (2)
Non-binary	66.7% (4)	33.3% (2)	0% (0)	0% (0)	0% (0)
Ethnicity					
White	30.2% (16)	56.6% (30)	1.9% (1)	9.4% (5)	1.9% (1)
Racialized	37.5% (18)	41.7% (20)	6.2% (3)	12.5% (6)	2.1% (1)
Sexuality					
Heterosexual	30% (15)	46% (23)	6% (3)	16% (8)	2% (1)
Queer	37.3% (19)	52.9% (27)	2% (1)	5.9% (3)	2% (1)

Note: N=101. Candidates were asked: "Did you have any specific concerns about the news media as you prepared to run for elected office?" Eligibles were asked: "What concerns would you have about the news media if you were to run?"

and sexuality generally did not alter this pattern. Less than one-third of women and men were apprehensive about media behaviour when contemplating a bid for elected office, though women were less likely than men to claim they weren't worried. The same is true for racial minorities in comparison to white people. For their part, queer individuals appeared to be more conflicted about media scrutiny than heterosexuals, with a greater percentage expressing both misgivings and indifference. These findings suggest under-represented groups in Canadian politics are only slightly more concerned about media scrutiny.

Interview results thus raise the possibility that scholarly fears about women, racial minorities, and queer people being deterred from running because of media behaviour could be misplaced. While the previous chapter showed that one-quarter of research participants saw public scrutiny as a major drawback to political candidacy, no one viewed the news media that way. Media scrutiny simply did not generate anywhere near the same level of apprehension as voter scrutiny. "The media are less of a concern for me than the nasty people in the public like your average nasty citizen," said Ralph Carl Wushke, a white gay man who won't run because of public scrutiny. "I have a degree in journalism, so I kind of get the different political slants of media coverage and how the media try to have a quote 'balanced' unquote reportage. So, I'm less

concerned about the media than I am about the wackos in the public."
This is not to suggest research participants didn't have any misgivings
about how journalists might cover their campaigns, but journalists are
a known quantity in comparison to anonymous social media users, an
issue discussed in more length in the next chapter.

Perceptions of Media Behaviour

That half of eligibles were not concerned about media behaviour during a hypothetical campaign can be attributed to two main factors:
experience and knowledge. Some eligibles had either worked in the
news media as journalists or had extensive dealings with journalists
through their professional, volunteer, or partisan activities. As a consequence, they knew how the news media operated and had already
built strong working relationships with news professionals. Some eligibles had already developed strategies on how to deal with journalists, especially in a manner that ensured accurate news reporting on
the organizations with which they were involved. Such knowledge and
experience gave these individuals confidence in their ability to handle
the news media should they ever run for office. Eligibles who did not
indicate their level of media skills either expressed a positive opinion
of news outlets' ability to produce objective coverage or professed not
to have any skeletons in their closet that would attract negative media
attention. Others expected to encounter a certain degree of media bias
but would not let that deter them from promoting their views.

Candidates were not concerned about media bias because they had
experience with the news media or had received extensive media training in the lead-up to their bid for office. Candidate perspectives on
media behaviour, however, were strongly influenced by recollections of
their campaigns. Two candidates noted that strong relations with journalists established during their professional career suddenly changed
when they decided to pursue elected office. "I went to bed on October 7, 2013, as a fine upstanding citizen who was an advocate and had
integrity and did great things," said former provincial politician Joanne
Bernard, "and then went to bed the next night elected that day as someone who was in it for herself, a thief, a fraud, and every other adjective
that you can describe a politician these days. It was the weirdest thing
because I haven't changed and I still haven't." Like eligibles, some candidates expected the news media to behave professionally and prioritize objectivity, accuracy, and fairness. They were thus shocked at the
degree of media bias they saw during the election. If some candidates
were worried about media bias, others dreaded media inattention.

One candidate was willing to deal with media bias if it meant he got at least some publicity for his campaign. A small number of candidates and eligibles expressed greater concern about social media trolls than journalists.

The one-third of eligibles who did express concerns about the news media were more perturbed by general media behaviour and did not demonstrate the same confidence as other research participants in their ability to manage the news media. These eligibles argued that some media organizations take a sensationalist slant to covering the news because this approach is believed to attract a greater audience. This sensationalism can occur despite a genuine desire on the part of (some) journalists to inform the public about current affairs and to do so in a way that is objective and/or balanced. The eligibles added that news organizations habitually slant the news to suit a particular narrative or to create a story where none exists.

Candidates also pointed to news norms as a reason for being concerned about potential media behaviour during their campaigns. But unlike eligibles, they were not concerned about sensationalism as much as the degree to which the news media do not live up to professional standards of accuracy, objectivity, fairness, and balance. Candidates noted that the media do not always accurately present information or quote sources in news stories. One white heterosexual woman said the news media in her province behave like attack dogs rather than watch dogs, viewing themselves as the "real" official opposition and attacking everything the provincial government does. It is one reason why she refuses to talk to the news media, with the notable exception of one journalist with whom she has developed a professional rapport.

Candidates and eligibles assert that some news organizations are highly ideological or partisan in their reporting, failing in the process to provide all sides of an issue. An Indigenous gay man eligible regularly monitors the CBC, *Globe and Mail*, and *National Post* because they each have different political leanings. "If you read the same [story] from all three, they have different ways of viewing it, but then you can kind of put it together and figure out what is actually going on. But not everyone does that." A former federal Conservative candidate does not trust the news media because of what she perceived to be highly partisan reporting against former party leader Stephen Harper.

Not everyone took a negative view towards the news media. Some candidates and eligibles described local news reporting in their area as fair and balanced. Eligibles tended to base their assessment on observations of media performance and candidates drew upon their experiences with journalists either in or outside of politics. One candidate reported receiving positive coverage during his campaign. Tyler Murnaghan felt his status as a young bisexual man enabled him to stand out from the crowd during his unsuccessful run for Charlottetown city council in the 2014 Prince Edward Island municipal elections:

> INTERVIEWER: Did you feel that the coverage of you was fair or balanced?
> MURNAGHAN: Definitely. It was actually maybe even a little positive, I'd say. Even the media here was very excited about seeing someone who didn't fit into the traditional image of the Charlottetown city council run.
> INTERVIEWER: So, you felt that your distinctiveness – being young and whatnot – helped you to get media attention?
> MURNAGHAN: Yeah. It's a lot easier to write about the one youth that is running than it is to write about the 45 white men that are running.

Research participants' comments demonstrate that the Canadian news media are not a monolithic group. Considerable variation exists among news outlets regarding how they report on campaigns and candidates, with some journalists prone to sensationalist coverage and others intent on upholding the professional norms of neutrality and objectivity.

Dangers of Media Attention

Despite extensive research demonstrating that white women politicians receive highly gendered coverage (Ejaz 2018; Meeks 2013; Trimble and Everitt 2010; Wagner, Trimble, and Sampert 2019), media sexism was not a major concern for white women research participants. Only one white heterosexual woman anticipated having to face sexist coverage if she ever ran for elected office. Danielle Parrell said women politicians are more heavily scrutinized than men politicians. "You're expected to be the beautiful, 110-pound blonde with this perfectly straight teeth and beautiful smile. Unrealistic beauty standards, which are largely unachievable," said Parrell, who was thinking about a federal candidacy. "My personal image, I know for sure, would be heavily scrutinized while my male counterparts would be heard for their politics." As for other white heterosexual women research participants? Candidates and eligibles alike either didn't address the issue, claimed not to have noticed media sexism, or insisted they wouldn't let it bother them. None said it would prevent them from running.

Parrell's concern about media sexism was primarily shared by racialized women. A South Asian woman eligible cited the American media's obsession with Hillary Clinton's outfits when the latter was seeking the American presidency. Nisha Patel expected similar gendered coverage if she ran, especially if she was the only woman candidate in the race and her gender difference becomes the story. If she was also the only racialized candidate, she said her coverage would likely take on racial dimensions too. That was certainly Rana Bokhari's experience as leader of the Manitoba Liberals from 2013 to 2016. The news media struggled to cover the Muslim woman of South Asian descent because she didn't fit the norm for a Canadian party leader –a white, Christian, older man. "They took the difference, all the things that should have been perceived as a strength, [and] made it into my weakness," Bokhari said. This attitude came out in news coverage of her efforts to reform the party's internal organization. While a man would have been seen as a strong leader for taking on the party establishment, Bokhari said she was depicted as a weak leader facing internal fighting. "They create the narrative, they create the public perception, and they can pick and choose what they want to run with," she said. "It became quite problematic, actually."

Racialized women expected gender stereotypes to influence news coverage in numerous ways. A heterosexual woman of East Asian descent pointed to the belief in many countries that women politicians are, or should be, more honest and ethical than men politicians (Aaldering and van der Pas 2020; Adams 2010; Campus 2013; Huddy and Terkildsen 1993). She argued that women politicians who don't live up to this gendered standard will be judged more harshly by the news media: "Your mistakes are not easily forgiven." The extent to which this assertion is true remains to be determined. Most gendered mediation research focuses on the personalization of women politicians – their hair, hemlines, and husbands (Murray 2010; Trimble et al. 2013). Political psychology research, however, indicates that voters do hold negative opinions of women politicians seen as dishonest (Visser, Book, and Volk 2017).

People from marginalized communities are acutely aware of the complex nature of individual identities and how they can shape one's experiences with the news media. Change a single aspect of your identity – gender, race/ethnicity, or sexuality – and you can receive a completely different reception by journalists, which can in turn influence your ability to generate positive press, recruit volunteers, raise money, and maybe even win an election. Minority research participants highlighted this conundrum in their comments about media behaviour. Canadian news organizations might herald the candidacy of a

Southeast Asian woman of the Hindu religion, but they might advise caution if she is a hijab-wearing Muslim. Widespread distrust of the Islamic faith, especially in the aftermath of the 9/11 terrorist attacks in the United States, could lead some journalists to openly question what influence her faith might have on her policy positions. It wouldn't take a lot to raise doubts. They can be triggered by news coverage that constantly mentions the racialized woman's head covering, which, rightly or wrongly, is often taken as a sign of religious and social conservatism. Change the Muslim candidate's gender to man and the doubts are harder to raise through implicit cues. It is rare to a see a Muslim man in Canada wearing the male version of a head covering, a *ghutra* (also known as a *kuffiyeh* or *shemagh*), in everyday life. With few outward signs of their faith, Muslim men could escape the same level of scrutiny regarding the impact of religion on their politics because journalists wouldn't be able to use Islamic clothing as a subtle hint that they don't belong in Canadian politics. Such negative evaluations need to be explicit. Some journalists are certainly comfortable criticizing Islam and Muslims in general (Warman and Farber 2018), but others might be cautious to avoid accusations of racism. Change the racialized man candidate's religion to Sikhism and the subtle cues return. Newspaper coverage of Jagmeet Singh's ultimately successful bid to lead the federal NDP in 2017 was replete with references to his turban and beard. Columnists pointed to these visual representations of his Sikh faith as reasons why his leadership might make the NDP less viable in a federal election, especially in a secular Quebec that has tried to regulate religious symbols (Ibbitson 2017; Yakabuski 2017). Change the racialized man's religion to Christianity and the issue dissipates entirely for the mainstream media.

What might remain an issue for the mainstream media is a person's race, nationality, and/or sexuality. A Middle Eastern heterosexual man who someday plans to run for federal office claims the Quebec media discriminates against immigrants like him, and the best he could hope for is that they ignore his candidacy. Part of the problem could be that the white-dominated mainstream media are less familiar with non-white cultures, including the ways in which those cultures understand sexuality and gender. For example, some Indigenous people describe themselves as two-spirited, which "is an Indigenous-defined pan-Native North American term that refers to a diversity of Indigenous LGBTQ identities, as well as culturally specific non-binary expressions of gender" (Hunt 2018, 28; for an explanation of the complexities of gender, sexuality, and two-spirit identity in Indigenous nations, see

Robinson 2020). Eliza Knockwood, an Indigenous two-spirited person who ran for the Green Party in 2011, encountered such media confusion during her federal campaign:

> INTERVIEWER: What kind of concerns did you have [about the news media before you ran for office]?
>
> KNOCKWOOD: That they were going to jumble up my words or something, or use a statement against me. But also I remember doing a CBC interview, and this is a good example, and she wanted to know what two-spirited meant. I gave her the definition from a First Nations perspective, but it still wasn't good enough for her. She basically wanted to know, "Are you a lesbian or bisexual. I don't know what two-spirited is. We want the public to know what this means. If I don't know what it means, they're not going to know what it means." And she's like, "Well, are you in a relationship?" I'm like, "Yeah, I'm in a relationship." "With a woman?" I'm like, "Yeah, with a woman." She's like, "Okay, that's for the interview. Bye." And then on CBC they're like, "Eliza Knockwood, in a relationship with a woman." (Laughs) I was like, "That was kind of silly."
>
> INTERVIEWER: It's more the fact that they wouldn't necessarily understand certain aspects of Indigenous culture?
>
> KNOCKWOOD: Yeah.
>
> INTERVIEWER: Because if they don't understand it – I mean she's right, if she doesn't understand it, she can't explain it to someone else. But it sounds like she was trying to fit you within a framework that she understood instead of trying to understand yours.
>
> KNOCKWOOD: Yes. Exactly.

Indigenous cultural understandings aren't the only challenge for the mainstream media. An Indigenous gay man eligible doesn't expect homophobic coverage if he were to run, but he does anticipate strong pushback regarding his views on the Canadian state and on Indigenous-Canadian relations. "I'm sure I would get labelled as being media unfriendly because I have accosted them for some of their most ignorant and stupid comments on Indigenous things," he said. He added that white candidates often don't face the same backlash for making similar comments. Insights from Indigenous and racialized research participants thus alert us to the possibility that not all minority candidates will face the same type, or amount, of stereotyped news coverage depending upon their particular mix of gender, race/ethnicity, sexuality, religion, and nationality. Candidate experiences also indicate that some racialized politicians are subjected to very little discriminatory coverage (sometimes because of a lack of media attention) and others to a lot of it.

Racialized candidates also face challenges in how their complex social identities are received in their own ethnic communities. Ethnic media might criticize a candidate who does not conform to the community's gender, cultural, and/or religious norms, but the mainstream media would likely pay little attention. A racialized woman eligible cited the issue of hair. Sikh women are expected to have long hair, but hers was short at the time of our interview. Just months away from launching her first campaign for elected office, she anticipated the ethnic media would focus on the ways in which she deviated from cultural norms regarding her personal appearance. White journalists likely wouldn't pick up on this as short hair is common among white women, their cultural default. "The mainstream media's view may be completely different if I looked too ethnic," she said. While she didn't elaborate, it is not difficult to image that racialized candidates who don't adopt a European style of dress, such as a business suit, might be poorly received by white voters. Research has shown that a candidate's physical appearance can affect election outcomes (Mattes and Milazzo 2014; Praino and Stockemer 2018; Praino, Stockemer, and Ratis 2014). But the woman eligible added that not all racialized candidates are penalized by dressing in an ethnic or religious fashion. "If I was a man and I had a turban, everyone would be super excited about me running because then I would have the right symbols and the right cache to say who I am." Her comment reveals the complexities of how minorities can be perceived in the political sphere: a turban-wearing Sikh candidate can simultaneously be seen as an asset to equity-seeking efforts in democratic politics and as a threat to the dominant political order.

Regardless of race, ethnicity, or religion, some individuals expect their sexuality to be a major issue for ethnic media. A Black gay man eligible was dismayed when a Tamil radio station aired what was widely considered to be a homophobic commercial supporting Rob Ford for mayor in the 2010 Toronto municipal election. The following is a translation of the Tamil-language commercial (via City News 2010):

1ST PERSON: Mani Anna, who you voting for in the mayoral election?

2ND PERSON: [Laughs] What kind of question is this? I am Tamil. We have a religion and culture. Take Rob Ford for example, his wife is a woman.

That's not only it, he said he will reduce land transfer taxes and other taxes.

1ST PERSON: What about immigration?

2ND PERSON: [Laughs] That's a federal government issue. So, the white people can get our vote.

1ST PERSON: I am also going to vote for Rob Ford.

The Black gay man eligible, and many others, interpreted the commercial as a homophobic attack against Ford's main rival, George Smitherman (Stayshyn 2010). The commercial elicited a strong backlash, both from the Tamil community and the city at large, and was the subject of news stories by mainstream outlets such as the *Globe and Mail* newspaper and *Toronto Life* magazine (Grant and Paperny 2010; McGrath 2010). The Black gay man eligible hoped that homophobic treatment disappears over time as journalists and voters become familiar with queer politicians. Recent studies on media behaviour lend some support to this view (McLean 2019; Mundy 2013). Yet Smitherman, a white gay man who had been publicly out for years, was a former provincial politician and cabinet minister with a high profile in the city before he sought the mayorship. The Toronto media knew him well. Their decision to report on the controversy and, in some cases, describe the radio ad in negative terms does suggest a growing responsiveness to the challenges that queer individuals face in politics.

Unfortunately, members of the public can sometimes confuse the news media's editorial practices with their advertising activities. Commercials are paid ads placed by third parties. Journalists don't produce them. The advertising department deals with the ads and the advertiser, not publicly known in this case, is responsible for the content of the commercial. Even if a queer politician is well known to the electorate, opponents or their supporters might still try to stir up anti-gay sentiment through such ads to appeal to socially conservative voters. The problem is not how this ethnic radio station covered a queer candidate in its news stories, but rather that it agreed to air a thinly veiled anti-gay commercial.

The complexity of media behaviour makes it difficult for individuals of different genders, religions, and sexualities to navigate politics. Alter one aspect of a candidate's complex social identity and media perceptions alter along with it. But not all media experiences are negative. Two racialized candidates asserted that ethnic media organizations were highly supportive of their campaigns for elected office, likely out of a desire to see that ethnic community represented in Canadian politics. Sexuality even proved to be a non-issue in one case. Ethnic news outlets ignored the queer politician's sexual orientation, highlighting instead her ethnic identity.

Other candidates who expected to receive discriminatory coverage discovered their gender, race/ethnicity, or sexuality wasn't an issue at all for local journalists. It was their partisan affiliation or the media's own agenda that shaped coverage. Some queer candidates were even able to influence the news agenda. Ted Mouradian went to local outlets when his campaign signs were defaced with anti-gay slurs during a municipal election and the subsequent news coverage increased his voter support because some people were upset that his sexuality had been made an issue. Joanne Bernard also used the news media to combat discrimination. While a provincial cabinet minister, Bernard alerted a television reporter to homophobic treatment she was receiving from the public. He was at her office to do another story but promptly dropped it to focus on this issue. She recalls it being the lead story on that night's news program. The TV report was one of several stories produced by the Canadian news media in recent years about online and offline harassment that non-traditional politicians receive (Huncar 2015; McMillan 2016; Rumbolt 2016; Star Editorial Board 2018).

Some transgender eligibles believe they could use the news media in a similar fashion to educate the public about the challenges their group faces. Marni Panas, a white transgender woman in Alberta who might one day run for elected office, already has experience with the news media because of her activism and professional activities. She cited her accessibility, extensive networks, and communication skills as reasons why she has been able to develop a strong relationship with journalists. That has translated into positive coverage for the trans community. "What I've seen, certainly from my own personal experience in the trans community over the last few years, [is] that media have done a really, really good job actually and have been probably my biggest tool and ally in moving a lot of our issues forward." Across the country in Newfoundland and Labrador, Jennifer McCreath used her historic candidacy as the first transgender individual to run for federal office in Canada to generate awareness of her political party, the newly formed Forces et Democratie. The white transgender woman knew that her gender identity was going to attract media attention in the 2015 federal election, but "I also kind of adopted that ideology that there's no such thing as bad press when you're just trying to do a little bit of education and awareness." McCreath talked about the challenges that trans individuals face while emphasizing that her candidacy was about more than trans issues (CBC 2015). One of her goals as a public figure was to highlight the contributions that trans people can make to civic life.

However, before the news media can be used as a venue through which to educate voters, journalists must be challenged in how they write about different types of candidates. How can voters' misperceptions be dispelled if news coverage contains the same biases? Some eligibles insisted that, if they ran, they would call out journalists for any sexist, racist, or homophobic coverage of their campaigns. Racialized women, in particular, said they would stand up for themselves, pointing out problems with the news report and discussing what individuals like them can contribute to politics and public policy. Susan Rose, a white lesbian eligible, added that it would be an opportunity to open a dialogue about issues like sexism.

Efforts to educate journalists, however, are not new. Numerous organizations, institutes, centres, activists, and scholars around the world monitor media behaviour with an eye to transforming it. Their ability to draw public attention to grievous examples of media discrimination – and, more importantly, to demand corrective action – has been made easier by social media. Indigenous activists, for example, used Twitter in 2017 to criticize Canadian journalists for encouraging the cultural appropriation of Indigenous motifs, symbols, ideas, and stories by non-Indigenous authors (Dundas 2017). The digital firestorm sparked discussions about the general lack of Indigenous and marginalized voices in the mainstream media (Domise 2017).

Although the news media continue to struggle with issues of sexism and racism, they also have work to do regarding the accurate portrayal of gender and sexual minorities. Many journalists aren't up to date with evolving understandings of and practices related to gender identity, gender expression, and sexual orientation, hence the decision by advocacy organizations like GLAAD in the United States to create media reference guides to facilitate accurate and fair coverage of the LGBTQ community (GLAAD 2016). A gender-neutral eligible expects that they would have to educate journalists about their specific circumstances should they run for office but would insist any mistakes in coverage be fixed. Two gay eligibles were equally confident in their abilities to handle problematic campaign coverage, though they would take slightly different approaches. Christopher Matthews, a Black gay man, has developed a thick skin after years of experiencing racism and homophobia. He was confident that he could devise a strategy on how to address that problem, should it arise. Patrick Schertzer would take a more laissez-faire approach. As a libertarian, the white gay man said that everyone has the right to their own viewpoints: "I very much believe in freedom of speech, so if people want to print or write something, fine, go for it. It's not affecting me and I don't think it's bringing them up at all, and it's not going to help them. In general, we live in a broad and inclusive society."

In fact, societal attitudes in Canada have changed so much that some eligibles argue that the news media can no longer get away with sexist, racist, or homophobic coverage. Fadumo Robinson, a Black heterosexual woman who participated in a City of Edmonton program to encourage more women to get involved in municipal politics, doesn't expect stereotypical coverage if she ever ran for office. "I would be shocked if there's discriminatory news coverage or print media because I think most Canadians would be appalled by that. But that doesn't mean there's no discrimination in Canada. There's plenty," said Robinson. "It's not publicly supported, let's put it that way. It's smaller groups of people." While a news story might briefly mention a candidate's sexual orientation or gender identity, one eligible insisted the media wouldn't make it central to how they described the person. "I don't think they'd ever frame it like that because that's not the way that most people would be okay with the media running something," said a white queer woman with no plans to run.

Their views are rather optimistic. The news media have subtle ways of stereotyping politicians according to gender, race/ethnicity, and sexuality. It can be as simple as giving a white man front-page treatment but relegating a racialized man to the inside pages, where the story is less likely to be noticed by readers. A common approach, and one that some research participants noted, is to associate certain types of candidates with certain types of issues (see also Tolley 2016). News coverage of women politicians, for example, is likely to include discussion of abortion and childcare even when their campaign platforms don't mention them (Kahn 1996). This pattern repeats itself for racialized candidates (Tolley 2016) and LGBTQ candidates (Everitt and Camp 2009b). While blatant discrimination is less prevalent in today's political reporting, more subtle forms of discrimination persist in media depictions of non-traditional politicians (Tolley 2016).

Dangers of Media Inattention

While eligibles pointed to a variety of dangers that media attention would bring if they ran for elected office, candidates pointed to media *inattention* as the greater threat to a person's political ambitions. Before voters can cast a ballot in support of a candidate, they must first be aware that the candidate exists. In an ideal system, voters would have information about every candidate's qualifications, experience, and platform before heading to the polling station on election day. The news media have traditionally been a major source, if not *the* source, of that information, but their tendency to focus on party leaders, mayoral hopefuls, and a few high-profile politicians means voters get precious little information about the scores of other candidates running for office. To cope with this, voters might opt to pick from among the candidates they do know or to rely on partisan affiliation (where available) as a cue on how to vote. Voters often prefer the devil they know to the devil they don't. That is one reason why incumbents typically get re-elected.

The low-information environment of many Canadian elections wasn't on the radar for most eligibles. Only two eligibles raised the issue of media inattention, and only briefly. It was left to candidates to highlight this concern for anyone considering a bid for elected office. They talked about the importance of, and difficulty in, getting news coverage. Catherine Meade, a Black lesbian who ran for the Liberals in the 2008 federal election, only caught the media's eye when vandals threw rocks into her campaign office. "And quite frankly, had I known all the publicity I would have gotten … I would have thrown a rock in there myself!" she said, laughing. Otherwise, the Liberal candidate found it hard to get news coverage in the Halifax riding of retiring incumbent Alexa McDonough, former leader of the federal NDP. Queer activist Megan Leslie went on to hold the riding for the NDP.

Municipal candidates were especially vocal about media inattention. They recognized that the sheer number of municipal elections taking place at one time in a province, as well as the number of candidates who run in each municipality, makes it extremely difficult for news organizations to cover every candidate. To rationalize resources, the news media focus on mayoral races with a particular emphasis on the front-running candidates. Individuals seeking a regular council seat are usually ignored. "I remember going to my first meeting, just an event, with all of the candidates and it was with everybody – trustees, councillors, mayoral candidates," recalled Donovan Martin, a Black heterosexual man whose first election campaign was for councillor in the 2014 Manitoba municipal elections. "I remember approaching one of the media reps and I was just, 'When will you do a story on council candidates?' Because at the time it was just the mayors. And the words were, 'We're only here for the mayor council candidates. You're not important.' They were right. We were not important at all." Candidates seeking a regular council seat are left to find other, potentially less effective ways to drum up voter support.

Two federal candidates had the misfortune of running against high-profile politicians who had once been party leaders and thus commanded significant media attention, both inside and outside the riding. The 2015 federal election saw former Bloc Québécois leader Gilles Duceppe try to win back his Laurier–Sainte-Marie riding from NDP MP Hélène Laverdière. While Duceppe lost, media fascination with that battle as well as the pregnancy of Liberal candidate Christine Poirier left Green candidate Cyrille Giraud struggling to get any coverage. "I was totally eclipsed." Media attention was even more narrowly focused in the 2008 federal election in Toronto Centre. NDP candidate El-Farouk Khaki ran against former Ontario NDP premier Bob Rae, who switched to the Liberals when he moved to federal politics. Journalists covering the riding focused on Rae to the exclusion of all others. "The media wouldn't even contact anybody else. They wouldn't contact me. They wouldn't contact the Green or the Tory [candidates], they just went to him. He was their go-to person," recalled Khaki. "They didn't bother [to] even mention our names sometimes." As a Black gay Muslim man, Khaki found this erasure difficult to process.

> ... if you are a newcomer, if you are from a racialized or some other minority community that does not have a history of political engagement, what kind of air time are you given if you are given any air time at all? This became very apparent – the straight white guy who was known, who was running for the Liberals, got a lot more air time. A lot of times the other candidates, myself included, weren't even asked to respond on a particular issue or on a particular announcement, but he was. That just ends up marginalizing candidates who come from non-traditional communities.

Other queer individuals tried to use the novelty of their candidacies to garner at least some news coverage for their campaigns, although that didn't always work out. Giraud was surprised that the news media didn't highlight the fact that he was a gay candidate, especially considering his Montreal riding was home to the city's Gay Village.

The experiences of these individuals demonstrate that prospective candidates must not only have a communications strategy for dealing with media bias but also with media inattention. Candidates need a firm plan on how to solicit news coverage when they are not the star candidate. Social media is an important venue through which to reach voters, but legacy media such as newspapers and television still have considerable power to raise a person's public profile.

Conclusion

Interviews with eligibles and candidates suggest the news media might not be the barrier to candidacy that many fear. No one listed the news media as a reason why they might not have, or would not, run for elected office. A national survey of Canadians is needed to confirm this result, but further comments from women, racialized individuals, and queer people indicated that they could not or would not be easily dissuaded from entering politics because of the potential for stereotypical coverage of their social identities. They were certainly aware that the news media can shape the local electoral environment in ways detrimental to their campaigns or reputation, that journalists continue to struggle to make sense of candidates whose social identities differ from their own, and that this challenge is evident with both mainstream and ethnic media. Racialized women were the most attentive to media bias, or how media treatment of a candidate depends upon one's unique mix of social characteristics. Yet, some research participants identified other media behaviours as more problematic. Eligibles were worried about the news media's tendency towards sensationalism, while candidates were more alert to violations of journalistic norms as well as media inattention. Municipal candidates were resigned to the lack of media coverage during their campaigns because of the sheer number of people who seek local office each electoral cycle, but they clearly didn't like it.

Whatever the concerns, media behaviour was not a deterrent to candidacy for two reasons: knowledge and experience with the news media. Both eligibles and candidates indicated that the news media were not a mystery to them. Some eligibles had either worked in the news media as journalists or had extensive dealings with journalists through their professional, volunteer, or partisan activities. Candidates had either dealt with the news media in the past or received extensive media training before the election. In both cases, they had forged strong relationships with local journalists, developing strong media skills in the process. They felt confident in their ability to handle media relations. Others were optimistic that local journalists would follow the norms of their profession and emphasize objectivity, accuracy, fairness, and balance above commercial interests or partisan bias.

For all the criticism of the news media and their coverage of municipal, provincial, and federal politics, both eligibles and candidates were far more concerned about the damage that online trolls could do to their campaigns. They know journalists are trained to be fair and balanced in their reporting, presenting only the facts in news stories and leaving opinions for editorials and columns. Many journalists remain committed to objectivity – or at least the appearance of it – despite enormous challenges brought on by constant technological and corporate changes in the news industry. Another professional norm requires journalists to identify their sources except in limited circumstances, reducing the amount of anonymous and unverified criticism of a candidate in news coverage (McCarten 2013, 28–30). Such gatekeeping is rare on social media.

Research participants believed that journalism's professional norms ensure some level of accuracy and reduce bias in news reporting. The news media can also be held accountable when they fail to live up to these standards. Critics routinely call them out for a sexist headline or racist photograph. The public conversation about media behaviour has even led individual journalists to evaluate their own reporting practices (LeFrance 2016). But not all biases are problematic. The news media are expected to be sites of public debate and routinely enter the fray on behalf of their preferred outcomes. Consequently, the ideological viewpoints of individual news organizations are well known. The news media's professional norms and ideological openness enable voters to evaluate the credibility of the information and opinion provided.

Social media platforms share the same democratic purpose as news organizations – to encourage and protect freedom of expression – but they are not bound by the same professional norms. Social media users don't have to be balanced in their commentary; they can say whatever they want. They can spread misinformation, falsehoods, or unfounded accusations, which can be especially damaging to candidates and politicians. Many platforms don't even require users to publicly identify themselves. This anonymity means users can attack, insult, demean, cajole, ridicule, and taunt other people online without being held accountable for their actions. Women are a popular target for online trolls, who use violent and sexual language to try to expel women from the online public sphere and maintain it as a space for men only (Mantilla 2015). The wild west nature of social media today is why research participants, especially eligibles, expressed far greater concerns about the negative uses of social media than they did about media behaviour. The next chapter explores perceptions of social media scandals and online harassment of politicians.

Chapter Eight

The Digital Calculation: Dangers of Social Media Scandals and Online Harassment

I spent a lifetime building up a reputation, being credible, and trying to be quote-unquote a good person, and when you have people who, throughout a campaign right from the beginning, are trying to discredit you, you wonder whether the prize is worth that fight.

> – Tash Taylor, a white heterosexual woman who ran for city council

Introduction[1]

Tash Taylor had been planning to run for elected office since the age of five, when she first became fascinated with the personalities and processes of politics. But she considered abandoning her childhood dream of becoming a politician because of the dark side of social media. Taylor was subjected to a well-coordinated campaign of online harassment from the moment rumours surfaced that she would run in a 2015 city council by-election. Opponents used Twitter, Facebook, and the local newspaper's online comment section to publicly attack the rookie candidate. At first, the trolls were not able to target her directly because a busy professional career had kept her off social media. But that changed once she set up her election sites. Her posts, purposely innocuous, constantly drew derisive commentary. "I tried to mitigate it and respond and say, 'I would love to have a discussion with you, please feel free to contact me.' But as soon as I said anything, it would just open it up to more [attacks]." The online harassment led her to shut down her Twitter account and even caught the attention of the local newspaper (Paterson 2015), which ran an editorial condemning the abuse

---

1 Parts of this chapter are adapted from Wagner 2022b, 32–47.

("Keep It Civil St. Albert" 2015). But the online tormenting did not stop until the by-election was over and she had lost. As the above quote notes, her experience with online negative campaigning compelled Taylor to re-evaluate whether being a municipal councillor was worth the grief. Thankfully it wasn't. Taylor was one of 25 non-mayoral candidates in the city's 2017 general election, placing ninth and missing out on a council seat by a little more than 200 votes.

Taylor's story is one of many cautionary tales about social media that emerged during interviews on factors shaping the decision to become a candidate for elected office. Many research participants were resigned to becoming targets for online trolls if they ran. Others expressed a deeper concern that deleted social media posts might be recovered by opponents to discredit them during an election. A few individuals whose old posts did, in fact, derail their candidacies were profoundly marked by the experience.

The various ways in which partisans use social media to attack opponents have made political candidacy more problematic for those considering a bid for elected office. Online attacks and social media scandals threaten a person's reputation and standing in the community. Yet digital barriers to candidacy aren't fully understood. Problems associated with campaign fundraising, political parties, and family responsibilities are well documented, but the political candidacy literature is just starting to grapple with social media as an obstacle to elected office. It first came to my attention when two young people highlighted social media histories as a problem during the pilot phase of this project, when potential questions were tested in interviews with politicians and party members. It was not until the main data collection was well underway that online attacks against politicians, and women politicians in particular, were flagged as issues. The interview protocol, or list of questions, was amended to ask people about whether they had any concerns about their social media histories being mined for potentially damaging information or about opponents using social media as a platform through which to attack them during a campaign.

This chapter explores perceptions of, and experiences with, social media scandals and online attacks in recent Canadian elections. Specifically, what impact do digital dangers have on individuals' willingness to seek or hold elected office in Canada? The aim is to understand how such digital dangers shape different stages of the political process, including candidate deterrence (the decision not to run), candidate emergence (the decision to run), and candidate selection (party permission to run). The ubiquitous nature of social media today, and its integral role in modern campaigning, means anyone considering a bid for elected office must figure out how to deal with online negativity before becoming a candidate. To understand the role of social media in political candidacy in the twenty-first century, this chapter begins by explaining what social media scandals are before outlining eligible and candidate views on the dangers they pose. The next section focuses on social media attacks, highlighting their gendered dimensions and threat to democratic equality. The third section investigates the strategies that people use to deal with digital dangers to their political aspirations.

Social Media Scandals: Resurrecting the Online Past

Scandals have long been a feature of democratic politics, though their occurrence and ramifications have grown alongside developments in information and communication technologies (Thompson 2000). In general, a scandal is an action that transgresses established moral codes and is seen as offensive once it becomes known. Political scandals typically revolve around moral transgressions such as marital infidelity (Mandell and Chen 2016; Sipes 2011) but also involve financial impropriety (Hammarlin and Jarlbro 2012; Ruderman and Nevitte 2015) and breach of political norms (Trottier 2018). Regardless of their nature, scandals have five key characteristics: (1) they involve some kind of transgression that (2) others would disapprove of and as such (3) it is kept secret or otherwise concealed, but once the transgression becomes known, (4) it is denounced by others and (5) harms the reputation of the individual(s) involved (Thompson 2000, 13–14).

Not all transgressions take place in secret or can be concealed. The increasing mediatization of politics (Strömbäck 2008) has led to the rise of talk scandals (Ekström and Johansson 2008). Talk scandals occur when a person makes a comment during a media event that is viewed as transgressing some kind of norm (Ekström and Johansson 2008, 62). Social media scandals are a type of talk scandal in that they originate in the mass media, but in this case, the offending behaviour either occurs online (in the form of a blog post or tweet) or is documented online (in the form of a posted photograph or video). The event is also not secret; it is simply not widely known. As with other scandals (Allern and Pollack 2012; Schudson 2004), the news media play an integral role in turning a potentially overlooked online post into a highly publicized controversy. Scandals only come to the public's attention because of journalistic decisions regarding whether, and how, to report on a transgressive event (Allern and Pollack 2012). In the case of social media scandals, the news media draw the public's attention to something that was already in the public domain.

Journalists are not the only, or perhaps even primary, actors responsible for bringing an online transgression to the public's attention. Scandals are typically triggered by tips from informed sources, whistleblowers, or opponents (Allern and Pollack 2012). The third group – opponents – are the most common tipsters in social media scandals involving political candidates (Jenssen and Fladmoe 2012; Trottier 2018). That is because the ease and affordability of digital media enable political operatives to conduct comprehensive opposition research on a candidate, otherwise known as scandal mining (Trottier 2018). And the pickings can be plentiful. Many individuals, and young people in particular, have an extensive online history that can be excavated for political gain. Opponents can scour the person's social media sites, as well as those of their friends, family, and associates, in search of potentially damaging comments and compromising images. Websites such as waybackmachine.org also make it possible to retrieve information from defunct sites, provided a snapshot was taken when a site was still in operation. If an individual is expected to become a candidate in the future, political operatives might even pro-actively archive online posts for future use.

When the time is right during the campaign, they release this information to the news media (Allern and Pollack 2012; Jenssen and Fladmoe 2012; Marland 2016) to create a media storm that engulfs the candidate (Nyhan 2014, 2017) and, in the case of parliamentary systems, their political party (Marland 2016). This tactic proved highly effective in Canadian elections, leading to the resignation or termination of several candidates (Trottier 2018). In response, political parties have intensified their vetting efforts, rejecting potential candidates based on their online histories and instructing green-lit candidates to scrub or delete their social media sites to eliminate the chances of a scandal, though this is not always successful because of diligent archiving by opponents (Marland and DeCillia 2020; Trottier 2018).

Social media scandals are thus a product of negative campaigning. Candidates need to convince voters that they have the character, experience, and qualifications to be elected leaders but that their opponents do not. To make the distinction, candidates must draw public and media attention to their opponents' shortcomings by highlighting their misdeeds, challenging their policy positions, and pointing to character flaws. Negative campaigning is therefore primarily about criticizing one's opponent (Lau and Pomper 2001). But it must be carefully done to be persuasive. In the case of political television ads, Jonathan Rose (2012) outlines four criteria that must be met for negative attacks to be seen as appropriate: they must be about issues, offer evidence, compare candidate positions, and be focused on topics relevant to governing. Candidates who do not meet these standards run the risk of damaging their own campaigns (Geer 2006, 6). Opponents do not face this problem in the case of social media scandals. If there is any concealment in a social media scandal, it typically relates to the identity of the individual(s) responsible for alerting the news media to the transgression. Anders Todal Jenssen and Audun Fladmoe argue that "scandals may be even more effective weapons when the part played by other politicians is less obvious from the public perspective" (2012, 52). Unlike political television ads, politicians are not forced to identify themselves as the source of information that leads to a social media scandal.

Social media scandals offer potentially positive and negative outcomes for democratic politics. One benefit of social media scandals is that they bring to light a pattern of behaviour that might not be viewed as appropriate for an elected representative. Candidates in Canadian elections have been sanctioned, dropped, or resigned because of old posts of a homophobic, sexist, racist, or otherwise offensive nature (Graham 2016; "Social Media Exposes the Dark Side" 2015; "Social Media's Long Reach" 2015). The attitudes that these comments reveal raise questions about the person's ability to acknowledge and respond to the needs of the country's diverse electorate. Negative views of such behaviour are likely why opponents target such posts in the first place. An attendant benefit is the contribution of social media scandals to the electoral information environment (Geer 2006; Rose 2012). To spark a social media controversy, opponents need to provide evidence that the online transgression actually occurred, such as a copy of the photograph or screenshot of the tweet. Voters can then decide for themselves if the transgression was serious or not.

A key drawback to social media scandals is the damage they can cause to reputations (Schudson 2004; Thompson 2000). Depending on the nature or severity of their case, targeted candidates can experience a high degree of notoriety that can be accompanied by a loss of, or difficulty in acquiring, employment and/or volunteer positions post-election. The possibility exists that opponents can see their own reputations damaged as much by the controversy as the targeted candidate (Schudson 2004), but this depends on the public being aware that they are the source of the revelation, which is not always the case in social media scandals. Of greater relevance in a parliamentary system, such as Canada's, is the impact on political parties. Social media scandals are typically timed to blindside an opposing party during an election, causing that party acute embarrassment and forcing them off message to perform damage control (Flanagan 2014, 180–5; Marland 2016, 193–4).

Table 8.1. Responses to question about whether the person is concerned about their social media histories being used against them during a (potential) run for elected office, by candidate status and personal characteristics.

Characteristic	Yes	No	No clear answer
Overall	23.2% (23)	67.7% (67)	9.1% (9)
Candidacy Status			
Candidate	16.3% (8)	73.5% (36)	10.2% (5)
Eligible	30% (15)	62% (31)	8% (4)
Gender			
Women	20% (10)	70% (35)	10% (5)
Men	26.7% (12)	64.4% (29)	8.9% (4)
Neither group	25% (1)	75% (3)	0% (0)
Ethnicity			
White	15.7% (8)	74.5% (38)	9.8% (5)
Racialized	31.3% (15)	60.4% (29)	8.3% (4)
Sexuality			
Heterosexual	14% (7)	76% (38)	10% (5)
Queer	32.7% (16)	59.2% (29)	8.2% (4)

Note: *N* = 99. Candidates were asked: "Did you have any specific concerns about your social media history as you prepared to run for elected office?" Eligibles were asked: "What concerns would you have regarding your social media history and how it might be used by others against you if you were to run?"

Canadian Perspectives on Social Media Scandals

Both candidates and eligibles were asked if they were concerned that their social media histories would be used against them by political opponents, critics, and journalists during an election. Candidates were asked "Did you have any specific concerns about your social media history as you prepared to run for elected office?" while eligibles were asked "What concerns would you have regarding your social media history and how it might be used by others against you if you were to run?" Two-thirds (67.7 per cent) of research participants professed not to have such fears. Table 8.1 shows that candidates (73.5 per cent) were generally more confident than eligibles (62 per cent) that their social media sites were clear of any potentially damaging content, raising the possibility that fear of a social media scandal might be one reason why some individuals have not run for office in this digital age. An intersectional analysis also found that individuals who fit the typical profile of a politician – white and heterosexual – were generally less concerned about their social media history than individuals from marginalized communities: 74.5 per cent of white research participants and 76 per cent of heterosexuals said 'no' compared to 60.4 per cent of racialized research participants and 59.2 per cent of queer individuals. Gender differences were also noted, with 64.4 per cent of men and 70 per cent of women expressing no fears.

Eligibles and candidates offered a variety of reasons, if any, for why they had no serious concerns that their Facebook, Twitter, or other accounts contained any fodder for a social media scandal. People who ran for office when social media platforms were still new had little to fear because they had little online history to mine. But as people's digital archive grew and others mined it for damaging information, they were either careful in what they posted or fearlessly expressed their views and accepted whatever backlash occurred. Their approaches to social media use are discussed in more detail below.

Even though many folks from diverse backgrounds were not concerned about their social media histories, an intersectional analysis of the individuals who were concerned found that they were typically people who did not fit the white, heterosexual norms of politics. Racialized individuals, queer people, and women were more likely than their respective counterparts to be worried that opponents would dig up potentially damaging posts or photos to discredit them. One possible explanation for this concern is that queer and racialized individuals might have alternative lifestyles, espouse critical perspectives, and/or violate group stereotypes. Individuals who did fear a social media scandal offered several explanations that, as a whole, suggest the primary concerns are social media's ability to publicly archive a person's opinions and the potential for others to take those words out of context.

Several individuals explained that their (past) practice of speaking out online about controversial topics has produced a digital archive that can be mined by opponents to their detriment. The individuals were not necessarily repentant about their comments and were even prepared to defend their stances, but they knew other individuals could take their words and spin them for whatever purpose they see fit. Outspokenness was especially problematic for younger people who had been on social media since their teens and often before they knew they wanted to pursue elected office. Although they might now reject opinions expressed as a youth, their earlier views might still be publicly available on their accounts or been archived by friends, family, or potential opponents. An Indigenous gay man eligible suspected that evolutions in his thinking on issues such as abortion would be deliberately played down as opponents tried to capitalize on earlier views that might suggest he was at odds with his party's official policy. "I know there's been times when I've used my social media to vent about party choices. I've used my social media to express opinions and stances that I've had that I no longer share," said the long-time party activist. But he added later that "I think it's good when you can see that politicians have changed their minds. I don't like it when people try to hold something that someone said 20 years [ago] against a politician who's had time to evolve."

Some eligibles and candidates identified digital media in general as problematic for aspiring politicians. Partisans have long conducted opposition research on candidates from other political parties, spending countless hours going through dusty paper archives searching for damaging information. Digital technology means government and news archives are now available at the touch of a keyboard. Two high-profile individuals interviewed for this study expected comments during old media interviews to be retrieved, and another person was involved in legal proceedings that he feared would be dredged up before his provincial campaign.

Unearthing a digital record of a person's comments or activities is the first step in the creation of a social media scandal. The next step is to publicize that information, a process that often includes putting a specific spin on what happened. As a racialized woman eligible noted, "everything's up for interpretation," and how information is framed can shape public reactions to it. Queer candidate Jeffrey Rock was constantly worried during the 2015 Canadian federal election about what socially conservative partisans would do with his online history:

> I think in the age of social media, I was absolutely terrified that some comment made 15 years ago on social media would come back to haunt me, as a couple dozen candidates had to resign throughout the course of the election [because of it]. You live in complete and utter terror that something that realistically innocuous is going to become through that dog-whistle politics and get twisted into something completely different.

While some individuals were anxious about the possibility of becoming the focus of a social media scandal, overall dismissal of this possibility is likely why few people cited it as a barrier to political candidacy. Online attacks against politicians and social media scandals were not enough to dissuade them from running. Women from diverse backgrounds were especially defiant, an encouraging result that suggests women in general are not letting digital dangers discourage them from seeking elected office. Overall, three-quarters of research participants did not offer any kind of assessment regarding social media's potential impact on their future ambition. Those individuals who said they were not deterred cited cautious posting practices and the optimistic belief that social media scandals are only temporary.

Social Media Scandals a Generational Issue?

Eligibles and candidates indicated that social media scandals might be driven, in part, by generational differences among voters. They argued that the ability of opponents to use old social media posts – especially from years ago – as fodder in election campaigns might wane in the future as a generational turnover takes place among the electorate, with today's young people becoming tomorrow's main voter base. Today's young people have spent most of their lives documenting their personal experiences and opinions through online platforms. Because of this, research participants argued that younger people are more accepting of online indiscretions than older generations of Canadians, who did not grow up under the digital spotlight. Jesse Hitchcock, a 26-year-old white heterosexual woman who had not yet run at the time of the interview, was among those who believe that generational differences in personal experiences with, and orientations towards, social media will eventually render social media scandals a thing of the past:

> Soon we're going to be getting into the realm of age where everybody that's running has had social media since they were 17. As soon as that happens, then immediately it's irrelevant because everybody has this social media history, whereas right now it's largely targeting young people because every other politician didn't have social media most of their youth. I'm sure they were doing questionable things when they were young, it just wasn't on social media.

Young adults were not the only ones to propose that the recent wave of social media scandals involving candidates has a generational undercurrent. Some older individuals indicated that common understandings of what is, and is not, appropriate when it comes to public disclosure have changed along with advancements in digital technologies. While younger people "live their lives fully exposed," many older individuals hold fast to the traditional idea that one does not air one's dirty laundry in public. "The danger here isn't so much the people who use social media," said a 68-year-old white heterosexual man who has been active in party politics for decades but has never run. "The problem is the people who haven't used the social media at all or very little. They're more old school, and they don't want any shocks or surprises. I think that is fading." He expected the change to take place within a few electoral cycles.

It is true that a person's opinion on societal issues can change over time and that social media records that evolution for all to see. But what most research participants overlooked is the fact that the old social media posts most likely to generate a media firestorm are those where the individual expresses an opinion at odds with mainstream societal attitudes or the ideals and goals of their party. The offending comments tend to be sexist, racist, and violent in nature (Canadian Press 2015; Urback 2015). While candidates getting into difficulties over old posts will, on its own, lose its novelty value for the news media, journalists will likely continue to view a candidate's online comments as another form of (controversial) political speech and thus remain interested in reporting on them. An evolution in the norms regarding public disclosure of personal information is unlikely to change that.

Implications of Social Media Scandals

Although the number of individuals whose candidacies have been ruined because of social media scandals is growing, these incidents are still low enough overall that we must be careful not to overstate the extent to which social media scandals might be a barrier to elected office. Most eligibles and candidates indicated that they had few concerns about the potential for their social media history to compromise them. Because of a generally conservative approach to posting, only a few individuals expressed fears that someone might uncover potentially damaging information about them online. Some individuals reported scrubbing their social media sites as a pre-emptive measure. The more important issue might thus be the extent to which a person's social media history factors into the candidate selection process for political parties.

In Canada, individuals who are prepared to seek a party nomination undergo a vetting process so that the central party organization can "attempt to screen out extreme candidates and potential problems before the election begins" (Pruysers and Cross 2016, 788; see also Marland and DeCillia 2020). A person's social media history can be one such problem. The Liberals, Conservatives, and NDP were all dealt embarrassing blows during the 2015 Canadian federal election when candidate gaffes drew national and, in one instance, international headlines (Koziol 2015; "Social Media Posts Spell the End of Federal Candidacies Across Canada" 2015). One federal candidate recalled the party's provincial campaign manager instructing candidates to delete all of their online accounts before the election: "He said, 'If something you've done takes the campaign off message for a day, you just cost us a million dollars.'" Instead of seeking media uptake of its message of the day, the party is forced into damage control to prevent a social media scandal from becoming a major threat (Flanagan 2014, 180–5). The firefighting effort consumes the party's precious, and limited, campaign resources. This fact has led parties to intensify their vetting process. Lewis Cardinal, an Indigenous heterosexual man who ran for the federal NDP, recalled being instructed to provide a copy of everything he had ever written or published when he sought the party nomination in his riding:

> I also had to let them have access to my Facebook and my Twitter accounts and everything so they could review everything before they vetted us. And it was *rigid*. I knew guys and gals out here who were seeking a federal nomination and they were turned down because they had made statements that countered the federal NDP policy on, let's say, Palestine or the Palestinians – that countered what the federal leadership was positioning itself as. They simply wouldn't be allowed to run. That's how rigid it was, and these were good people.

Party vetting efforts are not always this thorough. A woman whose candidacy came to an end because of old social media posts said she informed the vetting committee about the online comments, but a party official dismissed the likelihood that they would resurface during the campaign. The party's desire to have her as a candidate likely led the official to minimize the potential ramifications of the old posts. "They were doing anything to get me through everything," she said. "I definitely had better treatment than a lot of other candidates in the beginning." The closed-door nature of the vetting process (Marland and DeCillia 2020; Pruysers and Cross 2016) means it is difficult to determine the extent to which political parties are rejecting potential candidates based on their social media, or what impact it has in terms of the types of individuals who do and do not make it through that vetting process. For individuals who do make the cut, the next section shows that far more women than men expect to experience intense online harassment from trolls during an election campaign.

Social Media Harassment: Tackling the Trolls

Women politicians have long been the focus of gendered political discourses. Extensive research has found a distinct gendering in political reporting (Ejaz 2018; Falk 2008; Taylor and Pye 2019; Wagner, Trimble, and Sampert 2019; Zulli 2019). Journalists typically pay greater attention to women's physical appearance and family life but not as much to their policy ideas. For example, Erika Falk (2008) discovered that women presidential candidates in the United States were just as likely to see their looks noted in election coverage in 2004 as they were in 1872. While this gendered scrutiny is dissipating for regular women politicians (Hayes and Lawless 2016), it remains a feature of media representations of women politicians aspiring to or holding executive positions (Falk 2008; Trimble et al. 2015; Zulli 2019). Gendered political reporting therefore discursively constructs politics as a masculine realm where women do not belong. Charlotte Adcock argues that the absence, marginalization, or devaluation of women's voices in public debates has serious implications for "what counts as true, normal, representative or politically significant," putting the credibility of democracy itself at stake (2010, 151). Despite the threat that under-representation of women in political institutions poses to democratic legitimacy (Sawer, Tremblay, and Trimble 2006), journalists continue to have difficulty treating as credible those candidates who do not conform to the traditional notion of a politician as a white heterosexual man (Everitt and Camp 2009a, 2009b).

Many online trolls express a similar attitude. Non-governmental organizations were among the first to investigate the highly misogynistic nature of online attacks against women politicians (Dhrodia 2017). Examining online harassment in the six months leading up to the 2017 British elections, Amnesty International found that the average white woman MP received 0.59 abusive tweets per day, or 92 in total, compared to 0.83 tweets per day, or 132 in all, for an Asian woman MP and 13.12 tweets per day, or 2,781 in total, for a Black woman MP. The later result was strongly influenced by figures for Black MP Diane Abbott, who received about half (45.14 per cent) of all abusive tweets directed at women MPs. Without Abbott, the figure for a Black woman MP was 0.51 tweets per day, or 81 in total (Dhrodia 2017). Racism and sexism were intertwined in the online harassment of Abbott, as the following example shows: "Pathetic useless fat black piece of shit Abbott. Just a piece of pig shit pond slime who should be fucking hung (if they could find a tree big enough to take the fat bitch's weight)'" (Mason 2017).

However, academic research about online harassment of women politicians is contradictory. One study found that men politicians in Canada received more uncivil tweets than women politicians but that women who became cabinet ministers or provincial premiers were targeted the most (Rheault, Rayment, and Musulan 2019). A different pattern was found in Britain. Twitter users not only sent more uncivil tweets to women politicians but their messages also contained more gender stereotypes and challenges to these women's right to be elected representatives (Southern and Harmer 2019b). A separate analysis on a subset of tweets found that trolls reinforced the notion that women do not belong in politics by dismissing their ideas, questioning their intelligence, and demanding they shut up (Southern and Harmer 2019a). Academic and non-academic findings together demonstrate that women politicians can be subjected to intense and discriminatory online harassment.

Social media attacks against women politicians are part of a larger trend of online harassment of women (Citron 2014; Jane 2014a, 2014b; Megarry 2014; Mantilla 2015). Women have faced various forms of cyber harassment since the early days of the Internet (Halder and Jaishankar 2011). Gendered online harassment, or gendertrolling, typically involves sexist or misogynistic remarks that target a person based on their gender or sexuality (Chen et al. 2020). Karla Mantilla (2013, 2015) identifies seven characteristics of gendertrolling: (1) it is sparked by women expressing their opinions online; (2) involves graphic gender-based insults and (3) rape and/or death threats; (4) occurs across online platforms, (5) at a high rate of intensity, and (6) for a long period of time; and (7) can be perpetrated by many attackers working together. Mantilla's concept of gendertrolling provides an important context to understand gendered perceptions of online harassment of politicians.

What makes gendertrolling distinct from generic forms of online harassment is its purpose. While generic trolls often espouse opinions that they do not believe in order to get a reaction, Mantilla (2015) argues that gendertrolls are deeply committed to a conservative gender ideology and typically believe what they say. They target women in a bid to reassert traditional gender hierarchies that position men as the legitimate actors in the public sphere and relegate women to the private sphere of children and housekeeping (Mantilla 2015; Megarry 2014). Rather than calmly debate the merits of women's arguments, gendertrolls typically spew sexualized insults, creating a hostile online environment for women. For example, women who actively participate in online political debates are routinely objectified and trivialized by men Facebook users (Vochocová 2018). Gendertrolling thus serves to police and silence women's voices in the mediated public sphere (Nussbaum 2010), limiting "the possibility of an effective feminist movement forming in the online public sphere, and perpetuat[ing] the oppression of women as a social class" (Megarry 2014, 52–3). Gendertrolling is a backlash against women's involvement in male-dominated domains such as politics.

Researchers have examined the gendered underpinnings of online harassment. Claire Hardaker and Mark McGlashan (2016) conducted a linguistic analysis of Twitter users' reaction to British journalist Caroline Criado-Perez's campaign to return a woman to British banknotes. They found that women were often the target of sexually aggressive language and threats, with Twitter users engaging in low-risk behaviour such as insults, ridicule, and sarcasm to high-risk behaviour such as threatening harm or attempting to instil fear (Hardaker and McGlashan 2016, 88–91). African American comedian Leslie Jones was targeted by trolls and hackers after she co-starred in an all-woman reboot of the popular 1980s film *Ghostbusters*. Not only did she receive racist threats and saw her personal website hacked (Ohlheiser 2016) but she was also criticized for not embodying Eurocentric beauty norms (Madden et al. 2018).

Although women public figures are popular targets, ordinary women also face extreme online harassment. Danielle Keats Citron (2014) documents the case of a law student who was targeted on a university discussion board in 2005. Anonymous posters provided regular updates on her activities, made sexually explicit threats, and spread reputation-harming lies that made it difficult for her to find a summer position. Gendertrolling not only carries a psychological cost for its victims but also economic and professional ones. Some victims of cyber harassment have lost their jobs because employers do not want to risk their organization's reputation or other workers' productivity because of the incident (Citron 2014).

Gendertrolling poses a significant risk to women's participation and advancement in politics. Former Australian prime minister Julia Gillard argues that it might deter other women from becoming politically engaged:

> Our community would not consider it acceptable to yell violent, sexually-charged abuse at a female politician walking down the street. Why is it okay to let these voices ring so loudly in our online worlds? We don't yet know to what extent online abuse translates into physical violence. But I am certain the connection is real, that women feel and fear it, and that it is preventing women from standing up and serving in public life. (Hunt 2016)

Although many current woman officeholders have learned to deal with online harassment, gendertrolling might have hidden costs in terms of candidate deterrence and retention. Otherwise politically interested women might opt out of a career in politics to avoid becoming the next target. If they opt in, their careers could be derailed or denigrated because of gendertrolling. Some women politicians have even left

Table 8.2. Responses to question about whether the person is concerned about being attacked through social media during a (potential) run for elected office, by candidate status and personal characteristics.

Characteristic	Yes	No	No clear answer
Overall	50.7% (38)	33.3% (25)	16% (12)
Candidacy Status			
Candidate	43.8% (14)	40.6% (13)	16.7% (6)
Eligible	55.8% (24)	27.9% (12)	16.3% (7)
Gender			
Women	62.2% (23)	21.6% (8)	16.2% (6)
Men	38.9% (14)	44.4% (16)	16.7% (7)
Neither group	50% (1)	50% (1)	0% (0)
Ethnicity			
White	47.1% (16)	26.5% (9)	26.5% (9)
Racialized	53.7% (22)	39% (16)	7.3% (3)
Sexuality			
Heterosexual	51.3% (20)	38.5% (15)	10.3% (4)
Queer	50% (18)	27.8% (10)	22.2% (8)

Note: N = 75. Candidates were asked: "Did you have any concerns about being attacked through social media?" Eligibles were asked: "Would you have any concerns about being attacked through social media?"

politics because of harassment (Perraudin 2019). Gillard's claims, however, have not been subjected to empirical analysis and, as such, remain fearful conjecture. It is beyond the scope of this book to statistically establish the extent to which gendertrolling does or does not depress the political ambition of different social groups, especially women. Instead, this chapter explores the issue by identifying perceptions of online harassment of politicians.

Perceptions of Online Harassment

To explore perceptions of online harassment of politicians, I asked research participants whether they had, or would have, any concerns about being attacked through social media as a candidate. Table 8.2 presents the descriptive statistics. Their responses reveal strong concerns about the potential for opponents, critics, and others to attack via online platforms during an election. Half of the research participants (50.7 per cent) admitted to being apprehensive about being targeted by online trolls, with eligibles (55.8 per cent) more likely to express this concern than candidates (43.8 per cent). Women, racialized individuals, and sexual minorities were the most uneasy groups. Women were almost twice more likely than men to be concerned, a reflection of the high prevalence of cybersexism today. Racial differences were also strong, with racialized individuals more likely to express these concerns than their white counterparts. Heterosexuals were slightly more likely than sexual minorities to admit to fears about social media attacks, but almost twice as many queer individuals voiced this unease than queer individuals who did not.

In contrast, one-third (33.3 per cent) of participants reported not having any initial fears about opponents or critics using social media as a soapbox to disparage them during a campaign. (The remaining individuals did not provide a clear indication of their views.) This is not to say they did not expect social media to be used for this purpose, just that they were not afraid of what might happen should this come to pass. Candidates, men, and heterosexuals were more comfortable with this type of scrutiny than their respective counterparts. Surprisingly, more racialized research participants than white ones indicated they were *not* concerned with social media attacks. One potential explanation is that racialized individuals might have been socialized as children on how to cope with racism and are not easily dissuaded from pursuing their goals by the racist attitudes of others (Brown 2008; Brown and Tylka 2011). In contrast, queer people are an invisible minority and typically only experience homophobia after publicly disclosing their sexuality. For older generations, this disclosure came during adulthood, but younger generations are coming out during adolescence (Dunlap 2016). Queer people might be aware of homophobia from a young age, but they might not need to deal with it until their teens.

Despite strong concerns about social media attacks, most participants were not dissuaded from running because of a belief that attacks have become a normal part of the online experience. "I don't think it would discourage me," said a white heterosexual woman eligible, "but it would definitely be something I'd have to think about and have to prepare myself for, unfortunately." Most people refused to be scared off by online trolls. A South Asian heterosexual woman candidate refused to give trolls oxygen by responding to their comments. She would rather address people's concerns face-to-face: "Get the real story before you start trashing me. If you don't have the decency to do that, then I don't have the time or energy to waste on you."

Five individuals indicated that online vitriol could discourage or has discouraged them from seeking elected office. What is striking is that all are women. They come from a mix of racial/ethnic backgrounds, and all but one is an eligible. These women were concerned about the harm that such attacks could cause to their reputations, mental health, and family members. The small sample size means conclusions are tentative, but these findings suggest social media attacks are a gendered *issue*, with the potential to emerge into a gendered *barrier* in the future if efforts to combat online vitriol are not successful. The following sections examine two aspects of online attacks that concerned participants the most: (1) the anonymous nature of social media and (2) the misogynistic content of online attacks.

Dangers of Gendertrolling

Anonymity was identified as a key reason why online political discussions have become so toxic. In face-to-face interactions, politicians know who the accuser is because that person is standing in front of them. A traditional assumption of democratic deliberation is that citizens will engage in rational, thoughtful debate about public issues. Individuals who express their views in emotional, crude, or hateful terms risk censure, leading many people to choose their words carefully when their identity is known. The anonymity afforded by social media removes this inhibition. Hiding behind fake usernames, anonymous posters are free to express sexist, racist, or homophobic views with little fear of being held accountable for their comments. "It's easy to attack from behind the screen, you know what I mean?" said an East Asian lesbian candidate. "There's no name associated with them, there's no identity associated with them, so they can say whatever they want." Anonymity makes it difficult for the target of trolls to do anything to counteract or stop these attacks, which only emboldens the trolls. Research indicates that the more online posters believe they are anonymous and consequence-free, the more positively they view cyberbullying and the more likely they are to do it (Barlett, Gentile, and Chew 2016).

But not every research participant took issue with online anonymity. An Indigenous heterosexual man eligible defended the practice of anonymous posting. He felt free speech is "slowly being chipped away at all the time." He argued that anonymity enables people like him to express potentially unpopular views and contribute to overall debate without facing a public backlash. In his case, he posts anonymously for fear that people might not do business with him if they do not agree with his political views.

Another concern that participants have about online trolls is their tendency to target women politicians. More than one-quarter (28 per cent) of participants pointed to gendertrolling when discussing online attacks against politicians, especially those against former Alberta premier

Rachel Notley. This theme proved to be highly gendered: 16 women raised the issue but only four men did so. A roughly equal number of white and racialized women discussed gendertrolling, demonstrating it is a concern to all women considering a bid for elected office and not just one group of women. Gendertrolls also weighed more heavily on the minds of those who had yet to pursue a career in electoral politics: almost twice as many eligibles as candidates discussed the issue.

Many of the women's comments regarding social media attacks fit with Mantilla's (2015) concept of gendertrolling. Mantilla argues that women are harassed online because they are women and not because of anything they have said or done. Both candidates and eligibles talked about the violent, misogynistic rhetoric they have seen or experienced online, with trolls objectifying women through a focus on their body parts and terrorizing women with threats of sexual violence.

> They never say, "You know, I really disagree with how you voted on that bill." It's "You're fat so what do you know?" or "You're a dyke, what do you know?" or "You're Indian, what do you know?" It's people sitting in their underwear in the basement somewhere, right, with no life of their own that have the time to sit there and troll you online. (Indigenous queer woman eligible)

> The sexist ones will usually come when I've done something more publicly [in the] media. If there's a picture or there's a video [of me], some people seem to think it's okay to cross over from the "You don't know what you're talking about" to "You stupid woman" and descending from there. (White bisexual woman eligible)

Participants also recognized the misogyny at the heart of online harassment of feminists and repudiation of feminist sentiments. Jessica Quan, an East Asian heterosexual woman eligible, believed her feminist views would be attacked if she ever ran for elected office. "There is a lot of antagonism, especially in the Facebook comments about topics like feminism. I could definitely see how I could be attacked personally, and also based on my views about certain things." An Indigenous heterosexual woman eligible was alarmed that a woman friend constantly gets death and rape threats as the head of a feminist organization in the community.

Having already seen or experienced it in their personal and professional lives, eligibles were well aware that it would continue, and perhaps even worsen, if they were in politics. Joanne Bernard's experiences in provincial office bears this out. The former provincial cabinet minister was surprised at the crude language of some trolls: "I can remember, oh god, it's about maybe two years ago, some guy tweeted that I was a 'retarded cunt' and you know I had a visceral reaction to that because I've never been called these things in my life." Two other participants noted that crude language can evolve into actual physical threats. A federal politician explained that some of his colleagues have been threatened online, prompting a swift response from police. Politicians at other levels of government have also been the focus of threats (Rushowy 2017).

Racialized and queer candidates noted that the gendertrolling they experienced was heavily infused with racism, homophobia, and/or Islamophobia. One woman was surprised at the threatening language used by online attackers. Meanwhile, Bernard, who is a white lesbian, was shocked at the level of homophobia directed at her after launching her first campaign. Rana Bokhari, a heterosexual woman of South Asian descent, did not anticipate being targeted by trolls when she announced her intentions to seek the leadership of a provincial party. The attacks were especially vicious and did not stop after she became the first racialized woman to lead a provincial party in Canada. Abandoning her campaign was never an option, despite the deluge of online and offline attacks. "I never once thought, oh, well, why did I do this? I was just in a fight and I recognized I was in a fight and I was just trying to keep my head above water while all this was going on." Bokhari continued to receive sexist and racist messages even after stepping down as party leader in 2016 to start her own law firm.

Although the nature of online attacks might vary based on a woman's racial and/or sexual identity, their purpose is the same: to make the Internet, and the public sphere in general, unwelcoming for anyone who is not a white heterosexual man (Mantilla 2013, 2015). Women research participants did not *explicitly* attribute online harassment of women to a deep-seated misogyny in society, but that sentiment comes through in their comments on gendertrolling. A former municipal politician believed gendertrolling occurs because women are seen as easier to victimize than men. "But that's from a segment of our society that we just can't seem to get through to them that it's not appropriate, you know what I mean?" said the white heterosexual woman. "I don't believe society as a whole [does it], but the portion of society that attacks women like that, that's shameful and it's unfortunate and I think there's that element in every society. I don't know when that will quit." Participants remarked that feminists and feminist views attract intense backlash from online trolls.

Responses to Gendertrolling

Women politicians' experiences with gendertrolling acted as a cautionary tale for women thinking about becoming candidates. Several woman eligibles reported keeping abreast of news reports of social media attacks against women politicians such as Rachel Notley, and they knew that if they wanted a career in politics, they would have to prepare themselves for gendertrolls. Miranda Jimmy, an Indigenous heterosexual woman, saw the vicious online attacks against prominent women politicians and developed a game plan on how she would react if she experienced similar sexism, as well as racism, during her municipal campaign. Meanwhile, a Filipino heterosexual woman worked with a mental health counsellor to deal with past traumas and put her in a stronger mental head space to deal with potential trolls for when she went forward with plans to run for municipal office in the future. But not all women eligibles were willing to put up with gendertrolls. A South Asian bisexual woman said she might become a political staffer or civil servant rather than a politician to avoid online harassment and other negative aspects of public scrutiny.

Current women politicians were viewed as having an important role in combatting gendertrolling and making online political participation less hostile to future generations of women. An East Asian bisexual woman spoke out about the online harassment she experienced when she ran for university student office. "There were a few sexist comments and I just kind of stood up for all the women instead of even just myself," said Crystal Lau. "This is why we need more women to be out there, to speak up, and to represent people because … it's very sexist." Her actions followed in the footsteps of provincial women politicians who have drawn public attention to gendertrolling. In 2016, Cheri DiNovo told the Ontario provincial legislature about the misogynistic, homophobic, and violent online comments that she had received (DiNovo 2016). The white lesbian, who did not run for re-election in 2018, was inspired to share her experiences after seeing Sandra Jansen do the same thing in the Alberta legislature two days earlier:

> I thought that was brave and a really excellent thing to do so I did it here too. I talked about how I've been threatened with rape, had death threats, everything's happened really. You name what can be said, it's been said to me on social media. And after I went over some of the things that had been said to me in the House and got picked up by the press a little bit, some of the males came over, cabinet ministers, high-profile folks, and said, "Wow,

I've never had that experience." No kidding. I think this is a particularly female experience on social media. I think the trolls attacking women in public office on social media are far worse and more virulent than those that attack men, and they do it in a particular way and a particularly personal way.

Rather than standing up in the Nova Scotia provincial legislature, Joanna Bernard showed her support by doing media interviews about her experiences with online homophobia, sexism, and fat-shaming (McMillan 2016). Bernard also publicly shamed gendertrolls by retweeting their comments for everyone else to see. European politicians are going further in the battle to combat online harassment of elected officials. The United Kingdom has banned anyone guilty of intimidating candidates, campaigners, or elected officials from seeking public office for a period of five years (Buchan 2018; UK Electoral Commission 2023), and the European Union has called on Facebook to take concrete steps to combat online hate speech or face sanctions (Boffey 2018). Efforts to combat gendertrolling are still in the early stages, but it is clear from research participants and news coverage that women are increasingly refusing to accept online harassment as a *permanent* part of contemporary politics.

Managing Digital Dangers

The growing number of social media scandals during Canadian elections and the increasing prevalence of online incivility have meant that people need to be strategic in how they approach online posting, both in their current careers and in preparation for a possible run for elected office. Eligibles and candidates indicated that they engaged in one or more of five main strategies: self-regulation, defence, resignation, openness, and online cleanse.

Self-Regulation

Awareness of scandal mining and social media attacks is one reason why most candidates and eligibles reported taking a cautious approach to their social media activities. Research participants indicated that they carefully managed their online presence for professional, personal, and political reasons. Eligibles, women, heterosexuals, and white people were more likely than candidates, men, queer individuals, and ethnic minorities to engage in self-regulation to make it more difficult for their critics. Some people were already adults when social media arrived on the scene and quickly realized that misuse of the digital technology could hurt their reputations. Other people learned it the hard way and eventually changed their posting practices to ensure their sites presented a professional face to the cyberworld.

People with high-profile jobs were especially careful about the opinions they expressed online because their comments could cause trouble for their organizations, and others were keen to project an "appropriate" image on their personal sites to maintain their professional reputations and possibly set themselves up for a future political run. Some individuals argued that their conservative approach to posting is necessary because social media does not afford much room, literally or figuratively, to explain the nuances of one's political stance. Tweets, for example, have a character limit. "I think twice or maybe a third time before I post something online because I think it is very dangerous," explained Magda Popeanu, a white heterosexual woman who was first elected a Montreal city councillor in 2013. "I don't believe you can express yourself in a few words and to give the shades of grey." The speed of social media makes such self-restraint prudent. The publication of a tweet or post is immediate: once a person presses the send button, their thoughts are in the public domain. People who quickly post their thoughts run the risk of letting their emotions dictate their words. "I find that's really where people start getting tied up in these tricky social media issues, when they're calling people out with derogatory terms and stuff, just anger towards the issues that maybe is just misguided," said Tyler Murnaghan, a white bisexual man who ran unsuccessfully for municipal office.

Defence

Individuals also said they (would) take a defensive stance against any politically motivated cyberattack, but it is an approach more heavily favoured by women than men. Candidates and eligibles were equally likely to take a defensive stance, suggesting it is a common approach when dealing with online criticism. No major differences were found based on race/ethnicity or sexuality. Many people were prepared to stand by whatever comments they had posted online in the past. "I think I do have some things that are not necessarily inflammatory but slightly controversial, but they're things I would feel comfortable standing behind and would even want to stand behind if it veered slightly off of the official party line," said a white queer woman eligible. Some research participants were willing to apologize and change their opinions if presented with evidence. In addition to self-defence, women spoke of the desire to see other people come to their defence when problematic posts resurfaced or others attacked them online. Three women candidates were disappointed that their supporters or political party didn't come to their defence when they faced online attempts to discredit them. Both candidates and eligibles acknowledged the need to have a strong campaign team who can run interference between candidate and online trolls.

Resignation

Participants were resigned to the fact that they could be the target of online incivility during an election campaign. "I don't know how you prepare yourself for that or don't let it weigh on you too much," said a white heterosexual woman eligible, "but it's definitely something that unfortunately is part of the political landscape here right now." Research participants argued that anyone who wants to get involved in politics needs to have a thick skin. Christopher Matthews, a Black gay man eligible, said criticism is simply par for the political course:

> If you don't have that backbone, then you're in the wrong job because regardless of what you do or how you do it or even if you think you're doing it for the best, somebody is going to disagree with you. And if you can't handle that criticism or even that wild comment, it would be a difficult job for you as a politician. That's something that I had to think about: can I do that?

Criticism of politicians has long been a feature of politics, but social media provides the public with an unfiltered avenue through which to publicly express concerns about a politician's policy stances or political views. In the past, the only public outlet that citizens had was the news media, often through letters to the editor. Journalists acted as gatekeepers, determining which individuals were granted access to speak publicly and which ones were excluded. Social media has removed these gatekeepers, allowing citizens to publicly express their views in a tweet or post whenever they want. Research participants felt that prospective candidates need to develop a plan on how to deal with the online trolls.

Openness

Although most research participants censored themselves online, some individuals were much more open about their lives and opinions. Derrick Biso, a white genderqueer individual who ran unsuccessfully for provincial office, is not ashamed of anything they had posted or was posted about them on social media, including photographs of a potentially controversial nature. Biso argued that society needs to come to terms with the fact that young people today document all aspects of their lives online as part of a life fully lived:

> If they're going to try to make me feel shame or guilt for being a human, fuck 'em. I don't have time for that. I live shamelessly. I don't believe in trying to live up to people's standards or norms. I actually have a lot of things to say about the fact that we can be denied employment because we like to have friends and party and that sometimes we take pictures and they're obnoxious and they're vulgar and they're gross and they're messy. That's the human condition, baby.

Other individuals see value in being politically outspoken, even if that means they are the target of public criticism. It allows them the opportunity to express their political beliefs, promote their policy ideas, and push for change in societal attitudes. Jennifer McCreath, a white transgender woman who ran both municipally and federally, was prepared to offer "a strong and reasonable explanation" for anything she has said online. However, she did struggle during her municipal campaign between trying to avoid controversy and trying to challenge stereotypical ideas about trans individuals and issues.

Online Cleanse

Several candidates admitted to going through their social media accounts and erasing any potentially offensive comments or photographs before running for office. Catherine Meade, a Black lesbian who unsuccessfully sought federal office, encourages prospective candidates to do this deep scrub. "Before you go embarrassing your party, look through all your social media, look for anything and decide [if you should remove it]. Really, you might be a great candidate today, but if there's something from your past that's going to actually scuttle a campaign – but anyways." These housekeeping efforts well in advance of any involvement in politics can help save the candidate, and their party, a lot of headaches during an election campaign.

Conclusion

The recent advent and constant evolution of social media means that any understanding of their role in the candidacy process depends on a person's age and the timing of a decision to seek elected office. Candidates who first ran before Facebook was launched in 2006 had fewer qualms with how social media could be used to discredit them during an election than did people who ran, or might run, afterwards. These older individuals did not use social media (that much) or have been cautious from the start in what they posted. In contrast, younger people have not only been more active online but also more frank, making them more exposed to political operators who are much savvier now about how to mine the Internet for potentially damaging information about opponents. Younger eligibles and candidates thus expressed more concerns than their older counterparts about becoming the focus of a social media scandal and took more steps to mitigate this potential. Nevertheless, eligibles of all ages who joined social media after they knew they wanted to seek elected office one day are more guarded in their public comments to limit the possibility that they will become the target of a social media scandal.

Although age is a factor in social media scandals, gender is more important when it comes to social media abuse. Online harassment of women politicians is a deeply troubling phenomenon that has the potential to become a gendered barrier to political participation, both online and offline. Online abuse is, of course, a problem that all politicians confront, but women politicians face especially vicious attacks with several research participants noting the sexist, racist, and homophobic aspects of online vitriol. This observation was highly gendered as well, with women more likely than men to highlight the issue of online harassment of politicians. Women participants also reported having first-hand experience with online abuse: women eligibles as well as candidates talked about the hateful rhetoric they had received or witnessed friends or colleagues receive. Minority women candidates in particular noted that they not only received sexist abuse but also racist or homophobic commentary during their campaigns.

Even though social media platforms have been political tools since the 2000s, they remain a moving target in terms of their impact on candidacy. New Internet-based applications are constantly being created, each one with its own set of features, social practices, and potential for politicking. Societal understandings of and cultural practices around social media are evolving alongside technological innovations, making it difficult for politicians to know how to respond to the increasingly complex ways in which other actors use them to engage in politics. The hazards of social media might make it more difficult to both recruit and retain candidates, especially from historically excluded groups in Canadian politics. Social media scandals and online harassment also have the potential to affect a candidate's mental and physical health. The next chapter identifies the health-related issues associated with political candidacy.

Chapter Nine

The Health Calculation: Threats to Physical and Mental Safety in Politics

It's a sacrifice of time, money, mental health and probably physical health to do this job. If stress is hard on your body, and I think there's ample evidence to say that, then you better have damn fine reasons for doing it in your mind because you know there isn't a day – no, there isn't a month – that goes by where you haven't had a day where you go, "Why the hell am I doing this?"

– Scott McKeen, Edmonton city councillor from 2013 to 2021

Introduction

Politics is a stressful job. Politicians are expected to be highly knowledgeable, skilfully debating government proposals, actively participating in committee meetings, eagerly developing policy expertise in one or two areas, and thoughtfully communicating with journalists and citizens alike about the big issues of the day. Politicians must also be dedicated constituency representatives, attending community events and helping individual residents resolve government-related problems. Federal and provincial politicians are further required to be loyal partisans, offering unfailing support for the party leader and participating in party affairs. Politics is thus a 24x7 job. The workload of an elected representative is so overwhelming that politicians often have little time for their families. Maintaining a healthy diet and regular exercise can be equally difficult. Politicians also face psychological stress. The rise of social media, for example, has intensified public scrutiny: mistakes that would have been overlooked in the past today generate online firestorms that can affect a person's career and reputation. As Scott McKeen notes in the epigraph, politics is a demanding job.

The mental and physical health of politicians matters because they exercise considerable power over our daily lives. Elected representatives are responsible for government services such as health care, education, policing, immigration, trade, and environmental regulation. Federal politicians, in particular, can declare war against foreign countries or terrorist organizations. Yet, politicians experiencing ill health are thought to run the risk of making harmful decisions – or none at all if incapacitated (Gilbert 1995; Robins and Post 1995). Such a failure of leadership could have damaging repercussions for a country, province, or municipality. That is why politicians often face scrutiny over health-related issues (Abrams 1995; Anderson et al. 2017; Bresnahan et al. 2016; Conroy 2018; Neville-Shepard and Nolan 2019; Roehling et al. 2014). Citizens expect government leaders like prime ministers, premiers, and mayors to be super-human: "We assume that leaders, for example, are well-furnished with capabilities, experience and support systems to carry out their role and to cope with the inevitable pressures their responsibilities bring" (Weinberg 2017, 2). Ongoing stigma around mental health provides additional motivation for politicians to keep quiet about any conditions.

Secrecy is one reason why scholars know little about how political life affects, and is affected by, the physical and mental health of politicians. Fortunately, several research participants felt comfortable enough to speak openly about the role of health in political candidacy, including their own health challenges, how these challenges can shape the candidacy and representative experience, and what they did to address these challenges. The participants come from various social backgrounds, indicating that health is a factor that all potential candidates must consider, though LGBTQ and racialized people also identified issues specific to their social groups. This chapter explores how eligibles and candidates perceive the physical and psychological factors that could limit political candidacy in Canada.

The Physical Health Challenges of Politics

Politics takes physical fortitude. Even though newspaper ads, TV commercials, and social media help candidates reach large audiences, politicians continue to put a lot of stock in traditional activities like door-knocking to build electoral support (Kahn and Kenney 1997; McKenna and Han 2014; Nielsen 2012). Door-knocking involves candidates walking from one residence to another, hoping to catch voters at home so they can discuss their platform and qualifications for elected office. It is a solitary activity for many candidates, especially at the municipal level. Candidates with well-staffed campaigns might be accompanied by a team of volunteers, who fan out ahead of the candidate, knocking on doors until someone answers. The candidate then steps forward to talk to that voter while the volunteers fan out again. This approach enables the candidate to spend their time talking to voters; the volunteers do the grunt work. Because of the larger number of missed contacts, it is not unusual for candidates to canvass a neighbourhood more than once during an election campaign.

The size of many constituencies makes door-knocking a herculean effort, even with help (Kenny and McBurnett 1997). Candidates spend weeks, and sometimes months, walking countless miles across the constituency to talk to voters, leading to sore feet and, in some cases, dramatic weight loss. Candidates also encounter crumbling sidewalks and dilapidated buildings that pose a risk of physical injury. "I've fallen on my butt" while campaigning for a candidate, said a white heterosexual man eligible. "You come up to all kinds of houses where the steps are falling apart, the house is falling apart. Or you get to an apartment building where you're uncertain about even your safety." The emotional hazards are equally troubling. Some voters can be rude, hostile, and downright aggressive when candidates come knocking.

Younger candidates have an advantage over their older competitors in terms of canvassing. Tyler Murnaghan, a 20-something white bisexual man who ran unsuccessfully for municipal office in Prince Edward Island, saw his youthfulness as a physical asset during his campaign. "I would say I easily had 20 years under most of [my competitors], so my ability to hit more doors than anyone else was definitely something that I thought would bring in some votes," he said, adding later: "Whereas some of my opponents, I don't know if they would have been able to walk to, say, every door. I know there were times when I went to doors and they'd say, 'I haven't seen this guy, and it's just a few weeks away from the election. I haven't heard anything. I don't think any of our neighbours have seen them.'"

Several candidates in their 50s and 60s noted that physical health would play an important role in any decision on whether to seek election, or re-election, to public office in the future. Whether involved in politics as an elected official or volunteer, these individuals were well aware of the physical toll that politics takes. Paul Harris, a former municipal councillor in Alberta who unsuccessfully ran for the NDP in the 2015 federal election, noted how American presidents such as Barack Obama and George W. Bush turned grey during their terms in office. "There's got to be a way not to take it all on, but I don't know what it is," said the white gay man. "I try to do my best not to." The stresses of being a candidate convinced Lewis Cardinal of the importance of self-care. He advised future candidates to "make sure that you have some personal tools to deal with stress, and that you have to find a way to release stress from yourself because there's real biological effects of living under stress after a prolonged amount of time," said the Indigenous heterosexual man, who ran unsuccessfully for municipal and federal office in Alberta. "Make sure that your health comes first in terms of making sure that you do your exercises or your meditation or whatever it is. That's the most important thing." He knows what he is talking about. Burnout eventually led Cardinal to step down as a federal NDP candidate.

Health concerns don't disappear once a person gets elected. Politics is a stressful occupation. Politicians need to work hard to maintain a healthy lifestyle. The emphasis that Canadian prime minister Justin Trudeau put on health is an example to one white heterosexual man and long-time federal politician:

> I remember one of the first days we were there [in Ottawa] and he was speaking to us and says, "You gotta check in with each other and make sure that everyone's doing okay. This is a very unique lifestyle. Things like eating habits can change. There's all kinds of opportunities for bad habits like that to develop and it's important to support each other." To have a leader that recognizes that and recognizes the importance of that balance is really, really important.

Not only are politicians constantly on the go to attend to legislative and constituency business but they also face a constant barrage of criticism. Elected office is a thankless job. Critiques are plentiful while praise is faint. McKeen, an Edmonton city councillor from 2013 to 2021, noted that the stress of the job can have dramatic physical and mental impacts on an individual. That is why the white heterosexual man noted in epigraph that "you better have damn fine reasons" for seeking elected office.

Some eligibles were already aware that their physical health might limit their ability to run in the future. But equally important was the health status of their close family members. A sick child or an elderly parent might delay or even prevent political candidacy. Limited childcare or family supports in political workplaces such as municipal councils, provincial legislatures, or the federal House of Commons make it harder for politicians with even more stressful caring duties to balance politics and family.

The Physical Safety Challenges of Politics

Although politics is physically challenging for many politicians, LGBTQ and racialized individuals also have to worry about their personal safety. Of the seven research participants who noted physical safety as an issue when considering a bid for elected office, five were either LGBTQ, racialized, or both. The main concern was their personal safety and those of family members. Widespread transphobia in Canadian society means transgender activist Marni Panas already lives with the fear of violence. "As a trans person … it's difficult to come out of a public washroom and wonder is this the day that somebody says you don't belong here and you get beat up for it?" Becoming a political candidate would only heighten the potential danger as even more people would know she is a transgender woman. A South Asian bisexual woman eligible is not out about her sexuality to family, colleagues, and acquaintances in part over fears about her safety. "I wouldn't be able, I think, to maintain the lifestyle I have right now or the safety level I feel right now if I were to be out," she said.

The potential for violence on the campaign trail is one reason why some gender non-conforming individuals act and dress in accordance with societal expectations for their assigned gender. "Sometimes you do have to pass … for safety," noted Derrick Biso, a white genderqueer candidate who dressed like a man to be more acceptable to voters. Meanwhile, an East Asian candidate limited the number of family photographs in campaign materials to protect her wife from potential homophobia in the wife's socially conservative workplace. Chapter 5 discussed how LGBTQ candidates perceive and respond to societal expectations regarding sex and gender.

Like queer people, racialized individuals pose a threat to the white heterosexist norms of Canadian politics and that can spark a violent backlash. A Black heterosexual woman eligible, who has taken a candidate training course, is alert to the potential for violence in politics against women in general and against racialized women in particular:

> People see you as a threat because you're a woman, because you're a Black woman, because you're a person of colour, because you're not like them, because you're different, because you have different ideas, because you're challenging their beliefs. People lash out.

Still, these people can roar all they want. This Black woman is not deterred from pursing her goals. "I've seen change by ploughing ahead" through this kind of backlash, she said. "There's always these ideas [that] you're not supposed to do these things. You just push." Panas is equally committed to her politics. If she opts not to run for elected office in the future, it won't be because of transphobia and the violence it can inspire.

The Psychological Challenges of Politics

Politics takes mental fortitude. As this book demonstrates, candidates experience enormous challenges on the campaign trail. They must navigate issues related to campaign fundraising, employment, news media, public scrutiny, and party politics, where relevant. Once elected, politicians have high workloads and limited family time, leading to mental and physical stresses that can be difficult to cope with over the long term. Symptoms of stress can include "difficulties in sleeping, headaches, indigestion, unexplained tiredness, a decrease in sexual interest, persistent low mood, lack of confidence and struggling to overcome problems," and chronic stress can lead to depression and anxiety (Weinberg 2015, 251–2). A series of British surveys between 1995 and 2010 found stress to be especially high for British MPs with long commutes, whose constituencies were located far away from the House of Commons, and who felt less control over their working lives. Parliamentary reforms to working hours did not reduce these stresses (Weinberg, Cooper, and Weinberg 1999; Weinberg and Cooper 2003; Weinberg 2015). Furthermore, politicians become deeply invested in their representational duties over time and can be emotionally devastated when they lose an election. Politicians who chose to retire are better off in that regard (Byrne and Theakston 2016).

The mental health impact of politics is thus a topic that many would-be candidates ponder when making the decision to run. Sixteen research participants – eight candidates and eight eligibles – voluntarily raised the topic of mental health when discussing the drawbacks to political candidacy. Only one person cited mental health as a barrier that almost kept them from running for office. The other participants viewed mental health as more of a challenge that needed to be addressed because of their previous emotional reactions to criticism or attacks, previous or current mental health conditions, or past trauma. Family members also broached the subject when candidates first thought about running.

Mental fortitude matters because politicians are regular targets of public criticism. Their offices are inundated with phone calls, letters, and visits from angry voters, and their social media posts attract fierce rebuttals from opponents, critics, and trolls (Akhtar and Morrison 2019). Politicians can also be accosted in person, whether it be at a political event, community gathering, or grocery store (Byrne and Theakston 2016). Angry comments aside, politicians are also at risk of serious harassment. Vandalism of election posters and campaign headquarters are not uncommon. Politicians can also be stalked, physically attacked, threatened, and intimidated (Adams et al. 2009; Collignon and Rüdig

2020; James et al. 2007, 2016; Narud and Dahl 2015). A 1998 survey of Canadian federal and provincial politicians found that almost one-third had experienced harassment of a criminal nature (Adams et al. 2009).

Politicians need to know how to handle emotionally charged interactions with the public. Bridget Sterling, a school board trustee in Edmonton, was thankful she took crisis training while working for a sexual assault centre before going into politics. Those skills enabled the white woman to navigate the emotional reactions of constituents seeking help. "You have to have that front-line ability to listen and help people get through the immediate crisis, do some problem-solving, look for some ways to help," said Sterling, "and I think that's actually served me better than I would have expected in this role." A thick skin is vital for politicians.

Politicians also need to handle their own emotional responses. It wasn't unusual for research participants to say that they were easily hurt by criticism. Candidates tried to suppress these emotions, in part to avoid creating a negative impression with that voter or bystanders. Miranda Jimmy, an Indigenous heterosexual woman who unsuccessfully sought a seat on Edmonton city council in 2017, expected to experience racism on the campaign trail and knew those moments would be emotionally charged for her. "Even in … mentally preparing for this, when the first [racist] comment came I was dumbfounded," she recalled. "It totally caught me off guard. I probably stood there stunned for a moment and then the guy kind of laughed and pretended that he was joking." Her response needed to be measured because her behaviour would influence the opinion of people within earshot of the conversation. Thankfully, Jimmy prepared for the emotional aspects of campaigning by accepting a psychologist friend's offer to hear her vent about and then strategize on how to deal with such incidents throughout the election. "I don't think most candidates think about their mental health supports going into this," said Jimmy. Having a mental health professional as a campaign volunteer is one idea that potential candidates could consider. Access to mental health resources could tip the scales in favour of candidacy.

Some research participants have mental health conditions that had them wondering whether candidacy was feasible for them. McKeen was worried that his depression and anxiety could "come rushing back" under the stress of politics and asked several politicians about their mental health experiences in elected office before eventually deciding to run himself. "That was kind of the final box I ticked when I decided I would run because I am a pretty sensitive guy and know that criticism will sting," said McKeen. "Unfair criticism especially will sting." Neuroatypical candidates also needed to figure out how to fulfil their political duties. One former politician has a learning disability, which made it difficult to absorb talking points in advance of political debates. "I don't have a strong working memory," they said. "If I memorize something I won't remember it, but if I learn it, I will know it."

Eligibles were more likely than candidates to admit to mental health or neurological conditions. They wondered if they could handle politics. Gurpreet Kaur Sodhi, a South Asian heterosexual woman eligible with no plans to run for office, has a learning disability that was not diagnosed until she was a young adult. Her dyslexia made it extremely challenging to graduate from high school and pursue a university education. Despite eventually earning a master's degree, Sodhi found it difficult to drop "the impression of myself that I'm not smart." Confidence issues aside, Sodhi felt opponents would use her history of depression to discredit her during a campaign, a realistic fear considering voters more harshly evaluate politicians with depression than those with a physical ailment (Loewen and Rheault 2021). A white queer woman eligible, who has an invisible disability but declined to identify it, added that individuals with any impairments or limitations would have to work significantly harder "to be half as respected in the political sphere." Negative public perceptions of psychological or neurological issues are an extra barrier to candidacy or electoral success for some individuals.

Family members also expressed reservations about the psychological impact of politics. A South Asian heterosexual woman considering a bid for local office faced questions from her husband and mother such as: "What kind of toll will it take on your health? It's a very public position. Can you handle the criticisms in the newspapers, in the media?" She struggled with this issue, and many others, before eventually deciding to run.[1]

Public criticism isn't the only reason why politics are emotionally challenging for politicians. Governments must address difficult problems. Sexual harassment, for example, has long been a feminist issue but received heightened public attention because of the #MeToo movement, which gained international prominence in 2017 after sexual assault accusations were levied against American film producer Harvey

---

1 The South Asian woman is considered an eligible for the purposes of this research because she did not make the decision to run until shortly before her interview. Furthermore, she didn't publicly announce her plans to run or file her nomination papers until several months after our interview.

Weinstein. Revelations soon spread to other industries, occupations, and workplaces, including the Canadian House of Commons (Collier and Raney 2018). Individuals seeking high-profile offices such as the American presidency have seen their sexual behaviours and views on sexual assault subjected to intense public scrutiny.

These public debates can be triggering for eligibles who have experienced sexual violence. Giselle General, who took candidate training geared for municipal office, was sexually assaulted before immigrating to Canada from the Philippines several years ago. She didn't realize she needed to address this past trauma before running for office until the 2016 US presidential election, when a 2005 *Access Hollywood* tape surfaced showing Republican candidate Donald Trump talking about his sexual aggression towards women (Rhodes et al. 2020). "It caught me off guard how devastated I was by the election of the US president Trump, particularly because I am a survivor of sexual assault," said General. This scandal, and her reaction to it, led her to sign up for therapy. The Filipino heterosexual woman completed a course of therapy on sexual assault trauma shortly after our interview and reached out later via email to say she felt empowered by the experience. "The most important piece that I learned is that if I am attacked and hurting, that it is okay to react, to heal, and to ask for help," General said. "I feel braver about the idea of getting more involved politically." Insights from research participants have demonstrated the importance of addressing the mental and physical health needs of (would-be) politicians.

Conclusion

Health is an overlooked issue in political candidacy. Both eligibles and candidates expressed concerns about the physical toll that campaigning takes on the body. Door-knocking is vital for reaching out to potential supporters, but it takes tremendous energy and stamina to canvass thousands of voters during a short election campaign. Weight loss, sore feet, and pulled muscles are not unusual. Younger candidates have an advantage over older candidates in this regard. They are less likely to feel the physical effects of campaigning, and if they do, they are likely to bounce back more quickly. One's physical condition also matters when it comes to the length of a political career: stress or failing health deters some older individuals from seeking election or re-election. More disturbing, however, is the potential for violence on the campaign trail. LGBTQ individuals and racialized folks identified this aspect of physical safety as important to them. Members of marginalized groups already fear for their physical safety because of the violence that transphobia, homophobia, and racism inspire. Political candidacy, and the public profile that comes with it, is likely to increase the threat of that violence. Consequently, the health calculation for LGBTQ and racialized individuals includes an assessment of the propensity for hate-driven violence in a community.

Although physical health is a factor in political exits, mental health is a factor in candidate emergence. Sixteen research participants identified mental health issues as a drawback to political candidacy. Eligibles and candidates alike were concerned that they didn't have the thick skin necessary to withstand public criticism and that public life might trigger a pre-existing condition such as anxiety and depression or dredge up an old trauma. Some eligibles also wondered if they would be taken seriously in politics if people knew they had a learning disability or mental health issue. These insights indicate that individuals need to ponder the following questions when considering political candidacy: Do they have the physical stamina and mental fortitude to be an elected representative in Canada? Do the reasons for getting into politics outweigh the drawbacks? As Scott McKeen suggested, the answer needs to be yes, otherwise politics will not be worth the cost.

Chapter Ten

The Final Calculations: Theoretical and Practical Insights into Political Candidacy

Young people need to stop being viewed as people who have the right to vote but not the right to run for office because the Constitution very clearly says that all Canadians have the right to public office subject only to those laws in a free and open society. Does a free and open society tell people under the age of 35 that you're not fit for politics and that you shouldn't bother? No, it doesn't.
– Jasmine Leicester, a white transgender woman
who has run municipally

What Does It All Mean?

This research project began during a two-year postdoctoral fellowship at the Centre for the Study of Democratic Citizenship in Montreal. Based at McGill University but involving scholars from universities around Quebec, the Centre is a hotbed of research on political attitudes and behaviour in Canada. Members routinely present their research findings at Centre-sponsored events. One such affair stood out for me: a two-day conference on youth political participation. It was unusual because of the large number of practitioners there to hear the presentations. Aside from the usual academics, conference attendees included officials from Elections Canada, provincial election agencies, and nonprofit organizations. The civil servants and activists would politely listen as scholars pondered the theoretical implications of research results. How does this information allow us to better understand how the political world works? When it was their turn to ask questions, the practitioners asked a very different question: How can we use this information to make the political process work better? For election officials, *theorizing* how current voting practices make it difficult for some individuals to vote is not enough; they wanted to know what *actions* they could take to improve the voting process.

I have often thought back to that conference when considering the implications of my own research findings on political candidacy. What *actions* can various actors take to make candidacy more feasible for under-represented groups in Canadian politics? This concluding chapter offers suggestions on how aspiring candidates, political parties, advocacy organizations, and governments can address issues related to candidacy raised by 101 individuals of diverse social and political backgrounds. For ease of presentation, I take a thematic approach to answering this question, first reviewing the main conclusions for each factor highlighted in this book and then discussing the implications for scholars and practitioners alike. I conclude the chapter with an overview of the theoretical, empirical, and methodological contributions of this study to our understanding of political candidacy in Canada.

Challenge #1: Candidates Seek Ways to Juggle Family and Politics

One of the most fundamental calculations that a candidate needs to make is how to achieve work–life balance, both during an election campaign and, if elected, in public office. The challenges of maintaining some semblance of a private life despite the all-consuming nature of political life depend on each individual's personal circumstances. Are they single, married, or divorced? Do they have adolescent or adult children? Can they rely on extended family members to help out? Family support for an individual's personal ambitions is crucial if they are to combine family responsibilities with political duties. Only those individuals who are single and childless – typically young people – escape this calculation, although only temporarily. As personal circumstances change, so do the calculations.

A notable finding from this study is that both women and men struggle to figure out how to combine a political career with family responsibilities. Early research on gender and political ambition identified family as a gendered barrier that keeps more women than men from pursuing elected office, but more recent studies – including this one – question that assumption. My interviews with politicians, candidates, and eligibles revealed that some men adjust and even sacrifice their political ambitions because of their families. These men want to be engaged fathers and know that high-level politics would mean long hours away from home. Fathers who are still keen to get involved in politics wait until their children are grown to leap from local to provincial or federal politics. Conversely, the interviews revealed that some women plough ahead with their candidacies despite family challenges because they want to achieve something in the political realm. Many women have also found a way to manage childcare. Consequently, family responsibilities might not be the gendered barrier it once was. To monitor any changes in the strength of this barrier, scholars need to continually reassess the role of family responsibilities in the willingness of women *and* men to become candidates. They also need to take a closer look at the reasons why mothers and fathers opt not to run for office and whether any variations among each group exist in terms of race/ethnicity, sexuality, age, and class.

Of greater relevance to practitioners are the candidate versus eligible findings related to how work–life balance can be achieved in politics. Many (men) candidates saw it as the responsibility of the individual to figure out a solution to the family calculation, and they admitted it would be their (primarily women) partners who would have to take care of the children while they engaged in politics. In contrast, (women) eligibles were far more likely to identify institutional and structural issues that make it difficult for individuals to combine politics and family. Eligibles wanted to see political parties and legislatures put a greater effort into making politics more family friendly. To that end, my recommendations for practitioners revolve around addressing institutional norms and practices, echoing calls made by other scholars and activists (cf. Childs 2016). The ultimate goal is to make politics a more attractive endeavour for parents who want to contribute to good government in Canada.

Feminists have put forward several ideas for reforming politics to make it more family friendly, and most start with legislatures. Legislatures need to enable parent politicians to do their jobs while also taking care of their families. Some examples include having on-site daycare at the legislature, allowing babies into the legislative chambers, and changing the timing of legislative activities, such as meetings and votes, to a time more suitable to parents with care responsibilities. Reforming legislative norms will be a long and difficult process. These institutions were created when only men were allowed to be politicians, and their norms reflect the assumption that the politician has a wife at home to take care of the kids. Not all reforms will work as intended, but updating old institutions is a process. Meanwhile, governments should consider enabling candidates to claim childcare as a campaign expense and political parties should provide candidates with family support, such as helping to cover the cost of childcare and offering on-site childcare at party events. Even with institutional changes in legislatures and parties, aspiring candidates still need to regularly check in with their partner, children, and other family members to ensure they retain family support and to address any emerging challenges.

Challenge #2: Candidates Seek Ways to Pay for Politics

An equally important calculation in the decision-making process to become a candidate is figuring out how to pay for it all. Both eligibles and candidates worried about this aspect of electoral politics. However, as the political candidacy literature predicts, women were more likely than men to raise concerns about their ability to raise money for a campaign. Regardless of candidacy status, women were more reluctant or shy about asking people to donate to their campaign, but few men expressed such reservations. One man even said he enjoyed fundraising! Part of the challenge for women was inexperience. Women often didn't know whom to ask, how to ask, or when to ask for financial support. Men had more experience in this area. Women also expected to raise less money than men because their networks included more lower-income individuals and fewer wealthier folks. Moreover, women expressed concerns about how asking people for money would affect personal relationships, especially if they lost. Would friends and family feel they wasted their money if she didn't get elected? Add to that the ethical quandaries. For example, women were uneasy about the reciprocal relationship between politician and donor that is at the heart of campaign fundraising. Once in office, what would donors expect from them? Men didn't appear to give these issues much thought.

How can practitioners and activists help non-traditional candidates to overcome these financial hurdles? Some political parties have taken steps to improve women's fundraising capabilities. Three federal parties established special funds in the 1980s to help raise money for their women candidates: the Agnes MacPhail Fund (NDP), the Ellen Fairclough Fund (Progressive Conservatives), and the Judy LaMarsh Fund (Liberals). The LaMarsh fund is still operating, but the status of the other two is unclear. Provincial parties in Nova Scotia have similar funds for their women candidates (Nova Scotia Advisory Council on the Status of Women 2021). To my knowledge, no formal actions have been taken to help Indigenous, racialized, or LGBTQ candidates with fundraising. Meanwhile, governments have targeted political parties. New Brunswick offers parties a financial incentive to field more women candidates (Poitras 2017). In 2017, the provincial government changed the formula for its annual per-vote subsidy for parties to make women candidates' vote tally in the previous election now worth 1.5 times that of men's vote tally. More women candidates mean more government money. A House of Commons committee recommended in 2019 that the federal government do something similar (Wright 2019).

In the United States, feminist activists have used political action committees (PACs), to raise and distribute money to viable woman candidates at all levels of government, but especially for those running as Democrats. Emily's List (www.emilyslist.org) has been the most effective in supporting women's candidacy in the United States. Its approach to recruitment, training, and fundraising has been mimicked by other organizations keen to increase the diversity of American politicians. The LGBTQ+ Victory Fund is a case in point (https://victory-fund.org/). Inspired by their southern neighbours, Canadian unions, business groups, and other organizations began to establish PACs around 2014 in a bid to influence federal and provincial elections. In response, the Trudeau government introduced new regulations in 2018 to limit what these third-party organizations can do during federal elections (Clark 2019). PACs are highly controversial in Canada, making it unlikely that a Canadian organization could use them in the way that American organizations do to financially support the candidacies of women and minorities.

The constant need for money in politics means that campaign schools routinely include information sessions on how to fundraise. But insights from women eligibles who took a City of Edmonton training course suggest campaign schools would have a stronger impact on increasing the diversity of representation in politics if they broadened their scope beyond candidacy. Not every individual is ready to become a candidate weeks or months after attending a campaign school. Individuals need time to prepare for an eventual run, including learning how to fundraise. One way to acquire these skills is to first volunteer on other people's campaigns. Yet women indicated that the Edmonton organizers failed to see the training course as an opportunity to build a network of women volunteers and donors willing to help other women run for elected office. "It could have been an extremely powerful networking opportunity where you form connections with up to 50 women who are interested in political governance," said Nisha Patel, a woman eligible of South Asian descent. These women could form a pool of campaign volunteers for the few women who do opt to jump into electoral politics right away. Not only would volunteers get an inside look at fundraising and campaigning but women candidates would also get some financial and human resources necessary to have a chance at winning. "We knew there were some women willing to run," said a Black heterosexual woman, "but I felt that there was an opportunity there for those individuals to better connect with other women who had skills and may not want to run right away but might have something to contribute to their campaign." By encouraging women to volunteer for other women's campaigns, campaign school organizers would not only dramatically increase the electoral chances of those women who do run but also expand the number of women who get involved in politics behind the scenes as campaign managers and volunteers.

An unexpected finding of this research project is that campaign fundraising is not the only financial challenge related to candidacy. Both candidates and eligibles revealed that employment-related issues before, during, and after an election can matter more in terms of who is willing to run for public office. Here one's socio-economic status, or class, matters more than one's gender. Individuals usually have to reduce their hours at work, take a leave of absence, or quit their job to run for office, and not everyone can afford the lost wages. For many people, their ability to save up money for an eventual run is limited. Personal expenses such as mortgages or rent also cannot be claimed as campaign expenses. What is the solution? Many working-class individuals opt not to become a candidate even though the remuneration for politicians is typically much higher than the salary they are earning now. Wealthier individuals can weather the loss of a month or two of wages but are far more concerned about politician pay. Becoming an elected representative would involve a large pay cut that would make it difficult for them to sustain their current lifestyle. Only the truly rich could afford to do that. Because wealthier individuals are over-represented in our legislatures (many clearly do take the pay cut), my recommendation for addressing this financial issue focuses on working-class individuals. One way to lower the money barrier for this under-represented group in Canadian politics would be for all governments to expand the list of allowable campaign expenses to include living expenses such as rent, utilities, food, and childcare during the election period. This approach would increase the ability of working-class individuals to run for elected office, enabling them to bring their specific set of life experiences to bear on governance and public policy.

Challenge #3: Candidates Seek the Right Political Party

As gatekeepers to elected office in partisan systems, political parties are a common focus of scholarly attempts to explain the under-representation of women and minority groups in democratic legislatures. Party recruitment practices and how they reinforce the dominance of white heterosexual men as candidates usually garner the most attention. But findings from this book suggest we need to step back from party practices and begin our assessment of the candidacy process by looking at ideological alignment. Before party gatekeepers even have the chance to decide whom to admit into their organization, eligibles must figure out which party they are interested in joining. Individuals thinking about one day running for office will survey the field of political parties operating at their desired level of government, comparing each party's ideology and platform against their own policy preferences. If they can't find a party that closely aligns with their values, they aren't likely to put themselves forward as candidates or respond favourably to recruitment attempts.

Why does ideological alignment matter? Simply put, many individuals won't subject themselves to the strict party discipline characteristic of the Canadian political system if they don't support at least three-quarters of a party's platform. Eligibles don't want to go into politics to become trained seals. They have to believe in the party's goals. Because scholarly research tends to assess ideological alignment between voters and parties, we don't know how individuals who self-select out of politics because of a lack of ideological fit differ from those individuals who do find a political home. Future research needs to identify the extent to which party ideology is a deterrent to candidacy overall but especially for members of which social groups. If party platforms typically reflect the policy preferences of white heterosexual men, a lack of ideological fit could help explain why more women and minorities choose not to become candidates at the federal or provincial levels. They are making a rational decision not to run because they don't see their policy priorities prioritized by any existing party.

The problem of ideological alignment is not one that can be solved by practitioners or activists. Eligibles either find a political party to join or they don't. No party can ever appeal to everyone (though some parties have certainly tried). Yet it is important to remember that party platforms are not static. Although a party's ideology tends to be consistent, its platform can shift over time depending on changes in the party leader, voter priorities, and party member preferences. Political parties can also become more attractive to eligibles who generally share their ideological bent by making sure their platforms reflect the policy interests of these potential partisans. That means moving beyond the superficial ("hey, we have racialized candidates!") to the substantive ("we will push for recognition of foreign credentials so immigrants can work in the professions for which they have been trained in their countries of origin").

Likewise, organizations keen to recruit more diverse individuals to run for elected office need to create opportunities for eligibles to learn about and connect with political parties. More knowledge about a party's ideology, platform, and officials might help some individuals to find their political home. Yet partisanship is a dicey issue for many advocacy organizations in Canada, which need to be non-partisan in their candidate training programs to maintain funding and/or political support. Parties certainly engage in their own outreach efforts, but eligibles would find it time consuming to attend several events held by different parties. A speed-dating or trade-fair approach, whereby individuals can talk to officials from several parties at one event, could provide a soft introduction to political parties and help people figure out which party or parties to investigate further. Even if many of these individuals don't end up becoming candidates, they might get involved behind the scenes as party members or campaign volunteers. We need to increase the diversity of not only political candidates but also party officials to ensure parties reflect the needs and interests of Canadian society as a whole, not those of just one social group.

Challenge #4: LGBTQ Candidates Seek Ways to Survive Public Scrutiny

An unexpected finding from this research is that public scrutiny is a barrier to candidacy for LGBTQ individuals. Although eligibles of all social backgrounds expressed concern about losing their privacy and facing a constant barrage of public criticism if they ran for office, LGBTQ eligibles were also worried about encountering moral regulation of their sexual and/or gender expression. Canadian attitudes towards sexual and gender minorities might have improved in recent decades, but the recent resurgence of the anti-LGBTQ movement in North America means LGBTQ individuals can still face intense backlash. To avoid dealing with that on a larger scale, some LGBTQ eligibles have chosen not to run for elected office despite a strong interest in public affairs. Their fears of public scrutiny are well grounded. LGBTQ candidates were candid about their struggles with moral regulation and the emotional toll that public criticism of their lifestyles and identities exacted.

Candidate experiences demonstrate that LGBTQ eligibles possess a clear understanding of the ways in which their identities will come under more intense scrutiny if they seek elected office. Because I didn't learn of this barrier until I interviewed LGBTQ eligibles at the very end of the data collection process, I wasn't able to ask LGBTQ candidates how they overcame a fear of public scrutiny to pursue a political career, a line of questioning that would have produced important insights into how LGBTQ individuals can prepare for and navigate this aspect of political life in ways that enable them to remain true to who they are. Future research should explore LGBTQ politicians' strategies for addressing public scrutiny. This information would help advocacy organizations that seek to boost LGBTQ representation in Canadian politics, like ProudPolitics, to refine their training programs to meet the specific needs of this politically marginalized community.

Interestingly, LGBTQ eligibles were not the only research participants who identified moral regulation of sexuality and gender expression as important challenges. Among the heterosexual participants, racialized candidates noted that they faced pressure to change their appearance to match Eurocentric beauty norms, and racialized eligibles didn't want past mistakes or indiscretions to be used to discredit them. That heterosexual individuals also experienced moral regulation suggests scholars should explore the role of public scrutiny in shaping the political environment for all candidates, but especially for those from various marginalized communities.

Scholars also need to explore how political context shapes the nature of public scrutiny that candidates experience. By investigating the candidacy process in Canada, this study reveals that public scrutiny is not only an issue in the candidate-focused US political system but also in party-centric systems where much of the news media's attention is focused on party leaders, cabinet ministers, and star candidates. Rank-and-file candidates receive little media attention, but they do spend countless hours interacting with voters on doorstops and at community events. Interviews with candidates reveal that these public interactions are a major source of moral regulation. Scholars need to explore the nature of these interactions to better understand how public scrutiny concerns limit the political advancement of sexual and gender minorities in democratic politics. In the meantime, political parties and advocacy organizations should focus on strengthening the communication skills of LGBTQ candidates by providing them with training sessions tailored to this community's unique challenges.

Challenge #5: Candidates Seek More (Objective) News Coverage

Although one-quarter of research participants saw public scrutiny as a major drawback to candidacy, none viewed the news media that way. Many eligibles weren't worried about how the news media might treat them during a hypothetical campaign because of prior experience with and knowledge of how the news media operate. A strong understanding of media behaviour gave these individuals confidence in their ability to handle journalists should they ever run for office. Still, research participants did critique the news media. Both candidates and eligibles expected the news media to prioritize objectivity, accuracy, and fairness when covering politics, but journalists don't always achieve these professional ideals. Participants argued that some news organizations are highly ideological and/or partisan in their reporting, and as such, fail to provide all sides of an issue. Candidates in particular were shocked at the degree of media bias they saw during elections. But not everyone took a harsh view. Some candidates and eligibles assessed their local news media as being fair and balanced. The variety of perspectives that came across in the interviews demonstrates that the news media are not a monolithic group. Considerable variation exists between news outlets regarding how they report on campaigns and candidates, with some journalists prone to sensationalist coverage and others intent on upholding the professional norms of objectivity.

That no one mentioned the news media as a barrier to candidacy means scholarly fears that women, racial minorities, and LGBTQ people might be deterred from running because of media treatment of politicians are probably misplaced. Research on stereotypical media depictions of women politicians, for example, would lead us to expect that at least one woman eligible would point to media sexism as a reason not to run, but that didn't happen. Media sensationalism and unprofessional behaviour were of far greater concern, but they did not hamper women's political ambitions. Again, this finding doesn't mean women and minorities didn't take issue with media coverage of non-traditional politicians. People from marginalized communities were acutely aware of the complex nature of individual identities and how they can shape one's experiences with the news media. Change a single aspect of a politician's identity – gender, race/ethnicity, sexuality – and they can receive a completely different reception by journalists that can influence their ability to generate positive press, recruit volunteers, raise money, and maybe even win an election.

The complexity of media behaviour can make it difficult for individuals of different genders, religions, and sexualities to navigate politics. But not all media experiences were negative. Two racialized candidates found their respective ethnic media to be highly supportive of their campaigns, likely out of a desire to see that ethnic community represented in Canadian politics. Other candidates who expected to receive discriminatory coverage discovered that their gender, race/ethnicity, or sexuality wasn't an issue at all for local journalists. It was their partisan affiliation or the media's own agenda that shaped election coverage. Consequently, a winning media strategy requires potential candidates to have a solid understanding of the local news industry and its approach to covering politics.

Activists have long been working to modify media behaviour to make news coverage less problematic for non-traditional candidates. For example, feminists monitor news coverage of women politicians and use social media to draw public attention to especially egregious examples of media sexism. Recent American election cycles have even seen journalists calling out other journalists for how they have covered women candidates. Advocacy organizations like GLAAD in the United States have also published media guides to advise journalists on the use of fair and accurate language, especially when covering women and minority candidates. The purpose of this activism is to pressure the news media to abandon stereotypical coverage of politicians. For their part, political parties and campaign schools routinely offer training sessions to help future candidates improve their media skills. Journalism schools are also becoming more self-critical in how the media report on marginalized populations in a bid to improve the quality of journalism in the future. All of these efforts need to continue, and intensify, to ensure the news media cover all politicians in a fair manner.

Challenge #6: Candidates Seek a Less Vitriolic Social Media

Social media is of far greater concern than the news media to eligibles because of the potential for online platforms to be the source of scandals and harassment. Younger people were attentive to the ways in which political opponents might search through their online past to find potentially embarrassing posts, photographs, or videos to discredit them during an election campaign, causing a media firestorm that could throw their political party off message and force them to resign. This fear is a realistic one. Young people have grown up with social media and regularly post their views and activities online. In contrast, older generations did not encounter social media until they were adults and are typically more cautious about their online communications. They also don't take up new platforms such as TikTok as readily as younger people, further diminishing their online exposure. Consequently, a digital record of past indiscretions is more prevalent for younger rather than older folks.

Because future voters will probably have their own digital pasts, younger eligibles are hopeful the electorate will be more understanding of mistakes and not judge aspiring politicians based on something they said or did years ago. But as much as campaign schools can train people on the professional uses of social media, it is up to individuals to be careful about what they say or do online. Eligibles therefore discussed some of the strategies they use to prevent a social media scandal from felling their future political ambitions, including scrubbing their sites long before getting involved in politics and being more careful about what they post. Some folks even left social media entirely. Individuals thinking about getting involved in politics, whether as a campaign volunteer or a candidate, need to avail themselves of whatever social media training and scrubbing services are available to help them navigate the dangerous roads of the information super highway.

Increasing awareness of the dangers of social media has led governments around the world to intensify efforts to regulate online platforms. Initiatives to protect digital privacy typically focus on government, consumer, and criminal uses of personal information. As part of that process, regulatory agencies and privacy activists are pushing for the "right to be forgotten" or the "right to erasure," which would enable citizens to request their personal data be erased under certain conditions. The European Union included such provisions in its General Data Protection Regulation (gdpr-info.eu). This aspect of digital privacy has yet to be resolved as it conflicts with commercial realities and democratic interests. Companies need to create a digital infrastructure to be able to erase data on demand, and that work will be costly. Data erasure also challenges democratic expectations of freedom of expression, transparency, and accountability. Resolving these tensions will take time. Because the digital regulation is still evolving, individuals need to find other strategies for protecting themselves from a social media scandal.

A second way in which social media poses a challenge to candidacy is online harassment. Women eligibles in particular were concerned that political opponents, critics, and anonymous trolls would use social media platforms, especially Facebook and Twitter, to launch attacks against them as individuals and as candidates. Criticism of one's policy ideas and political activities is to be expected, but attacks related to one's gender, race/ethnicity, sexuality, and religion are beyond the pale. Yet gendertrolls routinely send sexually explicit and violent messages to women politicians (Atalanta 2018; Dhrodia 2017), with minority women politicians also receiving racist, homophobic, and ableist commentary (Al-Rawi, Chun, and Amer 2022; Southern and Harmer 2019a). Among the research participants in this project, women eligibles of all social backgrounds were acutely aware of the online hostility that women politicians are more likely to experience than men politicians, and they knew they needed to prepare for this problem if they ever ran for office, but they would not allow it to deter their political ambitions. Online harassment of politicians is therefore a gendered *problem* – but not yet a gendered *barrier* to candidacy – in that women know they need to develop a strategy on how to address it while men don't have to give it much thought.

What steps can candidates take to protect themselves from online trolls? Both eligibles and candidates talked about having campaign staff deal with the online harassment rather than the candidate, but this approach simply transfers the psychological distress to campaign staff. It is difficult to read abusive comments, even if they are meant for someone else. Other research participants talked about having a thick skin and not letting the comments have the troll's desired psychological impact.

Whatever the strategy, it is grossly unfair to expect the target of these attacks to address the problem (Wagner and Young 2024). Other actors need to take steps to address online harassment of politicians. As they do with other social issues, governments and non-governmental organizations could launch general awareness campaigns to draw attention to the issue of cyberbullying and encourage citizens to be respectful when engaging others online. Companies and sporting organizations are already doing so. Canadian telecoms giant Telus has spent millions promoting its #EndBullying campaign. Among other initiatives, it is working with the Canadian Football League (CFL) and Hockey Canada to hold TELUS Wise workshops that teach elementary students about how to use technology responsibly. Notable sports figures such as National Hockey League (NHL) player Jordan Eberle and Olympic gold medallist Jillian Saulnier have backed the campaign. Provincial governments could follow the lead of business and civil society by incorporating modules on social media use into the educational curriculum. Finally, political parties and other political operatives need to set an example by not engaging in online negativity themselves. Partisans are behind some of the online harassment that politicians experience, and changes to their posting habits would go a long way towards improving the tone of Canadian politics today. Together, awareness campaigns, educational programs, and online professionalism could change the online environment.

Challenge #7: Candidates Seek Mental and Physical Well-Being

Health-related issues are an overlooked barrier to political candidacy. Although it is widely acknowledged that politics is a time-consuming occupation, little scholarly attention is paid to the physical and mental strains the job places on elected representatives. Politics is stressful, and stress manifests in numerous physical ailments. A proper diet and regular exercise can alleviate stress, but the non-stop demands of politics make it difficult for individual politicians to follow a healthy lifestyle. Constant partisan, public, and media scrutiny can also have a psychological effect, leading to new or aggravating pre-existing mental health issues. Some candidates might not run again while some eligibles might not become candidates because of less-than-ideal physical or mental well-being. Candidates didn't feel up to the physical challenges of campaigning anymore while eligibles feared voters would discriminate against them because of prior mental health issues. Social taboos around depression, anxiety, and other mental health issues are one reason why health is an overlooked barrier to candidacy. Research demonstrates that voters are more reluctant to support candidates with mental health issues than those with a physical injury (Loewen and Rheault 2021). Real or imagined physical frailty is also viewed as a serious shortcoming for politicians, especially those seeking the most powerful positions (Anderson et al. 2017; Neville-Shepard and Nolan 2019). That is why politicians keep health issues under wraps when running for or holding elected office (Russell 2011). This secrecy coupled with limited scholarly interest in politicians' health result in a lack of knowledge about the extent to which elected representatives experience physical or mental health issues while in office.

Thankfully, many resources exist to help would-be candidates prepare for the physical and mental challenges of politics. Individuals can work with health care professionals to devise strategies on how to maintain a healthy diet, regular exercise, and mental well-being. Depending on one's personal connections, candidates should consider asking a mental health professional if they would volunteer for the campaign and counsel the candidate during the election. One Indigenous woman municipal candidate found such assistance invaluable for dealing with racism, sexism, and other challenges on the campaign trail. Campaign schools can do their part by offering training sessions on how to maintain a healthy lifestyle in politics as well as identify health resources that candidates can use before, during, and after an election. Political parties should also make health care fundamental to their institutional norms. For example, they can make sure healthy food is always available at political functions, including items that can be easily taken on the go if the politician has to rush off (which is often the case). They should also make gym facilities available and allocate time for politicians to workout. Furthermore, parties must adjust workplace norms to protect this time: no interruptions should be allowed when the person is exercising. The goal is to institutionalize a healthy lifestyle that can sustain politicians throughout their term in office.

Concluding Thoughts

How do public perceptions of political candidacy shape the willingness of different types of Canadians to seek elected office? Answering this question is key to advancing our understanding of why political institutions in Western liberal democracies like Canada continue to be dominated by white heterosexual men. Research typically focuses on demand-side factors such as party recruitment and candidate selection, but studies on supply-side factors such as individuals' perceptions of candidacy are equally important to understanding why more diverse people choose not to run for elected office. By interviewing individuals of diverse social backgrounds and political ideologies, this book has identified new and previously overlooked barriers to candidacy as well as provided a more nuanced understanding of traditional ones and how these barriers can be higher for some social groups more than others. A desire to avoid the moral regulation that underlines public scrutiny is one reason why LGBTQ individuals decide not to run, and online harassment of politicians is of concern to women of all social backgrounds. More women are finding a way to combine politics and family while some men put family before politics, but the workplace norms of political institutions don't make it easy for any politician to be a parent. Women continue to view campaign fundraising as more challenging than men do. Many working-class folks cannot afford to take time off from their jobs to run for office – even if an election win leads to the highest-paying job they have ever had – while some wealthy individuals don't want to take the pay cut that comes with elected office. Meanwhile, difficulty finding a partisan home is preventing individuals of all backgrounds from becoming candidates despite a strong interest in public affairs. Taken together, these findings reveal that individual calculations regarding candidacy are far more complex than previously believed.

Five innovative features of this research project have made these insights possible. First, a major strength of this book is its focus on the Canadian context. Scholarly understandings of the pitfalls of candidacy are mainly derived from research on the United States, yet the American political system is relatively unique among Western liberal democracies. Differences in terms of political institutions and processes, party and electoral systems, and political cultures make it difficult to generalize findings from the American context to other countries. More non-American, comparative, and cross-national research is needed to determine which factors matter for which individuals and in which political contexts. Because most Western countries use a parliamentary system, findings from this Canadian study can be generalized to and/ or empirically tested in other national contexts.

Second, by comparing insights from eligibles and candidates, this project assesses the relative importance of various factors on the political ambition of Canadians. Eligibles were far more likely to cite partisanship, public scrutiny, nature of politics, and lifecycle as drawbacks to political candidacy while work–life balance weighed heavily on the minds of candidates before running. Comparing eligible and candidate responses also provided insights into how, and why, factors matter at different stages of the candidacy process. For example, although everyone was worried about money, eligibles were more focused on the costs of campaigning while candidates warned about post-politics employment issues.

Third, by employing a feminist intersectional research paradigm, this project identifies which factors are important to everyone and which factors matter to specific social groups. These intersectional insights can help advocates to tailor campaign training for the needs of different types of candidates. Fourth, by moving beyond a focus on federal politics to include the provincial and municipal levels, this study explores the degree to which institutional variations matter for political candidacy. Finally, this study demonstrates the importance of employing qualitative methods when investigating potential barriers to elected office for different types of individuals. The conversational nature of semi-structured interviews enabled LGBTQ individuals to raise public scrutiny as an issue, an opportunity not afforded in close-ended survey questions that require participants to choose between one of several options. For this reason, surveys are not well suited to uncovering new or previously overlooked factors shaping political candidacy. This project therefore makes an important contribution to our understanding of why descriptive representation in Canadian political institutions remains an elusive goal in the twenty-first century.

Appendix: Interview Schedules

Before we begin, I would like to remind you that participation in this study is voluntary. You can choose not to answer any question that you wish. You can also stop the interview at any time. I would also like to remind you that you are being audio-recorded for note-keeping purposes only.

Questions for Candidates

Can you tell me the story behind how you decided to run for [federal/ provincial/municipal] office?

Were your parents involved in politics? Was politics a regular topic in your household as you were growing up?

You must have considered the pros and cons about getting into politics before finally making the leap. What were the pros? Why did you want to get involved in politics?

What resources and/or skills did you have that you thought would serve you well as a candidate? What resources and/or skills did you think you were lacking?

What were the cons? What gave you pause about running for elected office?

If not mentioned:

- What did you think the challenges would be in terms of dealing with your preferred political party? What challenges did you expect to face in terms of getting the party nomination? What role did your evaluation of the party leader play in your decision to run?
- What did you think the challenges would be in raising money for your campaign? What do you see as the other potential financial implications of running for elected office?

- Did you have any specific concerns about your social media history as you prepared to run for elected office? Do you have any concerns about being attacked through social media?
- Was there anything about [federal/provincial/municipal] politics itself that you didn't like?
- Do you have any concerns about the time commitment needed to pursue elected office?
- How important was family support to your decision to run for [federal/provincial/municipal] office? How did your family react to your decision to become a candidate? Did you have any concerns about the potential impact on your family of your decision to run for elected office? Do you think [federal/provincial/municipal] office is compatible with family responsibilities?
- Did you have any specific concerns about the news media as you prepared to run for elected office?
- Were you concerned about how your [age/gender/race or ethnicity/sexual orientation] would be perceived by the party and/ or voters?
- Do you believe you faced any challenges to becoming a candidate because you are a [woman/man]?

If you had to do everything over again, how would you have addressed these challenges today?

- How would you recommend other candidates address them?
- What do you think a candidate needs to do today to make a credible run for elected office in Canada at the [federal/provincial/ municipal] level?

What do you believe needs to be done to encourage more diverse types of people to run for elected office in Canada?

Have you ever considered running for office at another level of government?

If yes:

- What other office have you considered pursuing?
- Why are you interested in seeking that office?
- When have/are you considering making the move?
- How would you assess your chances?
- What would you need in terms of resources, skills, support, and so on to mount a credible campaign for that office?

If no:

- Why aren't you interested in seeking office at another level of government?

Do you have any final comments on the topics we have discussed today?

Questions for Eligibles

Are you interested in politics? Why or why not?

- Do you follow politics at the federal, provincial, and municipal levels?
- Which level of politics do you follow the most?
- What is your impression of [federal/provincial/municipal] politics?
- What qualities do you believe an elected representative should have?
- Were your parents involved in politics?
- Was politics a regular topic in your household as you were growing up?

Have you ever thought about running for public office?

If yes:

- When did you first think about becoming a candidate?
- Have you thought about running for a particular level of government?
- What might encourage you to become involved in politics?
- What resources and/or skills do you have that might serve you well in a campaign?
- What resources and/or skills did you think you lack at this point to make a run for elected office?
- When do you think you will run? Why then?
- Would you be willing to run even if you thought your likelihood of winning was low?

If no:

- Why don't you see yourself as a potential politician?
- When you say you've never considered running, does that mean it's something you could never see yourself doing? Why or why not?

Why haven't you run for elected office? What do you view as the drawbacks to running for elected office?

If not mentioned:

- What do you think the challenges would be in terms of dealing with your preferred political party? What challenges would you expect to face in terms of getting the party nomination? What role would your evaluation of the party leader play in a decision to run?
- What do you think the challenges would be in raising money for a campaign? Would you have an easy or difficult time raising money for a campaign? What would you see as the other potential financial implications of running for elected office?
- What concerns would you have regarding your social media history and how it might be used by others against you if you were to run? Would you have any concerns about being attacked through social media?
- Is there anything about the nature of politics that might put you off running for elected office?
- Would you have any concerns about the time commitment needed to pursue elected office?
- How important would family support be any decision to run for elected office? How do you think your family would react to a decision to become a candidate? Would you have any concerns about the potential impact on your family of a decision to run for elected office? How compatible do you think elected office is with family responsibilities?
- What concerns would you have about the news media if you were to run?
- Would your [age/gender/race or ethnicity/sexual orientation/ immigrant status] be an issue for voters or journalists if you were to run?

What do you think a candidate needs to do today to make a credible run for elected office in Canada?

What do you believe needs to be done to encourage more diverse types of people to run for elected office in Canada?

Do you have any final comments on the topics we have discussed today?

References

Aalberg, Toril, Jesper Stromback, and Claes H. de Vreese. 2012. "The Framing of Politics as Strategy and Game: A Review of Concepts, Operationalizations and Key Findings." *Journalism* 13 (2): 162–78. https://doi.org/10.1177/1464884911427799.

Aaldering, Loes, and Daphne Joanna Van DerPas. 2020. "Political Leadership in the Media: Gender Bias in Leader Stereotypes During Campaign and Routine Times." *British Journal of Political Science* 50 (3): 911–31. https://doi.org/10.1017/S0007123417000795.

Abrams, Herbert L. 1995. "Presidential Health and the Public Interest: The Campaign of 1992." *Political Psychology* 16 (4): 795–820. https://www.jstor.org/stable/3791894.

Adams, Brian E., and Ronnee Schreiber. 2011. "Gender, Campaign Finance, and Electoral Success in Municipal Elections." *Journal of Urban Affairs* 33 (1): 83–97. https://doi.org/10.1111/j.1467-9906.2010.00508.x.

Adams, James, and Zeynep Somer-Topcu. 2009. "Modern Now, Win Votes Later: The Electoral Consequences of Parties' Policy Shifts in 25 Postwar Democracies." *Journal of Politics* 71 (2): 678–92. https://doi.org/10.1017/S0022381609090537.

Adams, Melinda. 2010. "Ma Ellen: Liberia's Iron Lady?" In *Cracking the Highest Glass Ceiling: A Global Comparison of Women's Campaigns for Executive Office*, edited by Rainbow Murray, 159–76. Santa Barbara: Praeger. https://doi.org/10.5040/9798400632815.ch-008.

Adams, Susan J., Tracey E. Hazelwood, Nancy L. Pitre, Terry E. Bedard, and Suzette D. Landry. 2009. "Harassment of Members of Parliament and the Legislative Assemblies in Canada by Individuals Believed to Be Mentally Disordered." *Journal of Forensic Psychiatry and Psychology* 20 (6): 801–14. https://doi.org/10.1080/14789940903174063.

Adcock, Charlotte. 2010. "The Politician, the Wife, the Citizen, and Her Newspaper: Rethinking Women, Democracy, and Media(Ted)

Representation." *Feminist Media Studies* 10 (2): 135–59. https://doi.org
/10.1080/14680771003672254.

Akhtar, Shazia, and Catriona M. Morrison. 2019. "The Prevalence and Impact
of Online Trolling of UK Members of Parliament." *Computers in Human
Behaviour* 99: 322–7. https://doi.org/10.1016/j.chb.2019.05.015.

Allen, Peter, David Cutts, and Madelaine Winn. 2016. "Understanding
Legislator Experiences of Family-Friendly Working Practices in Political
Institutions." *Politics and Gender* 12 (3): 549–72. https://doi.org/10.1017
/S1743923X16000040.

Allern, Sigurd, and Ester Pollack. 2012. "Mediated Scandals." In *Scandalous!
The Mediated Construction of Political Scandals in Four Nordic Countries*, edited
by Sigurd Allern and Ester Pollack, 9–28. Göteborg: Nordicom. https://
norden.diva-portal.org/smash/get/diva2:1534752/FULLTEXT01.pdf.

Al-Rawi, Ahmed, Wendy Hui Kyong Chun, and Salma Amer. 2022.
"Vocal, Visible and Vulnerable: Female Politicians at the Intersection of
Islamophobia, Sexism and Liberal Multiculturalism." *Feminist Media Studies*
22 (8): 1918–35. https://doi.org/10.1080/14680777.2021.1922487.

Andersen, Robert, and Tina Fetner. 2008. "Cohort Differences in Tolerance
of Homosexuality: Attitudinal Change in Canada and the United States,
1981–2000." *Public Opinion Quarterly* 72 (2): 311–30. https://doi.org/10.1093
/poq/nfn017.

Anderson, Jennifer, Yi Zhu, Jie Zhuang, Joshua C. Nelson, Mary J. Bresnahan,
and X. Yan. 2017. "Metaphors That Communicate Weight-Based Stigma
in Political News: A Case Study of New Jersey Governor Chris Christie."
Revue européeanne de psychologie appliquée 67 (3): 139–46. https://doi
.org/10.1016/j.erap.2016.12.007.

Arneil, Barbara. 2017. "Lactating Mothers in Parliament: Beyond
Accommodation." In *Mothers and Others: The Role of Parenthood in Politics*,
edited by Melanee Thomas and Amanda Bittner, 46–63. Vancouver: UBC
Press. https://doi.org/10.59962/9780774834605-005.

Arrington, Theodore S., and Gerald L. Ingalls. 1984. "Race and Campaign
Finance in Charlotte, N.C." *Western Political Quarterly* 37 (4): 578–83.
https://doi.org/10.1177/106591298403700405.

Ashe, Jeanette, and Kennedy Stewart. 2012. "Legislative Recruitment: Using
Diagnostic Testing to Explain Underrepresentation." *Party Politics* 18 (5):
687–707. https://doi.org/10.1177/1354068810389635.

Atalanta. 2018. "(Anti)Social Media: The Benefits and Pitfalls of Digital
for Female Politicians." www.atalanta.co/s/AntiSocial_Media_Report
-FINAL2-lowres.pdf.

Atkeson, Lonna Rae, and Nancy Carrillo. 2007. "More Is Better: The Influence
of Collective Female Descriptive Representation on External Efficacy."
Politics and Gender 3 (1): 79–101. https://doi.org/10.1017/S1743923X0707002X.

Atkins-Sayre, Wendy. 2009. "Governor Mom: Jane Swift and the Body Politic." In *Gender and Political Communication in America: Rhetoric, Representation, and Display*, edited by Janis L. Edwards, 129–47. Lanham: Rowman & Littlefield Publishers.

Auer, Meagan, Linda Trimble, Jennifer Curtin, Angelia Wagner, and V.K.G. Woodman. 2022. "Invoking the Idealized Family to Assess Political Leadership and Legitimacy: News Coverage of Australian and Canadian Premiers." *Feminist Media Studies* 22 (2): 338–53. https://doi.org/10.1080 /14680777.2020.1790627.

Azari, Julia R., and Benjamin A. Stewart. 2015. "Surrogates or Competitors? Social Media Use by Independent Political Actors." In *Controlling the Message: New Media in American Political Campaigns*, edited by Victoria A. Farrar-Meyers and Justin S. Vaughn, 53–73. New York: New York University Press. https://doi.org/10.18574/nyu/9781479886357.003.0003.

Barlett, Christopher P., Douglas A. Gentile, and Chelsea Chew. 2016. "Predicting Cyberbullying from Anonymity." *Psychology of Popular Media Culture* 5 (2): 171–80. https://doi.org/10.1037/ppm0000055.

Barman, Jean. 2008. "Writing Women in to the History of the North American Wests, One Woman at a Time." In *One Step Over the Line: Toward a History of Women in the North American Wests*, edited by Elizabeth Jameson and Sheila McManus, 99–127. Edmonton and Athabasca: The University of Alberta Press and Athabasca University Press. https://doi.org/10.15215/aupress /9780888645012.01.

Bateson, Regina. 2020. "Strategic Discrimination." *Perspectives on Politics* 18 (4): 1068–87. https://doi.org/10.1017/S153759272000242X.

Beail, Linda, and Rhonda Kinney Longworth. 2013. *Framing Sarah Palin: Pit Bulls, Puritans, and Politics*. New York: Routledge. https://doi.org /10.4324/9780203806791.

Beck, Susan Abrams. 2001. "Acting as Women: The Effects and Limitations of Gender in Local Governance." In *The Impact of Women in Public Office*, edited by Susan J. Carroll, 49–67. Bloomington: Indiana University Press.

Benoit, William L., and John P. McHale. 2004. "Presidential Candidates' Personal Qualities: Computer Content Analysis." In *Presidential Candidate Images*, edited by Kenneth L. Hacker, 49–63. Lanham: Rowman & Littlefield Publishers. https://search.library.wisc.edu/catalog/999975342802121.

Besco, Randy, and Erin Tolley. 2022. "Ethnic Group Differences in Donations to Electoral Candidates." *Journal of Ethnic and Migration Studies* 48 (5): 1072–94. https://doi.org/10.1080/1369183X.2020.1804339.

Bird, Karen. 2003. "Who Are the Women? Where Are the Women? And What Difference Can They Make? Effects of Gender Parity in French Municipal Elections." *French Politics* 1 (1): 5–38. https://doi.org/10.1057/palgrave .fp.8200014.

Bittner, Amanda. 2010. "Personality Matters: The Evaluation of Party Leaders in Canadian Elections." In *Voting Behaviour in Canada*, edited by Cameron D. Anderson and Laura B. Stephenson, 183–207. Vancouver: UBC Press. https://doi.org/10.59962/9780774817851-011.

Bittner, Amanda. 2014. "Party Leaders in the NDP." In *Reviving Social Democracy: The Near Death and Surprising Rise of the Federal NDP*, edited by David Laycock and Lynda Erickson, 197–217. Vancouver: UBC Press. https://doi.org/10.59962/9780774828512-010.

Bittner, Amanda. 2018. "Leaders Always Mattered: The Persistence of Personality in Canadian Elections." *Electoral Studies* 54: 297–302. https://doi.org/10.1016/j.electstud.2018.04.013.

Black, Jerome H. 2008. "The 2006 Federal Election and Visible Minority Candidates: More of the Same?" *Canadian Parliamentary Review* 31 (3): 30–6. www.revparl.ca/31/3/31n3_08e_Black.pdf.

Black, Jerome H. 2011. "Visible Minority Candidates and MPs." *Canadian Parliamentary Review* 34 (1): 30–4. www.revparl.ca/34/1/34n1_11e_Black.pdf.

Black, Jerome H. 2013. "Racial Diversity in the 2011 Federal Election: Visible Minority Candidates and MPs." *Canadian Parliamentary Review* 36 (3): 21–6. www.revparl.ca/36/3/36n3e_13_Black.pdf.

Black, Jerome H., and Lynda Erickson. 2003. "Women Candidates and Voter Bias: Do Women Politicians Need to Be Better?" *Electoral Studies* 22 (1): 81–100. https://doi.org/10.1016/S0261-3794(01)00028-2.

Blocker, Jr., Jack S. 1985. "Separate Paths: Suffragists and the Women's Temperance Crusade." *Signs* 10(3): 460–76. https://doi.org/10.1086/494155.

Boffey, Daniel. 2018. "EU Threatens to Crack Down on Facebook Over Hate Speech." *The Guardian*, 11 April. https://www.theguardian.com/technology/2018/apr/11/eu-heavy-sanctions-online-hate-speech-facebook-scandal.

Bogart, Nicole. 2021. "Despite Low Number of Election Victories, Advocates Say Canada's LGBTQ2S+ Candidates Are Becoming More Diverse." *CTV News*, 21 September. https://www.ctvnews.ca/politics/federal-election-2021/despite-low-number-of-election-victories-advocates-say-canada-s-lgbtq2s-candidates-are-becoming-more-diverse-1.5594524?cache=gszlebujvvuylyge.

Boily, Frédéric, and Ève Robidoux-Descary. 2019. "LGBT Groups and the Canadian Conservative Movement." In *Queering Representation: LGBTQ People and Electoral Politics in Canada*, edited by Manon Tremblay, 157–78. Vancouver: UBC Press. https://doi.org/10.59962/9780774861830-009.

Bouchard, Joanie, and Sabrina Bourgeois. 2024. "An Unheard Confidence Crisis? An Analysis of Indigenous Peoples' Perceptions of Settler

Institutions and Politics." *Representation* 60 (4): 559–81. https://doi.org /10.1080/00344893.2023.2265930.

Bratton, Kathleen A., Kerry L. Haynie, and Beth Reingold. 2006. "Agenda Setting and African American Women in State Legislatures." *Journal of Women, Politics and Policy* 28 (3–4): 71–96. https://doi.org/10.1300 /J501v28n03_04.

Bresnahan, Mary, Jie Zhuang, Yi Zhu, Jennifer Anderson, and Joshua Nelson. 2016. "Obesity Stigma and Negative Perceptions of Political Leadership Competence." *American Behavioral Scientist* 60 (11): 1362–77. https://doi .org/10.1177/0002764216657383.

Bristowe, Stephen L. 1980. "Women Councillors – an Explanation of the Underrepresentation of Women in Local Government." *Local Government Studies* 6 (3): 73–90. https://doi.org/10.1080/03003938008432878.

Brodie, Janine. 1985. *Women and Politics in Canada.* Toronto: McGraw-Hill Ryerson Limited. https://books.google.co.in/books/about/Women_and _Politics_in_Canada.html?id=ATIqAAAAYAAJ&redir_esc=y.

Brown, Danice L. 2008. "African American Resiliency: Examining Racial Socialization and Social Support as Protective Factors." *Journal of Black Psychology* 34 (1): 32–48. https://doi.org/10.1177/0095798407310538.

Brown, Danice L., and Tracy L. Tylka. 2011. "Racial Discrimination and Resilience in African American Young Adults: Examining Racial Socialization as a Moderator." *Journal of Black Psychology* 37 (3): 259–85. https://doi.org/10.1177/0095798410390689.

Buchan, Lizzy. 2018. "Online Trolls Who Torment Election Candidates Could Be Banned from Public Office Under Abuse Crackdown." *The Independent*, 29 July. https://www.independent.co.uk/news/uk/politics/election-trolls -social-media-abuse-ban-politicians-public-office-a8467831.html.

Burge, Camille D., Melissa J. Hodges, and Rio Rinaldi. 2020. "Family Matters? Exploring Media Coverage of Presidential Candidates' Families by Gender and Race." *Politics, Groups, and Identities* 8 (5): 1022–42. https://doi.org /10.1080/21565503.2019.1584748.

Burrell, Barbara C. 1985. "Women's and Men's Campaigns for the U.S. House of Representatives, 1972–1982: A Finance Gap?" *American Politics Quarterly* 13 (3): 251–72. https://doi.org/10.1177/1532673X8501300301.

Burrell, Barbara C. 1996. "Sex and Money: The Financing of Women's and Men's Campaigns for the U.S. House of Representatives, 1972–92." In *A Woman's Place is in the House.* Ann Arbor: University of Michigan Press. https://doi.org/10.3998/mpub.14231.

Burrell, Barbara. 2005. "Campaign Financing: Women's Experience in the Modern Era." In *Women and Elective Office: Past, Present, and Future*, 2nd ed., edited by Sue Thomas and Clyde Wilcox, 26–40. Oxford: Oxford University Press. https://doi.org/10.1093/oso/9780195180824.003.0002.

Burrell, Barbara C. 2014. "Financing Men's and Women's Campaigns for the U.S. House." In *Gender in Campaigns for the U.S. House of Representatives.* Ann Arbor: University of Michigan Press. https://doi.org/10.3998 /mpub.213944.

Burroughs, Benjamin. 2013. "Obama Trolling: Memes, Salutes and an Agnostic Politics in the 2012 Presidential Election." *The Fibreculture Journal* 22: 258–77. http://twentytwo.fibreculturejournal.org/fcj-165-obama -trolling-memes-salutes-and-an-agonistic-politics-in-the-2012-presidential -election/.

Byrne, Christopher, and Kevin Theakston. 2016. "Leaving the House: The Experience of Former Members of Parliament Who Left the House of Commons in 2010." *Parliamentary Affairs* 69 (3): 686–707. https://doi .org/10.1093/pa/gsv053.

Bystrom, Dianne G. 2005. "Media Content and Candidate Viability: The Case of Elizabeth Dole." In *Communicating Politics: Engaging the Public in Democratic Life,* edited by Mitchell S. McKinney, Lynda Lee Kaid, Dianne G. Bystrom, and Diana B. Carlin, 123–33. New York: Peter Lang.

Caesar-Chavannes, Celina. 2021. *Can You Hear Me Now?* Toronto: Penguin Random House. https://www.penguinrandomhouse.ca/books/622402 /can-you-hear-me-now-by-celina-caesar-chavannes/9780735279612.

Caliendo, Stephen M., and Charlton D. McIlwain. 2006. "Minority Candidates, Media Framing, and Racial Cues in the 2004 Election." *International Journal of Press/Politics* 11 (4): 45–69. https://doi.org/10.1177/1081180X06293551.

Campbell, David E., and Christina Wolbrecht. 2006. "See Jane Run: Women Politicians as Role Models for Adolescents." *Journal of Politics* 68 (2): 233–47. https://doi.org/10.1111/j.1468-2508.2006.00402.x.

Campbell, Rosie, and Sarah Childs. 2014. "Parents in Parliament: 'Where's Mum?'" *The Political Quarterly* 85 (4): 487–92. https://doi.org/10.1111 /1467-923X.12092.

Campbell, Rosie, and Sarah Childs. 2017. "The (M)otherhood Trap: Reconsidering Sex, Gender, and Legislative Recruitment." In *Mothers and Others: The Role of Parenthood in Politics,* edited by Melanee Thomas and Amanda Bittner, 25–45. Vancouver: UBC Press. https://doi.org/10.59962 /9780774834605-004.

Campus, Donatella. 2013. *Women Political Leaders and the Media.* Basingstoke, Hampshire: Palgrave Macmillan. https://doi.org/10.1057/9781137295545.

Canada, House of Commons. 2021. *Frequently Asked Questions: Pension Plan, Pay and Benefits of Departing Members of Parliament and During Dissolution of Parliament.* Ottawa: Government of Canada. https://www.ourcommons .ca/Content/Newsroom/Articles/FAQsPensionSalariesBenefits -Dissolution2021-ENG%20(final).pdf.

The Canadian Press. 2015. "Hashtag Fails on the 2015 Campaign Trail."
    Maclean's, 9 September. http://www.macleans.ca/politics/ottawa
    /hashtag-fails-on-the-2015-campaign-trail/.
Carbert, Louise. 2006. *Rural Women's Leadership in Atlantic Canada: First-Hand
    Perspectives on Local Public Life and Participation in Electoral Politics.* Toronto:
    University of Toronto Press. https://doi.org/10.3138/9781442679511.
Carbert, Louise. 2009. "A Political Economic Analysis of Women's Political
    Leadership." In *The Ashgate Research Companion to Political Leadership*, edited
    by Joseph Masciulli, Mikhail A. Molchanov, and W. Andy Knight, 435–53.
    Farnham: Ashgate Publishing Limited. https://www.routledge.com
    /The-Ashgate-Research-Companion-to-Political-Leadership/Masciulli
    -Molchanov/p/book/9780754671824?srsltid=AfmBOorMU254l3RJHtoInce
    VnrQiu1f_kQW42kF6rFDg804BFr3OvfId.
Carbert, Louise. 2010. "Viewing Women's Political Leadership Through a
    Rural Electoral Lens: Canada as a Case Study." In *Gender and Women's
    Leadership: A Reference Handbook*, vol. 1, edited by Karen O'Connor, 137–50.
    Los Angeles: Sage. https://doi.org/10.4135/9781412979344.n15.
Carnes, Nicholas. 2018. *The Cash Ceiling: Why Only the Rich Run for Office –
    and What We Can Do About It.* Princeton, NJ: Princeton University Press.
    https://doi.org/10.1515/9780691184203.
Carrigan, Tim, Bob Connell, and John Lee. 1985. "Toward a New Sociology of
    Masculinity." *Theory and Society* 14 (5): 551–604. https://doi.org/10.1007
    /BF00160017.
Carroll, Susan J., and Kira Sanbonmatsu. 2013a. "Entering the Mayor's
    Office: Women's Decisions to Run for Municipal Positions." In *Women and
    Executive Office: Pathways and Performance*, edited by Melody Rose, 115–36.
    Boulder, CO: Lynne Rienner Publishers. https://doi.org/10.1515
    /9781685854560-008.
Carroll, Susan J., and Kira Sanbonmatsu. 2013b. *More Women Can Run: Gender
    and Pathways to the State Legislatures.* New York: Oxford University Press.
    https://doi.org/10.1093/acprof:oso/9780199322428.001.0001.
Catungal, John Paul, and Eugene J. McCann. 2010. "Governing Sexuality
    and Park Space: Acts of Regulation in Vancouver, BC." *Social and Cultural
    Geography* 11 (1): 75–94. https://doi.org/10.1080/14649360903414569.
CBC. 2015. "More Than a Transgender Activist, Candidate Jennifer McCreath
    Says." *CBC News*, 14 August. https://www.cbc.ca/news/canada
    /newfoundland-labrador/more-than-a-transgender-activist-candidate
    -jennifer-mccreath-says-1.3191354.
Celis, Karen, and Sarah Childs. 2020. *Feminist Democratic Representation.*
    Oxford: Oxford University Press. https://doi.org/10.1093/oso
    /9780190087722.001.0001.

Chaney, Paul. 2013. "Institutionally Homophobic? Political Parties and the Substantive Representation of LGBT People: Westminister and Regional UK Elections 1945–2011." *Policy and Politics* 41 (1): 101–21. https://doi.org/10.1332/030557312X645793.

Chen, Gina Masull, Paromita Pain, Victoria Y. Chen, Madlin Mekelburg, Nina Springer, and Franziska Troger. 2020. "'You Really Have to Have a Thick Skin': A Cross-Cultural Perspective on How Online Harassment Influences Female Journalists." *Journalism* 21 (7): 877–95. https://doi.org/10.1177/1464884918768500.

Cheng, Christine, and Margit Tavits. 2011. "Informal Influences in Selecting Female Political Candidates." *Political Research Quarterly* 64 (2): 460–71. https://doi.org/10.1177/1065912909349631.

Childs, Sarah. 2016. *The Good Parliament*. Bristol: University of Bristol. http://www.bristol.ac.uk/media-library/sites/spais/images/grc/GoodParliament%20SinglePage%20Report.pdf.

Childs, Sarah, and Mona Lena Krook. 2006. "Should Feminists Give Up on Critical Mass? A Contingent Yes." *Politics and Gender* 2 (4): 522–30. https://doi.org/10.1017/S1743923X06251146.

Childs, Sarah, and Mona Lena Krook. 2009. "Analysing Women's Substantive Representation: From Critical Mass to Critical Actors." *Government and Opposition* 44 (2): 125–45. https://doi.org/10.1111/j.1477-7053.2009.01279.x.

Citron, Danielle Keats. 2014. *Hate Crimes in Cyberspace*. Cambridge: Harvard University Press. https://doi.org/10.4159/harvard.9780674735613.

City News. 2010. "Smitherman Targeted by Homophobic Campaign Posters." *CityNews*, 24 October. https://toronto.citynews.ca/2010/10/24/smitherman-targeted-by-homophobic-campaign-posters/.

Clark, Campbell. 2019. "The Age of the PAC Is Here, But Who They Are Still Not Completely Clear." *Globe and Mail*, 7 July. https://www.theglobeandmail.com/politics/article-the-age-of-the-pac-is-here-but-who-they-are-still-not-completely/.

Colebrook, Claire. 2004. *Gender*. New York: Palgrave Macmillan. https://doi.org/10.1007/978-1-137-06185-0.

Coleman, Daniel. 1997. "Immigration, Nation, and the Canadian Allegory of Manly Maturation." *Essays on Canadian Writing* 61 (Spring): 84–103.

Collier, Cheryl N., and Tracey Raney. 2018. "Canada's Member-to-Member Code of Conduct on Sexual Harassment in the House of Commons: Progress or Regress?" *Canadian Journal of Political Science* 51 (4): 795–815. https://doi.org/10.1017/S0008423918000032X.

Collignon, Sofia, and Wolfgang Rüdig. 2020. "Harassment and Intimidation of Parliamentary Candidates in the United Kingdom." *The Political Quarterly* 91 (2): 422–29. https://doi.org/10.1111/1467-923X.12855.

Collins, Patricia Hill. (1990) 2009. *Black Feminist Thought: Knowledge, Consciousness, and the Politics of Empowerment*. New York: Routledge. https://www.routledge.com/Black-Feminist-Thought-Knowledge-Consciousness-and-the-Politics-of-Empowerment/HillCollins/p/book/9780415964722.

Comacchio, Cynthia. 1997. "'A Postscript for FATHER': Defining a New Fatherhood in Interwar Canada." *Canadian Historical Review* 78 (3): 385–408. https://doi.org/10.3138/CHR.78.3.478.

Conroy, Meredith. 2018. "Strength, Stamina, and Sexism in the 2016 Presidential Race." *Politics and Gender* 14 (1): 116–21. https://doi.org/10.1017/S1743923X17000642.

Cook, Timothy E. 1998. *Governing with the News: The News Media as a Political Institution*. Chicago: University of Chicago Press. https://press.uchicago.edu/ucp/books/book/chicago/G/bo3534630.html.

Crenshaw, Kimberle. 1989. "Demarginalizing the Intersection of Race and Sex: A Black Feminist Critique of Antidiscrimination Doctrine, Feminist Theory and Antiracist Politics." *University of Chicago Legal Forum* 139–67. https://chicagounbound.uchicago.edu/uclf/vol1989/iss1/8.

Crenshaw, Kimberle. 1991. "Mapping the Margins: Intersectionality, Identity Politics, and Violence Against Women of Color." *Stanford Law Review* 43 (6): 1241–99. https://doi.org/10.2307/1229039.

Crespin, Michael H., and Janna L. Deitz. 2010. "If You Can't Join 'Em, Beat 'Em: The Gender Gap in Individual Donations to Congressional Candidates." *Political Research Quarterly* 63 (3): 581–93. https://doi.org/10.1177/1065912909333131.

Cross, William P., and André Blais. 2012. "Who Selects the Party Leader?" *Party Politics* 18 (2): 127–50. https://doi.org/10.1177/1354068810382935.

Cross, William P., and Scott Pruysers. 2019. "The Local Determinants of Representation: Party Constituency Associations, Candidate Nomination and Gender." *Canadian Journal of Political Science* 52 (3): 557–74. https://doi.org/10.1017/S0008423919000064.

Crowder-Meyer, Melody. 2013. "Gendered Recruitment Without Trying: How Local Party Recruiters Affect Women's Representation." *Politics and Gender* 9 (4): 390–413. https://doi.org/10.1017/S1743923X13000391.

Crowder-Meyer, Melody, and Rosalyn Cooperman. 2018. "Can't Buy Them Love: How Party Culture Among Donors Contributes to the Party Gap in Women's Representation." *Journal of Politics* 80 (4): 1211–24. https://doi.org/10.1086/698848.

Dahlerup, Drude. 2006. "The Story of the Theory of Critical Mass." *Politics and Gender* 2 (4): 511–22. https://doi.org/10.1017/S1743923X0624114X.

Dash, Paul. 2006. "Black Hair Culture, Politics and Change." *International Journal of Inclusive Education* 10 (1): 27–37. https://doi.org/10.1080 /13603110500173183.

Day, Christine L., and Charles D. Hadley. 2002. "Who Contributes? Similarities and Differences Between Contributors to EMILY's List and WISH List." *Women and Politics* 24 (2): 53–67. https://doi.org/10.1300 /J014v24n02_03.

DeGagne, Alexa. 2019. "A True Match? The Federal New Democratic Party and LGBTQ Communities and Politics." In *Queering Representation: LGBTQ People and Electoral Politics in Canada*, edited by Manon Tremblay, 201–19. Vancouver: UBC Press. https://doi.org/10.59962/9780774861830-011.

Degelman, Douglas, and Nicole Deann Price. 2002. "Tattoos and Ratings of Personal Characteristics." *Psychological Reports* 90 (2): 507–14. https://doi .org/10.2466/pr0.2002.90.2.507.

De Vet, Benjamin, Monica Poletti, and Bram Wauters. 2019. "The Party (Un) faithful: Explaining Members' Defecting Voting Behaviour in Different Contexts (Belgium and Britain)." *Party Politics* 25 (5): 690–700. https://doi .org/10.1177/1354068819836046.

Devitt, James. 1999. *Framing Gender on the Campaign Trail: Women's Executive Leadership and the Press.* Washington, DC: Women's Leadership Fund.

Dhima, Kostanca. 2022. "Do Elites Discriminate Against Female Political Aspirants? Evidence from a Field Experiment." *Politics and Gender* 18 (1): 126–57. https://doi.org/10.1017/S1743923X20000227.

Dhrodia, Azmina. 2017. "Unsocial Media: Tracking Twitter Abuse Against Women MPs." *Medium.com*, 3 September. https://medium.com /@AmnestyInsights/unsocial-media-tracking-twitter-abuse-against -women-mps-fc28aeca498a.

DiNovo, Cheri. 2016. *Sexual Harassment.* Ontario: Legislative Assembly of Ontario. Hansard 34 (2). 41st Parliament, 2nd Session. Legislative Assembly of Ontario Website. https://www.ola.org/en/legislative -business/house-documents/parliament-41/session-2/2016-11-24/hansard.

Docherty, David C. 2001. "To Run or Not to Run? A Survey of Former Members of the Parliament of Canada." *Canadian Parliamentary Review* (Spring): 16–23.

Dolan, Kathleen. 2004. *Voting for Women: How the Public Evaluates Women Candidates.* Boulder, CO: Westview Press. https://doi.org/10.1093 /oso/9780195180824.003.0003.

Dolan, Kathleen. 2010. "The Impact of Gender Stereotyped Evaluations on Support for Women Candidates." *Political Behavior* 32 (1): 69–88. https:// doi.org/10.1007/s11109-009-9090-4.

Domise, Andray. 2017. "One Way Forward, After Canadian Media's 'Appropriation Award' Fiasco." *Maclean's*, 16 May. https://www.macleans

.ca/news/canada/one-way-forward-after-canadian-medias-appropriation
-award-fiasco/.

Dovi, Suzanne. 2002. "Preferable Descriptive Representatives: Will Just Any
Woman, Black, or Latino Do?" *American Political Science Review* 96 (4):
729–43. https://doi.org/10.1017/S0003055402000412.

Duerst-Lahti, Georgia. 2010. "The Consequences of Gender for Women's
Political Leadership." In *Gender and Women's Leadership: A Reference
Handbook*, vol. 1, edited by Karen O'Connor, 20–30. Los Angeles: Sage.
https://doi.org/10.4135/9781412979344.n3.

Duerst-Lahti, Georgia, and Rita Mae Kelly. 1995. "On Governance,
Leadership, and Gender." In *Gender Power, Leadership, and Governance*,
edited by Georgia Duerst-Lahti and Rita Mae Kelly, 11–37. Ann Arbor:
University of Michigan Press. https://doi.org/10.3998/mpub.10371.

Dundas, Deborah. 2017. "Editor Quits Amid Outrage After Call for
'Appropriation Prize' in Writers' Magazine." *Toronto Star*, 10 May. https://
www.thestar.com/entertainment/books/2017/05/10/editor-quits-amid
-outrage-after-call-for-appropriation-prize-in-writers-magazine.html.

Dunham, Jackie. 2021. "Highest Percentage Ever of Female and Gender-
Diverse Candidates Running in This Election." *CTV News*, 2 September.
https://www.ctvnews.ca/politics/federal-election-2021/highest
-percentage-ever-of-female-and-gender-diverse-candidates-running-in
-this-election-1.5570913.

Dunlap, Andy. 2016. "Changes in Coming Out Milestones Across Five Age
Cohorts." *Journal of Gay and Lesbian Social Services* 28 (1): 20–38. https://doi
.org/10.1080/10538720.2016.1124351.

Eagly, Alice H., and Linda L. Carli. 2007. "Women and the Labyrinth of
Leadership." *Harvard Business Review* (September): 62–71. https://doi
.org/10.1037/e664062007-001.

Ejaz, Khadija. 2018. "Good Manners and High Heels: Newspaper Coverage
of South Carolina's First Female Governor." *Journal of Gender Studies* 27 (7):
802–14. https://doi.org/10.1080/09589236.2017.1316247.

Ekström, Mats, and Bengt Johansson. 2008. "Talk Scandals." *Media Culture and
Society* 30 (1): 61–79. https://doi.org/10.1177/0163443707084350.

Enloe, Cynthia. 2000. "The Surprised Feminist." *Signs: Journal of Women in
Culture and Society* 25 (4): 1023–26. https://doi.org/10.1086/495513.

Enloe, Cynthia. 2004. *The Curious Feminist: Searching for Women in a New Age of
Empire*. Berkeley: University of California Press. https://doi.org/10.1525
/9780520938519.

Enloe, Cynthia. 2007. *Globalization and Militarism: Feminists Make the Link*.
Lanham, MD: Rowman & Littlefield Publishers. https://rowman.com
/ISBN/9781442265455/Globalization-and-Militarism-Feminists-Make-the
-Link-Second-Edition.

Everitt, Joanna, and Michael Camp. 2009a. "One Is Not Like the Others: Allison Brewer's Leadership of the New Brunswick NDP." In *Opening Doors Wider: Women's Political Engagement in Canada*, edited by Sylvia Bashevkin, 127–44. Vancouver: UBC Press. https://doi.org/10.59962 /9780774815659-010.

Everitt, Joanna, and Michael Camp. 2009b. "Changing the Game Changes the Frame: The Media's Use of Lesbian Stereotypes in Leadership Versus Election Campaigns." *Canadian Political Science Review* 3 (3): 24–39. https:// doi.org/10.24124/c677/2009140.

Everitt, Joanna, and Michael Camp. 2014. "In Versus Out: LGBT Politicians in Canada." *Journal of Canadian Studies* 48 (1): 226–51. https://doi.org/10.1353 /jcs.2014.0013.

Falk, Erika. 2008. *Women for President: Media Bias in Eight Campaigns*. Urbana: University of Illinois Press. https://doi.org/10.1080/15544770903501426.

Farrar-Myers, Victoria A., and Brent D. Boyea. 2013. "Campaign Finance: A Barrier to Reaching the White House?" In *Women and Executive Office: Pathways and Performance*, edited by Melody Rose, 209–29. Boulder, CO: Lynne Rienner Publishers. https://doi.org/10.1515/9781685854560-012.

Flanagan, Thomas. 2014. *Winning Power: Canadian Campaigning in the 21st Century*. Montreal and Kingston: McGill-Queen's University Press. https:// doi.org/10.1515/9780773590366.

Fortin-Rittberger, Jessica, and Christina Eder. 2013. "Towards a Gender-Equal Bundestag? The Impact of Electoral Rules on Women's Representation." *West European Politics* 36 (5): 969–85. https://doi.org/10.1080/01402382.2013 .796702.

Fowler, Linda L., and Jennifer L. Lawless. 2009. "Looking for Sex in All the Wrong Places: Press Coverage and the Electoral Fortunes of Gubernatorial Candidates." *Perspectives on Politics* 7 (3): 519–36. https://doi.org/10.1017 /S1537592709990843.

Fox, Richard L., and Jennifer L. Lawless. 2005. "To Run or Not to Run for Office: Explaining Nascent Political Ambition." *American Journal of Political Science* 49 (3): 642–59. https://doi.org/10.1111/j.1540-5907.2005.00147.x.

Fox, Richard L., and Jennifer L. Lawless. 2014. "Reconciling Family Roles with Political Ambition: The New Normal for Women in Twenty-First Century U.S. Politics." *Journal of Politics* 76 (2): 398–414. https://doi.org/10.1017 /S0022381613001473.

Francia, Peter L. 2001. "Early Fundraising by Nonincumbent Female Congressional Candidates." *Women and Politics* 23 (1–2): 7–20. https://doi .org/10.1300/J014v23n01_02.

Franklin, Bob, and David Murphy. 1998. "Changing Times: Local Newspapers, Technology and Markets." In *Making the Local News: Local Journalism in Context*, edited by Bob Franklin and David Murphy, 5–21. London: Routledge.

Geer, John Gray. 2006. *In Defense of Negativity: Attack Ads in Presidential Campaigns.* Chicago: University of Chicago Press. https://doi.org/10.7208 /chicago/9780226285009.001.0001.

Gerrits, Bailey, and Randy Besco. 2019. "Processes of Differentiation in the 2014 Toronto Mayoral Race." In *Gendered Mediation: Identity and Image Making in Canadian Politics,* edited by Angelia Wagner and Joanna Everitt, 87–105. Vancouver: UBC Press. https://doi.org/10.59962/9780774860574-006.

Gershon, Sarah Allen. 2013. "Media Coverage of Minority Congresswomen and Voter Evaluations: Evidence from an Online Experimental Study." *Political Research Quarterly* 66 (3): 702–14. https://doi.org/10.1177 /1065912912467851.

Gidengil, Elisabeth, and André Blais. 2007. "Are Party Leaders Becoming More Important to Vote Choice in Canada?" In *Political Leadership and Representation in Canada: Essays in Honour of John C. Courney,* edited by Hans J. Michelmann, Donald C. Story, and Jeffrey S. Steeves, 39–59. Toronto: University of Toronto Press. https://doi.org/10.3138/9781442684706-005.

Gilbert, Robert E. 1995. "The Political Effects of Presidential Illness: The Case of Lyndon B. Johnson." *Political Psychology* 16 (4): 761–76. https://www.jstor .org/stable/3791892.

GLAAD. 2016. *GLAAD Media Reference Guide,* 10th ed. http://www.glaad.org /sites/default/files/GLAAD-Media-Reference-Guide-Tenth-Edition.pdf.

Golebiowska, Ewa A., and Cynthia J. Thomsen. 1999. "Group Stereotypes and Evaluations of Individuals: The Case of Gay and Lesbian Political Candidates." In *Gays and Lesbians in the Democratic Process: Public Policy, Public Opinion, and Political Representation,* edited by Ellen D.B. Riggle and Barry L. Tadlock, 192–219. New York: Columbia University Press.

Goodyear-Grant, Elizabeth. 2010. "Who Votes for Women Candidates and Why? Evidence from Recent Canadian Elections." In *Voting Behaviour in Canada,* edited by Cameron D. Anderson and Laura B. Stephenson, 43–64. Vancouver: UBC Press. https://doi.org/10.59962/9780774817851-005.

Goodyear-Grant, Elizabeth. 2013. *Gendered News: Media Coverage and Electoral Politics in Canada.* Vancouver: UBC Press. https://doi.org/10.59962 /9780774826259.

Graham, Jennifer. 2016. "Saskatchewan NDP Loses 2nd Candidate in Provincial Election Over Online Posts." *The Canadian Press,* 11 March. https://www.cbc.ca/news/canada/saskatoon/sask-ndp-candidates -campaign-manager-dropped-1.3488750.

Grant, Kelly, and Anna Mehler Paperny. 2010. "Campaign Ends on a Hateful Note." *Globe and Mail,* 25 October, A15.

Green, Joanne Connor. 2003. "The Times…Are They a-Changing? An Examination of the Impact of the Value of Campaign Resources for Women and Men Candidates for the U.S. House of Representatives." *Women and Politics* 25 (4): 1–29. https://doi.org/10.1300/J014v25n04_01.

Green, Joyce A. 2000. "The Difference Debate: Reducing Rights to Cultural Flavours." *Canadian Journal of Political Science* 33 (1): 133–44. https://doi.org /10.1017/S0008423900.

Green, Joyce A., and Ian Peach. 2007. "Beyond 'Us' and 'Them': Prescribing Postcolonial Politics and Policy in Saskatchewan." In *Belonging? Diversity, Recognition and Shared Citizenship in Canada,* edited by Keith G. Banting, Thomas J. Courchene, and F. Leslie Seidle, 263–84. Montreal and Kingston: McGill-Queen's University Press. https://irpp.org/research /belonging-diversity-recognition-and-share-citizenship-in-canada/.

Greig, Christopher J. 2012. "Boys' Underachievement in School in Historical Perspective: Exploring Masculinity and Schooling in the Postwar Era, 1945–1960." In *Canadian Men and Masculinities: Historical and Contemporary Perspectives*, edited by Christopher J. Greig and Wayne J. Martino, 99–115. Toronto: Canadian Scholars' Press Inc.

Griffith, Andrew. 2015. *Visible Minority Candidates in the 2015 Election: Making Progress.* Ottawa: Multicultural Meanderings. https:// multiculturalmeanderings.files.wordpress.com/2015/07/2015-ridings -with-more-than-50-vismin-and-main-candidates.pdf.

Halder, Debarati, and K. Jaishankar. 2011. "Online Social Networking and Women Victims." In *Cyber Criminology: Exploring Internet Crimes and Criminal Behavior*, edited by K. Jaishankar, 299–316. Boca Raton: CRC Press. https://legislativediv.portal.gov.bd/sites/default/files/files /legislativediv.portal.gov.bd/page/4e003fd0_cd24_4826_a89c _f1e74fe3ad0f/Cyber%20Criminology%20Exploring%20Internet%20 Crimes%20and%20Criminal%20Behavior%20%281%29.pdf.

Hammarlin, Mia-Marie, and Gunilla Jarlbro. 2012. "From Tiara to Toblerone: The Rise and Fall of Mona Sahlin." In *Scandalous! The Mediated Construction of Political Scandals in Four Nordic Countries*, edited by Sigurd Allern and Ester Pollack, 113–32. Göteborg: Nordicom.

Hancock, Ange-Marie. 2007. "When Multiplication Doesn't Equal Quick Addition: Examining Intersectionality as a Research Paradigm." *Perspectives on Politics* 5 (1): 63–79. https://doi.org/10.1017 /S1537592707070065.

Hardaker, Claire, and Mark McGlashan. 2016. "'Real Men Don't Hate Women': Twitter Rape Threats and Group Identity." *Journal of Pragmatics* 91: 80–93. https://doi.org/10.1016/j.pragma.2015.11.005.

Hardin, Michael. 1999. "Mar(k)ing the Objected Body: A Reading of Contemporary Female Tattooing." *Fashion Theory* 3 (1): 81–108. https://doi .org/10.2752/136270499779165734.

Harding, Sandra. 1998. "Is There a Feminist Method?" In *Feminisms*, edited by Sandra Kemp and Judith Squires, 160–70. Oxford: Oxford University Press.

Harell, Allison, and Dimitrios Panagos. 2013. "Locating the Aboriginal Gender Gap: The Political Attitudes and Participation of Aboriginal Women in Canada." *Politics and Gender* 9 (4): 414–38. https://doi .org/10.10.80/15544770802367770.

Hayes, Danny, and Jennifer L. Lawless. 2016. *Women on the Run: Gender, Media, and Political Campaigns in a Polarized Era.* New York: Cambridge University Press. https://doi.org/10.1017/CBO9781316336007.

Henderson, James (Sakej) Youngblood. 2002. "Sui Generis and Treaty Citizenship." *Citizenship Studies* 6 (4): 415–40. https://doi.org/10.1080 /1362102022000041259.

Herrick, Rebekah. 1996. "Is There a Gender Gap in the Value of Campaign Resources?" *American Politics Research* 24 (1): 68–80. https://doi.org /10.1177/1532673X9602400104.

Hier, Sean P. 2011. "Tightening the Focus: Moral Panic, Moral Regulation and Liberal Government." *British Journal of Sociology* 62 (3): 523–41. https://doi .org/10.1111/j.1468-4446.2011.01377.x.

Hills, Jill. 1983. "Life-Style Constraints on Formal Political Participation – Why So Few Women Local Councillors in Britain?" *Electoral Studies* 2 (1): 39–52. https://doi.org/10.1016/0261-3794(83)90105-1.

Hinojosa, Magda. 2010. "'She's Not My Type of Blond': Media Coverage of Irene Saez's Presidential Bid." In *Cracking the Highest Glass Ceiling: A Global Comparison of Women's Campaigns for Executive Office,* edited by Rainbow Murray, 31–47. Santa Barbara: Praeger. https://doi.org/10.5040 /9798400632815.ch-002.

Hinojosa, Magda, and Susan Franceschet. 2012. "Separate but Not Equal: The Effects of Municipal Electoral Reform on Female Representation in Chile." *Political Research Quarterly* 65 (4): 758–70. https://doi.org/10.1177 /1065912911427449.

Hirczy de Mino, Wolfgang P., and Angelle M. Kergosien. 1997. "Of Elephants, Donkeys, and Black Sheep in Their Midst: State Action Doctrine Thwarts Log Cabin Republicans' Bid to Gain a Place in GOP's Tent." *Albany Law Review* 60 (5): 1695–700.

Hobson, Brittany. 2021. "Record Number of Indigenous Candidates Running in Federal Election." *CTV News,* 1 September. https://www.ctvnews.ca /politics/federal-election-2021/record-number-of-indigenous-candidates -running-in-federal-election-1.5570074.

Houle, René. 2020. *Changes in the Socioeconomic Situation of Canada's Black Population, 2001 to 2016.* Catalogue no. 89-657-X2020001. Ottawa: Statistics Canada. https://www150.statcan.gc.ca/n1/pub/89-657-x/89-657-x2020001 -eng.htm.

Huddy, Leonie, and Nayda Terkildsen. 1993. "The Consequences of Gender Stereotypes for Women Candidates at Different Levels and Types of

Office." *Political Research Quarterly* 46 (3): 503–25. https://doi.org /10.1177/106591299304600304.

Huncar, Andrea. 2015. "Alberta Female Politicians Targeted by Hateful, Sexist Online Attacks." *CBC News*, 20 October. https://www.cbc.ca/news /canada/edmonton/alberta-female-politicians-targeted-by-hateful-sexist -online-attacks-1.3281275.

Hunt, Alan. 1999. *Governing Morals: A Social History of Moral Regulation.* Cambridge: Cambridge University. https://doi.org/10.1093/bjc/40.4.771.

Hunt, Elle. 2016. "Julia Gillard Says Online Abuse Deters Women from Political Careers." *The Guardian*, 6 October. https://www.theguardian.com /world/2016/oct/12/julia-gillard-says-online-abuse-deters-women -from-political-careers.

Hunt, Sarah. 2018. "Embodying Self-Determination: Beyond the Gender Binary." In *Determinants of Indigenous Peoples' Health: Beyond the Social*, 2nd ed., edited by Margo Greenwood, Sarah de Leeuw, and Nicole Marie Lindsay, 22–39. Toronto: Canadian Scholars.

Ibbitson, John. 2017. "A Unifying Figure with Divisive Potential." *Globe and Mail*, 12 July, A10.

Ibroscheva, Elza, and Maria Raicheva-Stover. 2009. "Engendering Transition: Portrayals of Female Politicians in the Bulgarian Press." *Howard Journal of Communication* 20 (2): 111–28. https://doi.org/10.1080/10646170902869429.

James, David V., Frank R. Farnham, Seema Sukhwal, Katherine Jones, Josephine Carlisle, and Sara Henley. 2016. "Aggressive/Intrusive Behaviours, Harassment and Stalking of Members of the United Kingdom Parliament: A Prevalence Study and Cross-National Comparison." *Journal of Forensic Psychiatry and Psychology* 27 (2): 177–97. https://doi.org/10.1080 /14789949.2015.1124908.

James, David V., Paul E. Mullen, J. Reid Meloy, Michele T. Pathé, Frank R. Farnham, Lulu Preston, and Brian Darnley. 2007. "The Role of Mental Disorder in Attacks on European Politicians 1990–2004." *Acta Psychiatrica Scandiavica* 116: 334–44. https://doi.org/10.1111/j.1600-0447.2007.01077.x.

Jane, Emma A. 2014a. "'Your a Ugly, Whorish, Slut': Understanding e-Bile." *Feminist Media Studies* 14 (4): 531–46. https://doi.org/10.1080/14680777.2012 .741073.

Jane, Emma Alice. 2014b. "'Back to the Kitchen, Cunt': Speaking the Unspeakable About Online Misogyny." *Continuum* 28 (4): 558–70. https:// doi.org/10.1080/10304312.2014.924479.

Jansen, Harold J., and L.A. (Lisa) Lambert. 2013. "Too Little, Too Soon: State Funding and Electoral District Associations in the Green Party of Canada." In *Parties, Elections, and the Future of Canadian Politics*, edited by Amanda Bittner and Royce Koop, 211–30. Vancouver: UBC Press. https://doi.org /10.59962/9780774824101-013.

Jeffrey, Brooke. 2019. "Liberalism and the Protection of LGBT Rights in Canada." In *Queering Representation: LGBTQ People and Electoral Politics in Canada*, edited by Manon Tremblay, 179–200. Vancouver: UBC Press. https://doi.org/10.59962/9780774861830-010.

Jeffries, Judson L. 2002. "Press Coverage of Black Statewide Candidates: The Case of L. Douglas Wilder of Virginia." *Journal of Black Studies* 32 (6): 673–97. https://doi.org/10.1177/002234702032006003.

Jenkins, Shannon. 2007. "A Woman's Work Is Never Done? Fund-Raising Perception and Effort Among Female State Legislative Candidates." *Political Research Quarterly* 60 (2): 230–9. https://doi.org/10.1177/1065912907301682.

Jenssen, Anders Todal, and Audun Fladmoe. 2012. "Ten Commandments for the Scandalization of Political Opponents." In *Scandalous! The Mediated Construction of Political Scandals in Four Nordic Countries*, edited by Sigurd Allern and Ester Pollack, 51–71. Göteborg: Nordicom.

Johnson, Anna Elizabeth, Erin Tolley, Melanee Thomas, and Marc A. Bodet. 2021. "Dataset on the Demographics of Canadian Federal Election Candidates (2008–2019)." https://doi.org/10.7910/DVN/MI5XQ6,Harvard Dataverse, V1, UNF:6:l3XZtRo/Ob017+yomN//hw== [fileUNF].

Johnson, Gbemende, Bruce I. Oppenheimer, and Jennifer L. Selin. 2012. "The House as a Stepping Stone to the Senate: Why Do so Few African American House Members Run?" *American Journal of Political Science* 56 (2): 387–99. https://doi.org/10.1111/j.1540-5907.2011.00562.x.

Johnson-Myers, Tracy-Ann, and Joanna Everitt. 2022. "Breaking Through the Barriers: Black Candidates in Canadian Politics." Paper presented at the Canadian Political Science Association Conference, online, 30 May.

Jordan-Zachery, Julia S. 2007. "Am I a Black Woman or a Woman Who Is Black? A Few Thoughts on the Meaning of Intersectionality." *Politics and Gender* 3 (2): 254–63. https://doi.org/10.1017/S1743923X07000074.

Joshi, Devin K., and Ryan Goehrung. 2021. "Mothers and Fathers in Parliament: MP Parental Status and Family Gaps from a Global Perspective." *Parliamentary Affairs* 74 (2): 296–313. https://doi.org/10.1093/pa/gsaa003.

Jubas, Kaela, and Karla Jubas. 2006. "Theorizing Gender in Contemporary Canadian Citizenship: Lessons from the CBC's Greatest Canadian Contest." *Canadian Journal of Education* 29 (2): 563–83. https://doi.org/10.2307/20054177.

Kahn, Kim Fridkin. 1994. "Does Gender Make a Difference? An Experimental Examination of Sex Stereotypes and Press Patterns in Statewide Campaigns." *American Journal of Political Science* 38 (1): 162–95. https://doi.org/10.2307/2111340.

Kahn, Kim Fridkin. 1996.*The Political Consequences of Being a Woman.* New York: Columbia University Press.

Kahn, Kim Fridkin, and Patrick J. Kenney. 1997. "A Model of Candidate Evaluations in Senate Elections: The Impact of Campaign Intensity." *Journal of Politics* 59 (4): 1173–205. https://doi.org/10.2307/2998597.

"Keep It Civil St. Albert." 2015. *St. Albert Gazette*, 30 May, 26.

Kenny, Christopher, and Michael McBurnett. 1997. "Up Close and Personal: Campaign Contact and Candidate Spending in U.S. House Elections." *Political Research Quarterly* 50 (1): 75–96. https://doi.org/10.1177/106591299705000104.

King, Marvin. 2009. "Reluctant Donors: African Americans, Campaign Contributors, and the Obama Effect – or Lack of It." *Souls* 11 (4): 389–406. https://doi.org/10.1080/10999940903417177.

Kitchens, Karin E., and Michele L. Swers. 2016. "Why Aren't There More Republican Women in Congress? Gender, Partisanship, and Fundraising Support in the 2010 and 2012 Elections." *Politics and Gender* 12 (4): 648–76. https://doi.org/10.1017/S1743923X1600009X.

Koziol, Michael. 2015. "What a Mug: Canadian Conservative Party Candidate Jerry Bance Busted Urinating in Cup." *Sydney Morning Herald*, 7 September. http://www.smh.com.au/world/what-a-mug-canadian-consersative-party-candidate-jerry-bance-busted-urinating-in-cup-20150907-gjgyn3.html.

Kuhn, Raymond, and Erik Neveu, eds. 2002. *Political Journalism: New Challenges, New Practices.* New York: Routledge. https://doi.org/10.4324/9780203167564.

Kvale, Steinar. 2007. *Doing Interviews.* Los Angeles: Sage. https://doi.org/10.4135/9781849208963.

Ladner, Kiera L., and Michael McCrossan. 2009. "The Road Not Taken: Aboriginal Rights After the Re-Imagining of the Canadian Constitutional Order." In *Contested Constitutionalism*, edited by James Kelly and Chris Manfredi, 262–83. Vancouver: UBC Press. https://doi.org/10.59962/9780774816762-015.

Lafrance, Marc. 2012. "Building a Body, Building a Life: Men, Masculinity, and the Birth of Bodybuilding Magazines in Montreal." In *Canadian Men and Masculinities: Historical and Contemporary Perspectives*, edited by Christopher J. Greig and Wayne J. Martino, 345–60. Toronto: Canadian Scholars' Press Inc.

Lalancette, Mireille, and Manon Tremblay. 2019. "Media Framing of Lesbian and Gay Politicians: Is Sexual Mediation at Work?" In *Queering Representation: LGBTQ People and Electoral Politics in Canada*, edited by Manon Tremblay, 102–23. Vancouver: UBC Press. https://doi.org/10.59962/9780774861830-007.

Langer, Ana Inés. 2007. "A Historical Exploration of the Personalisation of Politics in the Print Media: The British Prime Ministers (1945–1999)." *Parliamentary Affairs* 6 (3): 371–87. https://doi.org/10.1093/pa/gsm028.

Langer, Ana Inés. 2010. "The Politicization of Private Persona: Exceptional Leaders or the New Rule? The Case of the United Kingdom and the Blair effect." *International Journal of Press/Politics* 15 (1): 60–76. https://doi.org/10.1177/1940161209351003.

Lau, Richard R., and Gerald M. Pomper. 2001. "Negative Campaigning by US Senate Campaign." *Party Politics* 7 (1): 69–87. https://doi.org/10.1177/1354068801007001004.

Lawless, Jennifer L., and Richard L. Fox. 2010. *It Still Takes a Candidate: Why Women Don't Run for Office.* Cambridge: Cambridge University Press. https://doi.org/10.1017/CBO9780511778797.

Lawless, Jennifer L., and Richard L. Fox. 2015. *Running from Office: Why Young Americans Are Turned Off to Politics.* Oxford: Oxford University Press. https://doi.org/10.1017/S1537592716002358.

Lawrence, Regina G., and Melody Rose. 2010. *Hillary Clinton's Race for the White House: Gender Politics and the Media on the Campaign Trail.* Boulder, CO: Lynne Reinner Publishers. https://doi.org/10.1515/9781685856830.

Lee, Marcia Manning. 1976. "Why Few Women Hold Public Office: Democracy and Sexual Roles." *Political Science Quarterly* 91 (2): 297–314. https://doi.org/10.2307/2148414.

LeFrance, Adrienne. 2016. "I Analyzed a Year of My Reporting for Gender Bias (Again)." *The Atlantic,* 16 February. https://www.theatlantic.com/technology/archive/2016/02/gender-diversity-journalism/463023/.

Lewis, Gregory B., Marc A. Rogers, and Kenneth Sherrill. 2011. "Lesbian, Gay, and Bisexual Voters in the 2000 U.S. Presidential Election." *Policy and Politics* 39 (5): 655–77. https://doi.org/10.1111/j.1747-1346.2011.00315.x.

Loch-Drake, Cynthia. 2008. "Jailed Heroes and Kitchen Heroines: Class, Gender, and the Medalta Potteries Strike in Postwar Alberta." In *One Step Over the Line: Toward a History of Women in the North American Wests,* edited by Elizabeth Jameson and Sheila McManus, 341–80. Edmonton and Athabasca: The University of Alberta Press and Athabasca University Press. https://doi.org/10.15215/aupress/9780888645012.01.

Loewen, Peter John, and Ludovic Rheault. 2021. "Voters Punish Politicians with Depression." *British Journal of Political Science* 51 (1): 427–36. https://doi.org/10.1017/S0007123419000127.

Loewen, Peter John, and Daniel Rubenson. 2011. "For Want of a Nail: Negative Persuasion in a Party Leadership Race." *Party Politics* 17 (1): 45–65. https://doi.org/10.1177/1354068810372564.

Loke, Jaime, Dustin Harp, and Ingrid Bachmann. 2011. "Mothering and Governing: How News Articulated Gender Roles in the Cases of Governors Jane Swift and Sarah Palin." *Journalism Studies* 12 (2): 205–20. https://doi.org/10.1080/1461670X.2010.488418.

Lombardo, Emanuela, and Petra Meier. 2019. "The Significance of Symbolic Representation for Gender Issues in Politics." *NORA Nordic Journal of Feminist and Gender Research* 27 (4): 231–44. https://doi.org/10.1080 /08038740.2019.1660404.

MacRae, Heather and Elaine Weiner. 2021. "Feminist Institutionalism." In *The Routledge Handbook of Gender and EU Politics,* edited by Gabriele Abels, Andrea Krizsán, Heather MacRae, and Anna van der Vleuten, 56–67. London: Routledge. https://doi.org/10.4324/9781351049955-6.

Madden, Stephanie, Melissa Janoske, Rowena Briones Winkler, and Amanda Nell Edgar. 2018. "Mediated Misogynoir: Intersecting Race and Gender in Online Harassment." In *Mediating Misogyny: Gender, Technology, and Harassment,* edited by Jacqueline Ryan Vickery and Tracy Everbach, 71–90. Cham, Switzerland: Palgrave Macmillan. https://doi.org/10.1007 /978-3-319-72917-6_4.

Major, Lesa Hatley, and Renita Coleman. 2008. "The Intersection of Race and Gender in Election Coverage: What Happens When the Candidates Don't Fit the Stereotypes?" *Howard Journal of Communication* 19 (4): 315–33. https://doi.org/10.1080/10646170802391722.

Malcolmson, Patrick, Richard Myers, Gerald Baier, and Thomas M.J. Bateman. 2016. *The Canadian Regime: An Introduction to Parliamentary Government in Canada,* 6th ed. Toronto: University of Toronto Press.

Mandell, Hinda, and Gina Masullo Chen. 2016. "Scandal-Suffering Politicians, Scorned Wives and Salacious News: Examining Public Response to the Scandal Press Conference." Interactions: Studies in Communication and Culture 7 (1): 85–98. https://doi.org/0.1386 /iscc.7.1.85_1.

Manning-Miller, Carmen L. 1996. "Carol Moseley-Braun: Black Women's Political Images in the Media." In *Mediated Messages and African-American Culture: Contemporary Issues,* edited by Venise T. Berry and Carmen L. Manning-Miller, 117–28. Thousand Oaks, CA: Sage.

Mansbridge, Jane. 1999. "Should Blacks Represent Blacks and Women Represent Women? A Contingent 'Yes'." *Journal of Politics* 61 (3): 627–57. https://doi.org/10.2307/2647821.

Mansbridge, Jane. 2003. "Rethinking Representation." *American Political Science Review* 97 (4): 515–28. https://doi.org/10.1017/S0003055403000856.

Mantilla, Karla. 2013. "Gendertrolling: Misogyny Adapts to New Media." *Feminist Studies* 39 (2): 563–70. https://www.jstor.org/stable/23719068.

Mantilla, Karla. 2015. *Gendertrolling: How Misogyny Went Viral.* Santa Barbara: Praeger. https://doi.org/10.5040/9798400656026.

Mara, David. 2012. "Reformulating Masculinities: Renegotiating Masculinity After a Spinal Cord Injury." In *Canadian Men and Masculinities: Historical and Contemporary Perspectives*, edited by Christopher J. Greig and Wayne J. Martino, 253–65. Toronto: Canadian Scholars' Press Inc.

Maras, Steven. 2013. *Objectivity in Journalism*. Malden, MA: Polity Press. https://catalogue.nla.gov.au/catalog/6186975.

Marland, Alex. 2016. *Brand Command: Canadian Politics and Democracy in the Age of Message Control*. Vancouver: UBC Press. https://doi.org/10.59962/9780774832052.

Marland, Alex, and Brooks DeCillia. 2020. "Reputation and Brand Management by Political Parties: Party Vetting of Election Candidates in Canada." *Journal of Nonprofit and Public Sector Marketing* 32 (4): 342–53. https://doi.org/10.1080/10495142.2020.1798857.

Marland, Alex, and Angelia Wagner. 2020. "Scripted Messengers: How Party Discipline and Branding Turn Election Candidates and Legislators into Brand Ambassadors." *Journal of Political Marketing* 19 (1–2): 54–73. https://doi.org/10.1080/15377857.2019.1658022.

Mason, Rowena. 2017. "Diane Abbott: Misogyny and Abuse Are Putting Women Off Politics." *The Guardian*, 14 February. https://www.theguardian.com/politics/2017/feb/14/diane-abbott-misogyny-and-abuse-are-putting-women-off-politics.

Mattes, Kyle, and Caitlin Milazzo. 2014. "Pretty Faces, Marginal Races: Predicting Election Outcomes Using Trait Assessments of British Parliamentary Candidates." *Electoral Studies* 34 (June): 177–89. https://doi.org/10.1016/j.electstud.2013.11.004.

McAllister, Ian. 2019. "The Gender Gap in Political Knowledge Revisited: Australia's Julia Gillard as a Natural Experiment." *European Journal of Politics and Gender* 2 (2): 197–220. https://doi.org/10.1332/251510818X15272520831148.

McAndrews, John R., Jonah I. Goldberg, Peter John Loewen, Daniel Rubenson, and Benjamin Allen Stevens. 2020. "Nonelectoral Motivations to Represent Marginalized Groups in a Democracy: Evidence from an Unelected Legislature." *Legislative Studies Quarterly* 46 (4): 961–94. https://doi.org/10.1111/lsq.12310.

McCall, Leslie. 2005. "The Complexity of Intersectionality." *Signs: Journal of Women in Culture and Society* 30 (3): 1771–800. https://doi.org/10.1086/426800.

McCarten, James, ed. 2013. *The Canadian Press Stylebook: A Guide for Writers and Editors*. Toronto: The Canadian Press.

McElroy, Justin. 2016. "NDP Candidate Reveals Bisexuality After Questions Over Party's Equity Rule." *CBC News*, 18 October. https://www.cbc.ca/news/canada/british-columbia/ndp-candidate-reveals-bisexuality-after-questions-over-party-s-equity-rule-1.3811299.

McGrath, John Michael. 2010. "End-Game: In Last Hours of Election, Things Get Even Uglier." *Toronto Life*, 25 October. https://torontolife.com/city /end-game-in-last-hours-of-election-things-get-even-uglier/.

McIlwain, Charlton D. 2011. "Racialized Media Coverage of Minority Candidates in the 2008 Democratic Presidential Primary." *American Behavioral Scientist* 55 (4): 371–89. https://doi.org/10.1177/0002764211398067.

McKay, Joanna. 2011. "'Having It All?' Women MPs and Motherhood in Germany and the UK." *Parliamentary Affairs* 64 (4): 714–36. https://doi .org/10.1093/pa/gsr001.

McKenna, Elizabeth, and Hahrie Han. 2014. *Groundbreakers: How Obama's 2.2 Million Volunteers Transformed Campaigning in America.* New York: Oxford University Press. https://doi.org/10.1093/acprof: oso/9780199394593.003.0001.

McLean, Karalena, Angelia Wagner, and Joanna Everitt. 2019. "Examining Mediation of Female and LGBTQ-Identifying Candidates." In *Gendered Mediation: Identity and Image Making in Canadian Politics*, edited by Angelia Wagner and Joanna Everitt, 145–62. Vancouver: UBC Press. https://doi .org/10.59962/9780774860574-009.

McMillan, Elizabeth. 2016. "MLAs Speak Out About Fat-Shaming, Death Threats and Homophobia." *CBC News*, 19 December. https://www.cbc.ca /news/canada/nova-scotia/mla-joanne-bernard-sexism-harassment -fat-shaming-legislature-1.3900518.

Meeks, Lindsey. 2013. "All the Gender That's Fit to Print: How the *New York Times* Covered Hillary Clinton and Sarah Palin in 2008." *Journalism and Mass Communication Quarterly* 90 (3): 520–39. https://doi.org/10.1177 /1077699013493791.

Megarry, Jessica. 2014. "Online Incivility or Sexual Harassment? Conceptualising Women's Experiences in the Digital Age." *Women's Studies International Forum* 47 (Part A): 46–55. https://doi.org/10.1016/j.wsif .2014.07.012.

Miller, Patrick R., Andrew R. Flores, Donald P. Haider-Markel, Daniel C. Lewis, Barry L. Tadlock, and Jami K. Taylor. 2017. "Transgender Politics as Body Politics: Effects of Disgust Sensitivity and Authoritarianism on Transgender Rights Attitudes." *Politics, Groups, and Identities* 5 (1): 4–24. https://doi.org/10.1080/21565503.2016.1260482.

Miruka, Simon Okumba, Grace Wamue-Ngare, and Pacificah Okemwa. 2021. "Passage of Family Laws in Kenya's National Assembly (11th Parliament – 2013 to 2017): The Impact of Women Legislators." *Journal of Social Welfare and Family Law* 43 (3): 272–90. https://doi.org/10.1080/09649069.2021 .1953858.

Mohanty, Chandra Talpade. 2003. "'Under Western Eyes Revisited: Feminist Solidarity Through Anticapitalist Struggles." *Signs: Journal of Women in Culture and Society* 28 (2): 499–535. https://doi.org/10.1086/342914.

Mügge, Liza M., Daphne J. van der Pas, and Marc van de Wardt. 2019. "Representing Their Own? Ethnic Minority Women in the Dutch Parliament." *West European Politics* 42 (40): 705–27. https://doi.org/10.1080/01402382.2019.1573036.

Mundy, Dean E. 2013. "Framing Saint Johanna: Media Coverage of Iceland's First Female (and the World's First Openly Gay) Prime Minister." *Journal of Interdisciplinary Feminist Thought* 7 (1): 1–21, Article 5. http://digitalcommons.salve.edu/jift/vol7/iss1/5.

Murray, Rainbow, ed. 2010. *Cracking the Highest Glass Ceiling: A Global Comparison of Women's Campaigns for Executive Office.* Santa Barbara: Praeger. https://doi.org/10.5040/9798400632815.

Narud, Kjersti, and Alv A. Dahl. 2015. "Stalking Experiences Reported by Norwegian Members of Parliament Compared to a Population Sample." *Journal of Forensic Psychiatry and Psychology* 26 (1): 116–31. https://doi.org/10.1080/14789949.2014.981564.

Neering, Rosemary. 2005. *The Canadian Housewife: An Affectionate History.* North Vancouver: Whitecap Books.

Nerone, John. 2013. "The Historical Roots of the Normative Model of Journalism." *Journalism* 14 (4): 446–58. https://doi.org/10.1177/1464884912464177.

Neveu, Erik. 2002. "Four Generations of Political Journalism." In *Political Journalism: New Challenges, New Practices*, edited by Raymond Kuhn and Erik Neveu, 22–43. New York: Routledge. https://doi.org/10.4324/9780203167564

Neville-Shepard, Ryan, and Jaclyn Nolan. 2019. "'She Doesn't Have the Stamina': Hillary Clinton and the Hysteria Diagnosis in the 2016 Presidential Election." *Women's Studies in Communication* 42 (1): 60–79. https://doi.org/10.1080/07491409.2019.1575301.

Newman, Jacquetta, and Linda A. White. 2006. *Women, Politics, and Public Policy: The Political Struggles of Canadian Women.* Oxford: Oxford University Press.

Nicholas, Jane. 2012. "Representing the Modern Man: Beauty, Culture, and Masculinity in Early-Twentieth-Century Canada." In *Canadian Men and Masculinities: Historical and Contemporary Perspectives*, edited by Christopher J. Greig and Wayne J. Martino, 42–60. Toronto: Canadian Scholars' Press Inc.

Nielsen, Rasmus Kleis. 2012. *Ground Wars: Personalized Communication in Political Campaigns.* Princeton: Princeton University Press. https://www.jstor.org/stable/j.ctt7rs6w.

Norris, Pippa and Joni Lovenduski. 1995. *Political Recruitment: Gender, Race and Class in the British Parliament.* London: Cambridge University Press. https://books.google.co.in/books/about/Political_Recruitment.html?hl=id&id=GlAbudeTSwQC&redir_esc=y.

Nova Scotia Advisory Council on the Status of Women. 2021. "Resources." https://women.novascotia.ca/sites/default/files/Campaign%20School%20 online%20training/Toolkit/6%20Resources_2021.pdf.

NPR, Robert Wood Johnson Foundation, and Harvard T.H. Chan School of Public Health. 2018. "Discrimination in America: Final Summary." https:// cdn1.sph.harvard.edu/wp-content/uploads/sites/94/2018/01/NPR-RWJF -HSPH-Discrimination-Final-Summary.pdf.

Nussbaum, Martha C. 2010. "Objectification and Internet Misogyny." In *The Offensive Internet: Speech, Privacy, and Reputation,* edited by Saul Levmore and Martha C. Nussbaum, 68–87. Cambridge: Harvard University Press. https://doi.org/10.2307/j.ctvjf9zc8.7.

Nyhan, Brendan. 2014. "Scandal Potential: How Political Context and News Congestion Affect the President's Vulnerability to Media Scandal." *British Journal of Political Science* 45 (2): 435–66. https://doi.org/10.1017 /S0007123413000458.

Nyhan, Brendan. 2017. "Media Scandals Are Political Events: How Contextual Factors Affect Public Controversies Over Alleged Misconduct by U.S. Governors." *Political Research Quarterly* 70 (1): 223–36. https://doi.org /10.1177/1065912916684403.

Ohlheiser, Abby. 2016. "The Leslie Jones Hack Used All the Scariest Tactics of Internet Warfare at Once." *The Washington Post,* 26 August 2016. https:// www.washingtonpost.com/news/the-intersect/wp/2016/08/26/the-leslie -jones-hack-used-all-the-scariest-tactics-of-internet-warfare-at-once/?utm _term=.83dcc088c6a3.

O'Neill, Brenda, and Elisabeth Gidengil. 2017. "Motherhood's Role in Shaping Political and Civic Participation." In *Mothers and Others: The Role of Parenthood in Politics,* edited by Melanee Thomas and Amanda Bittner, 268–87. Vancouver: UBC Press. https://doi.org/10.59962/9780774834605-015

Oyedemi, Toks. 2016. "Beauty as Violence: 'Beautiful' Hair and the Cultural Violence of Identity Erasure." *Social Identities* 22 (5): 537–53. https://doi .org/10.1080/13504630.2016.1157465.

Palmer, Maxwell, and Benjamin Schneer. 2015. "Capitol Gains: The Returns to Elected Office from Corporate Board Directorships." *Journal of Politics* 78 (1): 181–96. https://doi.org/10.1086/683206.

Palmieri, Sonia. 2019. "Feminist Institutionalism and Gender-Sensitive Parliaments: Relating Theory and Practice." In *Gender Innovation in Political Science,* edited by Marian Sawer and Kerryn Baker, 173–94. Cham, Switzerland: Palgrave Macmillan. https://doi.org/10.1007 /978-3-319-75850-3_9.

Paterson, Victoria. 2015. "The Ugly Side of Social Media: Online Engagement Can Lead to Political Vitriol." *St. Albert Gazette,* 23 May, 3.

Perraudin, Frances. 2019. "Alarm Over Number of Female MPs Stepping Down After Abuse." *The Guardian*, 31 October. https://www.theguardian.com/politics/2019/oct/31/alarm-over-number-female-mps-stepping-down-after-abuse.

Perrella, Andrea M.L., Steven D. Brown, and Barry J. Kay. 2012. "Voting Behaviour Among the Gay, Lesbian, Bisexual and Transgendered Electorate." *Canadian Journal of Political Science* 45 (1): 89–117. https://doi.org/10.10170S000842391100093X.

Philpot, Tasha S., and Hanes Walton, Jr. 2007. "One of Our Own: Black Female Candidates and the Voters Who Support Them." *American Journal of Political Science* 51 (1): 49–62. https://doi.org/10.1111/j.1540-5907.2007.00236.x.

Pitkin, Hanna Fenichel. 1967. *The Concept of Representation*. Berkeley: University of California Press.

Poitras, Jacques. 2017. "Political Parties to Get Financial Incentive to Run Female Candidates." *CBC News*, 22 March. https://www.cbc.ca/news/canada/new-brunswick/financial-incentive-women-candidates-1.4036359.

Polk, Jonathan, and Ann-Kristin Kölln. 2018. "Electoral Infidelity: Why Party Members Cast Defecting Votes." *European Journal of Political Research* 57 (2): 539–60. https://doi.org/10.1111/1475-6765.12238.

Praino, Rodrigo, and Daniel Stockemer. 2019. "What Are Good-Looking Candidates, and Can They Sway Election Results." *Social Science Quarterly* 100 (3): 531–43. https://doi.org/10.1111/ssqu.12540.

Praino, Rodrigo, Daniel Stockemer, and James Ratis. 2014. "Looking Good or Looking Competent? Physical Appearance and Electoral Success in the 2008 Congressional Elections." *American Politics Research* 42 (6): 1096–117. https://doi.org/10.1177/1532673X14532825.

Pruysers, Scott, and William Cross. 2016. "Candidate Selection in Canada: Local Autonomy, Centralization, and Competing Democratic Norms." *American Behavioral Scientist* 60 (7): 781–98. https://doi.org/10.1177/0002764216632820.

Public Policy Forum. 2017. *The Shattered Mirror: News, Democracy and Trust in the Digital Age*. Ottawa: Public Policy Forum. https://ppforum.ca/wp-content/uploads/2017/01/theShatteredMirror.pdf.

Reddy-Best, Kelly L. 2018. "LGBTQ Women, Appearance Negotiations, and Workplace Dress Codes." *Journal of Homosexuality* 65 (5): 615–39. https://doi.org/10.1080/00918369.2017.1328225.

Rheault, Ludovic, Erica Rayment, and Andreea Musulan. 2019. "Politicians in the Line of Fire: Incivility and the Treatment of Women on Social Media." *Research and Politics* 6 (1): 1–7. https://doi.org/10.1177/2053168018816228.

Rhodes, Jesse H., Elizabeth Sharrow, Jill Greenlee, and Tishe Nteta. 2020. "Just Locker Room Talk? Explicit Sexism and the Impact of the Access

Hollywood Tape on Electoral Support for Donald Trump in 2016." *Political Communication* 37 (6): 741–67. https://doi.org/10.1080/10584609.2020.1753867.

Roberts, Jane. 2017. *Losing Political Office*. Basingstoke: Palgrave Macmillan. https://doi.org/10.1007/978-3-319-39702-3.

Robins, Robert S., and Jerrold M. Post. 1995. "Choosing a Healthy President." *Political Psychology* 16 (4): 841–60. https://www.jstor.org/stable/3791896.

Robinson, Margaret. 2020. "Two-Spirit Identity in a Time of Gender Fluidity." *Journal of Homosexuality* 67 (12): 1675–90. https://doi.org/10.1080/00918369 .2019.1613853.

Rocha, Roberto, and Claire Loewen. 2017. "Immigrant Wages Rising, But Gaps with Canadian-Born Earners Persist." *CBC News*, 28 November. https:// www.cbc.ca/news/canada/montreal/immigrant-wages-canada-1.4421783.

Roehling, Patricia V., Mark V. Roehling, Ashli Brennan, Ashley R. Drew, Abbey J. Johnston, Regina G. Guerra, Ivy R. Keen, Camerra P. Lightbourn, and Alexis H. Sears. 2014. "Weight Bias in U.S. Candidate Selection and Election." *Equality, Diversity and Inclusion: An International Journal* 33 (4): 334–46. https://doi.org/10.1108/EDI-10-2013-0081.

Rogers, Mary F., and Phillip B. Lott. 1997. "Backlash, the Matrix of Domination, and Log Cabin Republicans." *The Sociological Quarterly* 38 (3): 497–512. https://doi.org/10.1111/j.1533-8525.1997.tb00489.x.

Rose, Jonathan. 2012. "Are Negative Ads Positive? Political Advertising and the Permanent Campaign." In *How Canadians Communicate IV: Media and Politics*, edited by David Taras and Christopher Waddell, 149–68. Edmonton: Athabasca University Press. https://doi.org/10.15215 /aupress/9781926836812.01

Ruderman, Nick, and Neil Nevitte. 2015. "Assessing the Impact of Political Scandals on Attitudes Toward Democracy: Evidence from Canada's Sponsorship Scandal." *Canadian Journal of Political Science* 48 (4): 885–904. https://doi.org/10.1017/S0008423915001055.

Rumbolt, Ryan. 2016. "Women in Politics Unite Against Bullying of Female Candidates." *Calgary Herald*, 10 November. https://calgaryherald.com /news/local-news/women-in-politics-unite-against-bullying-of-female -candidates.

Ruonavaara, Hannu. 1997. "Moral Regulation: A Reformulation." *Sociological Theory* 15 (3): 277–93. https://doi.org/10.1111/0735-2751.00035.

Rushowy, Kristin. 2017. "Twitter and Facebook Are a Minefield of Threats, Hate and Anger for Many Female Politicians." *Toronto Star*, 24 February. https://www.thestar.com/news/canada/2017/02/24/twitter-and-facebook -are-a-minefield-of-threats-hate-and-anger-for-many-female-politicians .html.

Russell, Gerald. 2011. "Psychiatry and Politicians: The 'Hubris Syndrome'." *The Psychiatrist* 35 (4): 140–45. https://doi.org/10.1192/pb.bp.110.031575.

Rutherdale, Robert. 2012. "Fathers in Multiple Roles: Assessing Modern Canadian Fatherhood as a Masculine Category." In *Canadian Men and Masculinities: Historical and Contemporary Perspectives*, edited by Christopher J. Greig and Wayne J. Martino, 76–98. Toronto: Canadian Scholars' Press Inc.

Salgado, Susana, and Jesper Strömbäck. 2012. "Interpretive Journalism: A Review of Concepts, Operationalizations and Key Findings." *Journalism* 13 (2): 144–61. https://doi.org/10.1177/1464884911427797.

Sanbonmatsu, Kira, and Kathleen Dolan. 2009. "Do Gender Stereotypes Transcend Party?" *Political Research Quarterly* 62 (3): 485–94. https://doi .org/10.1177/1065912908322416.

Sapiro, Virginia. 1982. "Private Costs of Public Commitments or Public Costs of Private Commitments? Family Roles Versus Political Ambition." *American Journal of Political Science* 26 (2): 265–79. http://www.jstor.org /stable/2111039.

Sawer, Marian, Manon Tremblay, and Linda Trimble. 2006. "Introduction: Patterns and Practice in the Parliamentary Representation of Women." In *Representing Women in Parliament: A Comparative Study*, edited by Marian Sawer, Manon Tremblay, and Linda Trimble, 1–23. New York: Routledge. https://doi.org/10.4324/9780203965672

Schudson, Michael. 2004. "Notes on Scandal and the Watergate Legacy." *American Behavioral Scientist* 47 (9): 1231–8. https://doi.org/10.1177 /0002764203262345.

Schwindt-Bayer, Leslie A., and William Mishler. 2005. "An Integrated Model of Women's Representation." *Journal of Politics* 67 (2): 407–28. https://doi .org/10.1111/j.1468-2508.2005.00323.x.

Scott, Jacqueline. 2010. "Quantitative Methods and Gender Inequalities." *International Journal of Social Research Methodology* 13 (3): 223–36. https:// doi.org/10.1080/13645579.2010.482258.

Seiter, John S., and Sarah Hatch. 2005. "Effect of Tattoos on Perceptions of Credibility and Attractiveness." *Psychological Reports* 96 (3_suppl): 1113–20. https://doi.org/10.2466/pr0.96.3c.1113-1120.

Serini, Shirley A., Angela A. Powers, and Susan Johnson. 1998. "Of Horse Race and Policy Issues: A Study of Gender in Coverage of a Gubernatorial Election by Two Major Metropolitan Newspapers." *Journalism and Mass Communication Quarterly* 75 (1): 194–204. https://doi.org/10.1177 /107769909807500118.

Sevä, Ingemar Johansson, and Ida Öun. 2019. "Conditional Representation: Gendered Experiences of Combining Work and Family Among Local Politicians." *Journal of Women, Politics and Policy* 40 (3): 367–84. https://doi .org/10.1080/1554477X.2019.1602992.

Shames, Shauna L. 2015. "American Women of Color and Rational Non-Candidacy: When Silent Citizenship Makes Politics Look Like Old White

Men Shouting." *Citizenship Studies* 19 (5): 553–69. https://doi.org/10.1080
/13621025.2015.1074348.

Shames, Shauna L. 2017. *Out of the Running: Why Millennials Reject Political
Careers and Why It Matters.* New York: New York University Press. https://
doi.org/10.2307/j.ctt1bj4rv1

Sipes, Carrie. 2011. "Men, Mistresses, and Media Framing: Examining
Political Scandals." In *Sex Scandals in American Politics: A Multidisciplinary
Approach to the Construction and Aftermath of Contemporary Political Sex
Scandals,* edited by Alison Dagnes, 94–112. London: Bloomsbury Academic.
https://doi.org/10.5040/9781501300660.ch-006.

Smith, Robert C. 1988. "Financing Black Politics: A Study of Congressional
Elections." *The Review of Black Political Economy* 17 (1): 5–30. https://doi
.org/10.1007/BF02900951.

Sobolewska, Maria, Rebecca McKee, and Rosie Campbell. 2018. "Explaining
Motivation to Represent: How Does Descriptive Representation Lead
to Substantive Representation of Racial and Ethnic Minorities?" *West
European Politics* 41 (6): 1237–61. https://doi.org/10.1080/01402382.2018
.1455408.

"Social Media Exposes the Dark Side." 2015. *Brampton Guardian,* 8 October, 1.

"Social Media Posts Spell the End of Federal Candidacies Across Canada."
2015. *This Week* (Clarington, Oshawa, Port Perry, Whitby, ON), 15 October, 1.

"Social Media's Long Reach." 2015. *Guelph Mercury,* 30 September, A8.

Somani, Indira S., and Natalie Hopkinson. 2019. "Color, Caste and the Public
Sphere: Black Journalists Who Joined Television Networks from 1994 to
2014." *Journalism Practice* 13 (3): 314–30. https://doi.org/10.1080/17512786
.2018.1426999.

Southern, Rosalynd, and Emily Harmer. 2019a. "Other Political Women:
Online Misogyny, Racism and Ableism Towards Women in Public Life."
In *Online Othering: Exploring Digital Violence and Discrimination on the Web,*
edited by Karen Lumsden and Emily Harmer, 197–210. Cham, Switzerland:
Palgrave Macmillan. https://doi.org/10.1007/978-3-030-12633-9_8.

Southern, Rosalynd, and Emily Harmer. 2019b. "Twitter, Incivility and
'Everyday' Gendered Othering: An Analysis of Tweets Sent to UK
Members of Parliament." *Social Science Computer Review* 1–17. https://doi
.org/10.1177/0894439319865519.

Stalsburg, Brittany L. 2010. "Voting for Mom: The Political Consequences of
Being a Parent for Male and Female Candidates." *Politics and Gender* 6 (3):
373–404. https://doi.org/10.1017/S1743923X10000309.

Stalsburg, Brittany L., and Mona S. Kleinberg. 2016. "'A Mom First and a
Candidate Second': Gender Differences in Candidates' Self-Presentation of
Family." *Journal of Political Marketing* 15 (4): 285–310. https://doi.org
/10.1080/15377857.2014.959684.

Star Editorial Board. 2018. "A Civil Election Campaign Is Vital to Encourage Women in Politics." *Toronto Star*, 25 March. https://www.thestar.com /opinion/editorials/2018/03/25/a-civil-election-campaign-is-vital-to -encourage-women-in-politics.html.

Statistics Canada. 2022a. *(Table) Census Profile: 2021 Census of Population.* Statistics Canada Catalogue no. 98-316-X2021001. Ottawa: Statistics Canada. Released 26 October. https://www12.statcan.gc.ca/census -recensement/2021/dp-pd/prof/details/page.cfm?Lang=E&SearchText =Whitby&DGUIDlist=2021A00053518009,2021S051235181251&GENDERlist =1,2,3&STATISTIClist=1&HEADERlist=0.

Statistics Canada. 2022b. "Study: Labour and Economic Characteristics of Lesbian, Gay, and Bisexual People in Canada." *The Daily*, 4 October. https://www150.statcan.gc.ca/n1/daily-quotidien/221004/dq221004d -eng.htm.

Stayshyn, Justin. 2010. "Who Is Behind the Anti-Gay Tamil Radio Ad?" *Dailyxtra.com*, 27 October. https://www.dailyxtra.com/who-is-behind -the-anti-gay-tamil-radio-ad-update-30039.

Steiner, Linda. 1998. "Newsroom Accounts of Power at Work." In *News, Gender and Power*, edited by Cynthia Carter, Gill Branston, and Stuart Allan, 145–59. London: Routledge. https://doi.org/10.4324 /9780203010631.

Stokes-Brown, Atiya Kai, and Kathleen Dolan. 2010. "Race, Gender, and Symbolic Representation: African American Female Candidates as Mobilizing Agents." *Journal of Elections, Public Opinions and Parties* 20 (4): 473–94. https://doi.org/10.1080/17457289.2010.511806.

Strömbäck, Jesper. 2008. "Four Phases of Mediatization: An Analysis of the Mediatization of Politics." *International Journal of Press/Politics* 13 (3): 228–46. https://doi.org/10.1177/1940161208319097.

Strong-Boag, Veronica. 1991. "Home Dreams: Women and the Suburban Experiment in Canada, 1945–60." *Canadian Historical Review* 72 (4): 471–504. https://doi.org/10.3138/CHR-072-04-03.

Summers, Anne. 2012. "Her Rights at Work: The Political Persecution of Australia's First Female Prime Minister." *Economic and Labour Relations Review* 23 (4): 115–26. https://doi.org/10.1177/103530461202300409.

Sutter, Daniel. 2006. "Media Scrutiny and the Quality of Public Officials." *Public Choice* 129 (1–2): 25–40. https://doi.org/10.1007/s11127-006-9025-0.

Sutton, Robert I., and D. Charles Galunic. 1996. "Consequences of Public Scrutiny for Leaders and Their Organizations." *Research in Organizational Behavior* 18: 201–50.

Swank, Eric. 2018a. "Who Voted for Hillary Clinton? Sexual Identities, Gender, and Family Influences." *Journal of GLBT Family Studies* 14 (1–2): 21–42. https://doi.org/10.1080/1550428X.2017.1421335.

Swank, Eric. 2018b. "Sexual Identities and Participation in Liberal and Conservative Movements." *Social Science Research* 74: 176–86. https://doi .org/10.1016/j.ssresearch.2018.04.002.

Takens, Janet, Wouter van Atteveldt, Anita van Hoof, and Jan Kleinnijenhuis. 2013. "Media Logic in Election Campaign Coverage." *European Journal of Communication* 28 (3): 277–93. https://doi.org/10.1177/0267323113478522.

Taras, David. 2015. *Digital Mosaic: Media, Power, and Identity in Canada.* Toronto: University of Toronto Press.

Taylor, Mary Anne, and Danee Pye. 2019. "Hillary Through TIME: The (Un) making of the First Woman President." *American Behavioral Scientist* 63 (7): 807–25. https://doi.org/10.1177/0002764217711801.

Teddlie, Charles, and Fen Yu. 2007. "Mixed Methods Sampling: A Typology with Examples." *Journal of Mixed Methods Research* 1 (1): 77–100. https://doi .org/10.1177/2345678906292430.

Terkildsen, Nayda, and David F. Damore. 1999. "The Dynamics of Racialized Media Coverage in Congressional Elections." *Journal of Politics* 61 (3): 680–99. https://doi.org/10.2307/2647823.

Tetlock, Philip E. 1985. "Accountability: The Neglected Social Context of Judgment and Choice." *Research in Organizational Behavior* 7: 297–332.

Tettey, Wisdom John. 2016. "Homosexuality, Moral Panic, and Politicized Homophobia in Ghana: Interrogating Discourses of Moral Entrepreneurship in Ghanaian Media." *Communication, Culture and Critique* 9 (1): 86–106. https://doi.org/10.1111/cccr.12132.

Theakston, Kevin. 2012. "Life After Political Death: Former Leaders in Western Democracies." *Representation* 48 (2): 139–49. https://doi.org /10.1080/00344893.2012.683494.

Thomas, Melanee. 2012. "The Complexity Conundrum: Why Hasn't the Gender Gap in Subjective Political Competence Closed?" *Canadian Journal of Political Science* 45 (2): 337–58. https://doi.org/10.1017 /S0008423912000352.

Thomas, Melanee. 2017. "Equality of Opportunity but Not Result: Women and FEDERAL Conservatives in Canada." In *The Blueprint: Conservative Parties and Their Impact on Canadian Politics*, edited by J.P. Lewis and Joanna Everitt, 129–49. Toronto: University of Toronto Press. https://doi .org/10.3138/9781487514020-006.

Thomas, Melanee, and Marc André Bodet. 2013. "Sacrificial Lambs, Women Candidates, and District Competitiveness in Canada." *Electoral Studies* 32 (1): 153–66. https://doi.org/10.1016/j.electstud.2012.12.001.

Thomas, Melanee, and Lisa Lambert. 2017. "Private Mom Versus Political Dad? Communications of Parental Status in the 41st Canadian Parliament." In *Mothers and Others: The Role of Parenthood in Politics*, edited by Melanee

Thomas and Amanda Bittner, 135–54. Vancouver: UBC Press. https://doi
.org/10.59962/9780774834605-009

Thompson, John B. 2000. *Political Scandal: Power and Visibility in the Media Age.*
Cambridge: Polity Press. https://doi.org/10.1353/sof.2003.0050.

Thomsen, Danielle M., and Michele L. Swers. 2017. "Which Women Can Run?
Gender, Partisanship, and Candidate Donor Networks." *Political Research
Quarterly* 70 (2): 449–53. https://doi.org/10.1177/1065912917698044.

Tolley, Erin. 2016. *Framed: Media and the Coverage of Race in Canadian Politics.*
Vancouver: UBC Press. https://www.ubcpress.ca/framed.

Tolley, Erin. 2019. "Who You Know: Local Party Presidents and Minority
Candidate Emergence." *Electoral Studies* 58 (April): 70–9. https://doi
.org/10.1016/j.electstud.2019.02.007.

Tolley, Erin. 2023. "Gender Is Not a Proxy: Race and Intersectionality in
Legislative Recruitment." *Politics and Gender* 19 (2): 373–400. https://doi
.org/10.1017/S1743923X22000149.

Tolley, Erin, Randy Besco, and Semra Sevi. 2022. "Who Controls the Purse
Strings? A Longitudinal Study of Gender and Donations in Canadian
Politics." *Politics and Gender* 18 (1): 244–72. https://doi.org/10.1017
/S1743923X20000276.

Törrönen, Jukka, Jenni Simonen, and Christoffer Tigerstedt. 2015. "'Disease'
of the Nation, Family and Individual: Three Moral Discourses of Alcohol
Problems in Finnish Women's Magazines from the 1960s to the 2000s."
Substance Use and Misuse 50 (4): 454–67. https://doi.org/10.3109/10826084
.2015.978186.

Tremblay, Manon. 2007. "Electoral Systems and Substantive Representation
of Women: A Comparison of Australia, Canada and New Zealand."
Commonwealth and Comparative Politics 45 (3): 278–302. https://doi.org
/10.1080/14662040701516870.

Tremblay, Manon. 2010. *Quebec Women and Legislative Representation.*
Translated into English by Kathe Roth. Vancouver: UBC Press. https://
www.ubcpress.ca/quebec-women-and-legislative-representation.

Tremblay, Manon. 2022. *LGBQ Legislators in Canadian Politics: Out to Represent.*
Cham, Switzerland: Springer. https://link.springer.com/book/10.1007
/978-3-030-91301-4.

Trimble, Linda. 1995. "Politics Where We Live: Women and Cities." In
Canadian Metropolitics: Governing Our Cities, edited by James Lightbody,
92–114. Toronto: Copp Clark.

Trimble, Linda. 2008. "Assembling Women, Gendering Assemblies." In
Gendering the Nation-State: Canadian and Comparative Perspectives, edited by
Yasmeen Abu-Laban, 79–96. Vancouver: UBC Press. https://doi.org
/10.59962/9780774856027-007

Trimble, Linda. 2009. "The Politics of Gender." In *Critical Concepts: An Introduction to Politics*, 4th ed., edited by Janine Brodie and Sandra Rein. Toronto: Pearson Prentice Hall.

Trimble, Linda. 2017. *Ms. Prime Minister: Gender, Media, and Leadership*. Toronto: University of Toronto Press. https://doi.org/10.3138/9781442662964.

Trimble, Linda, and Joanna Everitt. 2010. "Belinda Stronach and the Gender Politics of Celebrity." In *Mediating Canadian Politics*, edited by Shannon Sampert and Linda Trimble, 50–74. Toronto: Pearson Education Canada.

Trimble, Linda, Daisy Raphael, Shannon Sampert, Angelia Wagner, and Bailey Gerrits. 2015. "Politicizing Bodies: Hegemonic Masculinity, Heteronormativity, and Racism in News Representations of Canadian Political Party Leadership Candidates." *Women's Studies in Communication* 38 (3): 314–30. https://doi.org/10.1080/07491409.2015.1062836.

Trimble, Linda, and Manon Tremblay. 2003. "Women Politicians in Canada's Parliament and Legislatures, 1917–2000: A Socio-Demographic Profile." In *Women and Electoral Politics in Canada*, edited by Manon Tremblay and Linda Trimble, 37–58. Don Mills, ON: Oxford University Press.

Trimble, Linda, Angelia Wagner, Shannon Sampert, Daisy Raphael, and Bailey Gerrits. 2013. "Is It Personal? Gendered Mediation in Newspaper Coverage of Canadian National Party Leadership Contests, 1975–2012." *International Journal of Press/Politics* 18 (4): 462–81. https://doi.org/10.1177/1940161213495455.

Trottier, Daniel. 2018. "Scandal Mining: Political Nobodies and Remediated Visibility." *Media, Culture, and Society* 40 (6): 893–908. https://doi.org/10.1177/0163443717734408.

Trounstine, Jessica, and Melody E. Valdini. 2008. "The Context Matters: The Effects of Single-Member Versus at-Large Districts on City Council Diversity." *American Journal of Political Science* 52 (3): 554–69.

Turnbull-Dugarte, Stuart. 2020. "The European Lavender Vote: Sexuality, Ideology and Vote Choice in Western Europe." *European Journal of Political Research* 59 (3): 517–37. https://doi.org/10.1111/1475-6765.12366.

Uhlaner, Carole Jean, and Kay Lehman Schlozman. 1986. "Candidate Gender and Congressional Campaign Receipts." *Journal of Politics* 48 (1): 30–50. https://doi.org/10.2307/2130923.

UK Electoral Commission. 2023. "No Place for Candidate Intimidation Ahead of May Elections." https://www.electoralcommission.org.uk/media-centre/no-place-candidate-intimidation-or-abuse-ahead-may-elections.

Urback, Robyn. 2015. "How About We Just Burn Our Social Media Histories and Try Again Next Election?" *National Post*, 17 September. https://nationalpost.com/opinion/robyn-urback-how-about-we-just-burn-our-social-media-histories-and-try-again-next-election.

Van Zoonen, Liesbet. 1998. "'Finally, I Have My Mother Back': Politicians and Their Families in Popular Culture." *Press/Politics* 3 (1): 48–64. https://doi .org/10.1177/1081180X98003001005.

Van Zoonen, Liesbet. 2000. "Broken Hearts, Broken Dreams? Politicians and Their Families in Popular Culture." In *Gender, Politics and Communication*, edited by Annabelle Sreberny and Liesbet van Zoonen, 101–19. Cresskill: Hampton Press.

Vickers, Jill. 2006. "The Problem with Interests: Making Political Claims for 'Women'." In *The Politics of Women's Interests: New Comparative Perspectives*, edited by Louise Chappell and Lisa Hill, 5–38. London: Routledge. https:// doi.org/10.4324/9780203028216.

Visser, Beth A., Angela S. Book, and Anthony A. Volk. 2017. "Is Hillary Dishonest and Donald Narcissistic? A HEXACO Analysis of the Presidential Candidates' Public Personas." *Personality and Individual Differences* 106: 281–86. https://doi.org/10.1016/j.paid.2016.10.053.

Vochocová, Lenka. 2018. "Witty Divas, Nice Mothers and Tough Girls in a Sexist World: Experiences and Strategies of Female Influencers in Online Political Debates." *Media, Culture and Society* 40 (4): 535–50. https://doi .org/10.1177/0163443717729211.

Wagner, Angelia. 2019. "Not a Taboo Topic? Talking About Family on the Campaign Trail." In *Gendered Mediation: Identity and Image Making in Canadian Politics*, edited by Angelia Wagner and Joanna Everitt, 65–83. Vancouver: UBC Press. https://doi.org/10.59962/9780774860574-005

Wagner, Angelia. 2021. "Avoiding the Spotlight: Public Scrutiny, Moral Regulation, and Lbib_diGBTQ Candidate Deterrence." *Politics, Groups, and Identities* 1–18. https://doi.org/10.1080/21565503.2019.1605298.

Wagner, Angelia. 2022a. "Motivations for Federal Candidacy." In *Inside the Local Campaign: Constituency Elections in Canada*, edited by Alex Marland and Thierry Giasson, 65–84. Vancouver: UBC Press. https://www .ubcpress.ca/media/9780774868204_web_OA.pdf.

Wagner, Angelia. 2022b. "Tolerating the Trolls? Gendered Perceptions of Online Harassment of Politicians in Canada." *Feminist Media Studies* 22 (1): 32–47. https://doi.org/10.1080/14680777.2020.1749691.

Wagner, Angelia, and Joanna Everitt, eds. 2019a. *Gendered Mediation: Identity and Image Making in Canadian Politics*. Vancouver: UBC Press. https://doi .org/10.59962/9780774860574.

Wagner, Angelia, and Joanna Everitt. 2019b. "Introduction: Gendered Identities and Political Communication." In *Gendered Mediation: Identity and Image Making in Canadian Politics*, edited by Angelia Wagner and Joanna Everitt, 3–23. Vancouver: UBC Press. https://doi.org/10.59962 /9780774860574-002.

Wagner, Angelia, Linda Trimble, and Shannon Sampert. 2019. "One Smart Politician: Gendered Mediation Discourses of Political Leadership in Canada." *Canadian Journal of Political Science* 52 (1): 141–62. https://doi.org/10.1017/S0008423918000471.

Wagner, Angelia, Linda Trimble, Shannon Sampert, and Bailey Gerrits. 2017. "Gender, Competitiveness and Candidate Visibility in Newspaper Coverage of Canadian Party Leadership Contests." *International Journal of Press/Politics* 22 (4): 471–89. https://doi.org/10.1177/1940161217723150.

Wagner, Angelia, and Tayler Young. 2024. "Digital Dangers: Theorizing Online Harassment of Politicians." In *Gender-Based Violence in Canadian Politics in the #MeToo Era*, edited by Tracey Raney and Cheryl N. Collier, 45–64. Toronto: University of Toronto Press.

Wagner, Markus. 2017. "Why Do Party Members Leave?" *Parliamentary Affairs* 70 (2): 344–60. https://doi.org/10.1093/pa/gsw024.

Wamsley, Kevin B. 2006. "The Public Importance of Men and the Importance of Public Men: Sport and Masculinities in Nineteenth Century Canada." In *Sport and Gender in Canada*, edited by Philip White and Kevin Young, 75–91. Oxford: Oxford University Press.

Ward, Orlanda. 2016a. "Seeing Double: Race, Gender, and Coverage of Minority Women's Campaigns for the U.S. House of Representatives." *Politics and Gender* 12 (2): 317–43. https://doi.org/10.1017/S1743923X16000222.

Ward, Orlanda. 2016b. "Media Framing of Black Women's Campaigns for the U.S. House of Representatives." In *Distinct Identities: Minority Women in U.S. Politics*, edited by Nadia E. Brown and Sarah Allen Gershon, 153–70. New York: Routledge. https://doi.org/10.4324/9781315661018.

Warman, Richard, and Bernie M. Farber. 2018. "Calling Out the Toronto Sun's Islamophobia." *NOW Toronto*, 26 October. https://nowtoronto.com/news/calling-out-the-toronto-suns-islamophobia/.

Wehrkamp, Connie, and Judson L. Jeffries. 2014. "Press Coverage and Its Impact on Attitudes Toward a Black Republican for High Statewide Office: The 2006 Ohio Governor's Election." *Spectrum: A Journal on Black Men* 3 (1): 97–122. https://doi.org/10.2979/spectrum.3.1.97.

Weinberg, Ashley. 2015. "A Longitudinal Study of the Impact of Changes in the Job and the Expenses Scandal on UK National Politicians' Experience of Work, Stress and the Home-Work Interface." *Parliamentary Affairs* 68 (2): 248–71. https://doi.org/10.1093/pa/gst013.

Weinberg, Ashley. 2017. "The Mental Health of Politicians." *Palgrave Communications* 3 (17081): 1–4. https://doi.org/10.1057/palcomms.2017.81.

Weinberg, Ashley, and Cary L. Cooper. 2003. "Stress Among National Politicians Elected to Parliament for the First Time." *Stress and Health* 19 (2): 111–17. https://doi.org/10.1002/smi.965.

Weinberg, Ashley, Cary L. Cooper, and Anne Weinberg. 1999. "Workload, Stress and Family Life in British Members of Parliament and the Psychological Impact of Reforms to Their Working Hours." *Stress Medicine* 15 (2): 79–97. https://doi.org/10.1002/(SICI)1099-1700(199904)15: 2<79::AID-SMI788>3.0.CO;2-S.

Werner, Timothy, and Kenneth R. Mayer. 2007. "Public Election Funding, Competition, and Candidate Gender." *PS: Political Science and Politics* 40 (4): 661–7. https://doi.org/10.1017/S1049096507071053.

West, Emily A. 2016. "Descriptive Representation and Political Efficacy: Evidence from Obama and Clinton." *Journal of Politics* 79 (1): 351–5. https://doi.org/10.1086/688888.

Whitworth, Sandra. 2005. "Militarized Masculinities and the Politics of Peacekeeping: The Canadian Case." In *Critical Security Studies in World Politics*, edited by Ken Booth, 89–106. Boulder, CO: Lynne Rienner Publishers. https://doi.org/10.1515/9781685857356-006.

Wilford, Rick, Robert Miller, Yolanda Bell, and Freda Donoghue. 1993. "In Their Own Voices: Women Councillors in Northern Ireland." *Public Administration* 71 (3): 341–55. https://doi.org/10.1111/j.1467-9299.1993 .tb00978.x.

Wilson, Laura Merriefield. 2018. "Does Money Matter? The Impact of State Political Context on the Relationship Between Race/Ethnicity and Campaign Finance." *Journal of the Indiana Academy of the Social Sciences* 21 (1): 171–91. https://digitalcommons.butler.edu/jiass/vol21/iss1/47.

Wiltse, David L. 2018. "Subsidizing Equality: Female Candidate Emergence and Clean Elections." *Election Law Journal* 17 (2): 85–99. https://doi.org /10.1089/elj.2017.0435.

Worthen, Meredith G.F. 2020. "'All the Gays Are Liberal?' Sexuality and Gender Gaps in Political Perspectives Among Lesbian, Gay, Bisexual, Mostly Heterosexual, and Heterosexual College Students in the Southern USA." *Sexuality Research and Social Policy* 17 (1): 27–42. https://doi.org /10.1007/s13178-018-0365-6.

Wright, Teresa. 2019. "Cash Incentives for Parties Could Help Get More Women in Politics: MPs." *CBC News*, 12 April 2019. https://www.cbc.ca /news/politics/incentives-for-women-in-politics-1.5096660.

Würfel, Maximilian. 2018. "Life After the Bundestag: An Analysis of the Post-Parliamentary Careers of Germany MPs." *German Politics* 27 (3): 295–316. https://doi.org/10.1080/09644008.2017.1344642.

Yakabuski, Konrad. 2017. "Singh Complicates the NDP's Quebec Quandary." *Globe and Mail*, 13 July, A11.

Young, Iris Marion. 2000. *Inclusion and Democracy.* Oxford: Oxford University Press. https://doi.org/10.1057/9781137440976.

Young, Lisa, and Harold J. Jansen, eds. 2011. *Money, Politics, and Democracy: Canada's Party Finance Reforms.* Vancouver: UBC Press. https://doi.org /10.59962/9780774818933.

Zulli, Diana. 2019. "The Changing Norms of Gendered News Coverage: Hillary Clinton in the *New York Times*, 1969–2016." *Politics and Gender* 15 (3): 559–621. https://doi.org/10.1017/S1743923X18000466.

Index